FOr The F

NEXT

Generation:

A RESOURCE FOR MINISTRY LEADERS AND PARENTS

BY JULIE KURZ

WITH SCOTT TURANSKY, JOANNE MILLER,
CARRI TAYLOR, AND KIRK WEAVER

D6 FAMILY MINISTRY
114 BUSH RD · NASHVILLE, TN 37217 · 800.877.7030 · D6FAMILY.COM

DEDICATION

To all the parents, teachers, and children's workers
who welcome children in Jesus' name.

To the "*next generation...*[and] *all who are to come.*"
Psalm 71:18b (NIV)

To all my prayer partners and financial supporters
who made this book possible.

And to my Lord and Savior, Jesus Christ, who told me
"*I can do all things through Christ who strengthens me.*"
Philippians 4:13 (NKJV)

*Since my youth, God, you have taught me, and to this day I declare
your marvelous deeds.
Even when I am old and gray, do not forsake me,
my God, till I declare your power
to the next generation, your mighty acts to all who are to come.*
Psalm 71:17-18 (NIV)

ACKNOWLEDGEMENTS

My husband, Dave deserves so much credit for this book becoming a reality. He was my constant encourager, my editor (at times a ghost writer), and my "manager" when we reached the point of pursuing publishing. Dave has always been an avid reader, an excellent writer, and a brilliant summarizer. Many times throughout this process, I thanked God for giving me a husband with the skills I needed for a book I never dreamed I would be writing. I can truly say my book would not have reached fruition without him.

I am so grateful that Kirk Weaver, Carri Taylor, Scott Turansky, and Joanne Miller were each willing to write a chapter for my book. I have been recommending their materials—Family Time Training, Opportunities Unlimited, and the National Center of Biblical Parenting—since the beginning of my ministry, so it seemed very appropriate for their ministries to be included and their areas of expertise to be represented by each of them personally.

Steve Elliott, who invited me to join Church Assistance Ministries (CAM) when he was president and has been my biggest fan in ministry. Steve has always believed in my mission and has promoted my ministry to so many churches in California. He wanted my book to be published as if it were his own. A second edit of my book was done by Steve and his team, Jane Mach and Birda McLeod.

Our generous friends, Daniel and Debbie Choi, who allowed me to write at their vacation home in Sedona when I needed a change of scenery during the week. More accurately, they provided a place for me to write with no distractions or people to talk to when I was so desperate for a distraction☺. (I did manage to meet a neighbor lady and go to breakfast with her a couple times...but for the most part, it was a great place to make a lot of needed progress in my writing.)

And to all of you who have encouraged me to write this book—Rob Rienow, Visionary Families; Steve Elliott, CAM; Rita Nystrom, former Evangelical Free Church of America (EFCA) West Administrator; Merlin Bergen, supporter & friend; and Leslie Tripp, my dear friend and co-worker at Bethany Evangelical Free Church (EFC) who has always encouraged me to pursue publishing the materials that I developed when I was children's director in Littleton, Colorado.

Table of Contents

Introduction

What I Wish We Would Have Known

I remember well the day my journey to form Reconnect Ministries began to take shape. I had just received the news from a fellow children's director that another one of our "church-grown" kids had made a series of choices that would impact the rest of his life. This one was serious! There were consequences and memories that could not be erased. I sat at my desk, shocked by the news and overwhelmed with sadness. I could not help but ask myself if there was more we could do in children's ministries. Why, after years of being in Sunday School, learning about God's plan for their lives and seemingly making commitments to follow Jesus, couldn't we keep our children from falling away in such spectacular fashion? It's not that we were expecting that our kids would never make poor choices, and I knew that performance-based faith was not the answer. But deep in my heart I could not help but wonder; "How does the church develop kids spiritually so they understand God's love, escape the snares of the world, and reflect His love, inwardly and outwardly?" So began my journey to better understand how kids actually develop spiritually and how to better shepherd them into a life of faith.

The next pivotal event for me was a discussion that took place at a church staff meeting. This discussion came about because of our observation that by the time our kids were juniors and seniors in high school, a large percentage were no longer attending church or coming to youth group. These were teens who had been children in *my* children's ministries program—"THE DISCOVERY ZONE: Where Kids Seek, Know, and Serve God." They were kids I thought had been excited about Jesus and wanted to follow Him. I reflected on the vision, mission, values, and strategy document I had developed with my team several years prior, and noted particularly the desire I had stated for children's ministries to be a *"foundation for our kids' teen years."*

Wow! I began to wonder, "Could I really be responsible for the *spiritual foundation* of children growing up in our church?" It was suddenly very clear to me, that I was not successfully accomplishing this goal in my church program. Not only did I have questions about how that *foundation* could be developed, I knew we couldn't build it in just the one to three hours we had with the children each week! I reluctantly decided to remove the statement from our mission and vision document in order to continue exploring how children develop spiritually. I did this by going to workshops, conferences, and talking to my spiritual mentors in children's ministries about this area of concern.

The next event that served to change my way of thinking took place during one of our children's ministry team meetings. After having spent time evaluating our strategy and programs, deciding what worked and what didn't work, and completing our list of changes for the coming year, we went on to evaluate our adherence to our mission and vision statement. When we got to the part about how we were doing in our desired role to *partner with parents,* there was in general a shrug of the shoulders followed by blank stares. When it came to supplementing the teaching parents were doing at home, we realized we didn't have a clue how we were doing, how to do it, or how to find out! The only thing we knew for sure was that our "take-home papers" were often found on the floor all over the church and no one was asking us for them. There was one thing about those papers; they were expensive, so we decided to stop ordering them with our curriculum.

I certainly understood that "partnering with parents" was a very important factor in the spiritual development of our children, but I assumed, at least to some degree, this was also understood by our parents and they were doing something at home to teach their children the Bible and make it applicable in their daily lives. But our team didn't know how to help them in this area, and I didn't know how to lead in this area either. I told my colleagues I would work on understanding this additional dilemma, and we moved on.

I kept asking God for wisdom and help as I continued to read, and attend children's ministry conferences to further expand my knowledge and understanding of how children develop spiritually. It was at the Children's Pastor's Conference (CPC) that I became aware of a new book by George Barna. I had read other books by him, but his focus had always been research for pastors in different areas of ministry such as church growth. So, I was pleasantly surprised to see research focusing on children's ministries in his book—*Transforming Children into Spiritual Champions: Why Children Should Be Your Church's #1 Priority!*

You can imagine how curious I was to hear what he had to say on this subject. I dove into the book immediately and could quickly see that God was beginning to answer my prayers as He gave me an understanding of what children really needed. I also realized that Barna was confirming many of my thoughts. He said,

> *"Our national surveys have shown that more than 4 out of 5 parents (85 percent) believe they have the primary responsibility for the moral and spiritual development of their children, more than two out of three of them abdicate that responsibility to their church… In short, most families do not have a genuine spiritual life together."* (*Transforming Children Into Spiritual Champions*, George Barna, pp. 77-78)

[And more recent research shows this trend is even worse.]

I resonated with his message. It made sense spiritually.

It wasn't long before research was pouring in from several sources in addition to the Barna Group, including Search Institute, Lifeway Research, Josh McDowell Ministries, and Pew Research. All of the research pointed to the critical role of parents in the spiritual development of their children and that because this was not happening, it was one of the main reasons the church was not retaining a large percentage of our "church-grown kids." And then I was shocked to read that,

- Less than 10% of parents who regularly attend church read the Bible, pray together, or serve God together as a family. (*Transforming Children Into Spiritual Champions*, George Barna, p. 78)
- Only 33% (one in three) Evangelical Christian parents place a high priority on their children's spiritual life. (Lifeway Research)
- Four out of five parents believe they have the primary responsibility for their children's spiritual development, but more than two out of three abdicate that responsibility to their church. (*Transforming Children Into Spiritual Champions*, George Barna p. 77)
- Many have estimated that between 69% and 94% of their young people are leaving the traditional church after high school. (*The Last Generation*, Josh McDowell, p. 13)
- 33% of these "church-grown kids" returned in their mid-20's (Lifeway Research) and more recent studies indicate this percentage is declining.

I decided to do my own personal study of the Scriptures to answer this important question: "How did God intend for faith to be passed from one generation to another?" My conclusions from the Old and New Testaments confirmed that God designed parents and grandparents to be the primary teachers and communicators of God's story. The community of faith also had an essential, but different role, in the lives of the children in Old Testament communities and later in the house churches of the New Testament. I really felt God stirring in my heart. I began sharing these ideas with my team so we could get back on track by equipping parents to take the primary role in the faith development of their children. I knew we couldn't keep doing "programs" if they were not accomplishing the ultimate goal of spiritually developing children who would be strong in faith.

Throughout this time, I sensed God calling me to try to make a difference and to help solve a critical problem in our churches and in the lives of the children who attend our churches. I became convinced we should no longer do programming in children's ministries for children's ministries' sake. I could see we had been evaluating the wrong metrics, and if children's ministries as we were doing them, were not accomplishing our long-term goals, then I had to be a part of communicating the biblical approach to spiritually developing our "church-grown" kids and passing faith from one generation to the next. I could see that our focus needed to change to one of strengthening the home and transferring the responsibility of the spiritual development of children to parents, guardians, and grandparents instead of the church. The role of the church and the home needed to be clearly defined and communicated. Children's ministries could no longer be just a drop-off ministry where parents found the best church to do a job that really belongs to the home. Having already made as many of these changes as my church was willing to make, I told God I was willing to step out in faith, jump off the cliff, and do what I could to communicate this message to churches and parents beyond the walls of my own church. I felt compelled to share this message to whoever would listen!

In October 2006, with the blessing of my church, I followed God's call and launched Reconnect Ministries, whose mission is "to influence the culture of the church and the home to better reflect the biblical model for passing faith to the next generation; a model where the home becomes the primary source of spiritual development for children, and the church comes alongside with training, equipping, resources, and encouragement."

The foundational principles of my ministry have been these:

1. Parents are the primary spiritual influencers in the life a child.

2. The role of the church is to come alongside parents—supporting, teaching, and equipping them to disciple their children. The church also serves as an "extended family."

3. The Holy Spirit is the One who ultimately works in our children's lives to bring them into relationship with God through Jesus Christ.

As I moved from the role of children's ministry director to church consultant, God provided an amazing team of financial partners and prayer warriors to make this ministry possible. Under the banner of Reconnect Ministries, I have conducted workshops all over the USA (and in Trinidad-Tobago, Czech Republic, Ethiopia, Thailand, and Indonesia), and I have consulted with churches in strategies that better connect the ministries of the church to the home. I've coached and mentored children's directors as they incorporated parents into their programs or changed programs entirely. I have talked to countless parents and church leaders about the importance of having parent's disciple their children and I am constantly sharing resources to accomplish this challenging task.

Sixteen years later...we have come a long way in awareness but many are still struggling to implement this biblically-based philosophy of ministry.

The purpose of this book is to help us move from awareness to a greater measure of success in keeping our kids in the faith. My goal is to help parents and children's workers discover and understand the many factors that impact how faith is developed in children and provide them with an understanding of how to teach God's Word in ways that effectively impact children, helping them begin a spiritual journey, seeking, knowing, and serving God all of their lives.

This book encapsulates the material I've presented in training and coaching for the past 16 years, even though I don't see myself as a writer. My preference would be to sit across from you at a table with a cup of coffee and engage in a back-and-forth discussion on these important topics. So, I've tried to present this material more like a letter to a dear friend than a "book." I hope you will sense this and embrace my casual writing style. It's my hope and prayer that the message God has given me will influence parents and foster parents, guardians, grandparents, children's workers, pastors, everyone who has influence on the faith of the next generation—my heart's passion since the birth of my first child. If even one child remains in the faith as a result of someone reading this book, it will be worth it; and maybe one day soon, we can meet and share that cup of coffee. Until then, I invite you join me now as I share material from my workshops and more of my journey to become a more effective leader of children and parents.

Resources

Barna, George. *Transforming Children into Spiritual Champions*. Regal Books, 2003.

Freudenburg, Ben. *Family Friendly Church*. Group Publishing, 1998.

Holmen, Mark. *Faith Begins at Home*. Regal Books, 2005.

Holmen, Mark. *Building Faith at Home*. Regal Books, 2007.

Holmen, Mark. *Church + Home*. Regal Books, 2010.

McDowell, Josh. *The Last Christian Generation*. Green Key Books, 2006.

Rainer, Thom S. *The Bridger Generation*. Broadman & Holman Publishers, 2006.

TIME FOR A CHANGE?

The Best Children's Programs Ever

For many years the church has given parents a clear message: "Bring your children to our church where our programs will teach the Bible and provide your children with everything needed for their spiritual development." This message has been reinforced with a sincere and determined effort to provide children with dedicated teachers and great programs such as Sunday School, Children's Church, Awana, Vacation Bible School, music camps, sports camps, and more. Even back when I was a child in the '50s and '60s, the Sunday School and mid-week program were considered a vital part of spiritual development for all the children coming to church.

The majority of Christian parents want their children to know and follow Jesus, and they are often following the example of their own parents by taking their children to church for spiritual education. Outside of the church, we are accustomed to finding experts to teach our children in many areas—school, sports, music, dance, and more. So parents who truly know Jesus and want their children to know Him have been diligent in finding churches that offer the best possible programming for their children and the needs of their family. With encouragement from the church, it has been easy for us to accept the view that spiritual training of our children is one more area where maximum results can be achieved by leaving the training to the experts.

Indeed, we looked like experts as the Sunday School model of yesterday became increasingly professional and became known as Children's Ministries. Our programs have become very sophisticated, housed in attractive state of the art facilities with curricula that focus on different learning styles, being reinforced with the latest learning techniques gleaned from public education research. Churches are now staffed with well-trained children's directors or children's pastors with advanced degrees from Christian universities and seminaries.

In addition, for twenty-five years we have had children's ministries conferences all around the country providing lay leaders with excellent training in all aspects of children's ministries. There are abundant resources for teaching children and for training children's volunteers, far more plentiful than what was available in decades past. The end result has been a highly professional, highly sophisticated drop-off program within the church that, while very similar to programs offered in other areas of our culture, has failed to produce the results we expected.

Before we go any further, I want to make it clear that the existing model, the church-driven program model, is the result of the best intentions on both the part of the church and parents. As a children's director, my greatest desire was teaching and spiritually developing the children entrusted to my children's ministry. I wanted to do everything with the highest possible quality so children would want to come to church, learn about Jesus, and become stable, lifelong followers of Him. I know the dedicated team that worked with me had the same desire. Many volunteers in children's ministries have sacrificially taught for many years with the same goals.

Unfortunately, it is now clear that in spite of all the ministry advances mentioned above, there is an overwhelming amount of research that indicates we have been ineffective in transferring our faith to the next generation. This is the reality that has driven leaders such as me to take a hard look at the church-driven program model and call it fundamentally flawed. This model has not generated the results we expected and desired in the lives of the children who have grown up in the church!

Dr. Michael Sciarra, senior pastor of Grace Church of Orange, and former professor at Talbot Seminary concludes,

The Church today must face a sobering fact: The way it has operated has not worked as well as it has hoped. It has worked under the assumption that if you strengthen the parts of the family you will strengthen the whole family. This is foundational, but not enough. This reflects an incomplete understanding of Christian formation and education. (Sciarra, 2011, p. 69)

How Did We Get Here?

It is helpful at this point to take a look at the origins of the Sunday School movement. What was its purpose in the beginning? In the late 18th century, Robert Raikes saw the need for a school for street children in the slums of England. These children were illiterate and they worked six days a week, often for up to twelve hours per day, because their families were so poor. Sunday was their only day off, so Raikes began Sunday School in the mid-1780s to provide these children with a basic education in reading and writing. The Bible was the textbook. These schools were not associated with churches at first, but in the 19th century, Sunday School became an evangelistic outreach of the church with the intention of preparing children for conversion.

By the mid-1800s, the Sunday School concept spread quickly throughout Europe and America. Following the American Civil War, there was another shift. Sunday School became less a tool of evangelism and more a vehicle for teaching and nourishing the people in the church. For the past 100-150 years, the Sunday School (and now children's church) has been the only source of Bible and spiritual teaching for the majority of our children.

Even back in the 19th century, leaders of the church warned parents against depending solely on the church for the spiritual education of their children. Notice what Charles Spurgeon (1834–1892) said in his book *Spiritual Parenting*:

Nowadays, since the world has in it so few Christian mothers and grandmothers, the church has thought it wise to supplement home instruction by teaching held under her fostering wing. The church takes under her maternal care those children who have no such parents. I regard this as a very blessed institution. I am thankful for the many brothers and sisters who give their Sunday to teaching other people's children who somehow grow to be very much their own. They endeavor to perform the duties of fathers and mothers, for God's sake, to those children who are neglected by their own parents. In this, they do well.

Let no Christian parents fall into the delusion that the Sunday School is intended to ease them of their personal duties. The first and most natural condition of things is for Christian parents to train up their own children in the nurture and admonition of the Lord. Let holy grandmothers and gracious mothers with their husbands, see to it that their own boys and girls are well taught in the Word of the Lord." (pp. 59-60)

Recent generations have primarily understood Sunday School to be a teaching arm of the church and not an evangelistic program. Charles Spurgeon was warning Christian parents when Sunday School was developing that it was not meant to take their place in their role of training and nurturing their own children. In spite of excellent warnings like these, the church-driven program model has remained to the present day the dominant way to help children grow spiritually.

It's Time to Face the Facts

Research completed in the last 10-15 years has shown that somewhere between 68% to 94% of our church-grown children are not remaining in the church after leaving high school, and less than half (33%) of the young adults who leave return to church after college. Thom S. Rainer, founder & CEO of Church Answers and former president of LifeWay Christian Resources, wrote *The Bridger Generation* in 2007. This was the first research I looked at as a way to partially evaluate the effectiveness of the church and its current model of reaching its children for Christ. In this research, Rainer defines Bridgers as children born from 1977–1994. Now, we more commonly refer to them as "Millennials"—children who were born between 1982 and 2000. What the research revealed to me was that losing church-grown children to our faith is not a new phenomenon. We have been losing a large percentage of every generation, but either we did not realize what was happening, or we just weren't addressing it in the church. His findings include these:

Estimated Proportion of Each Generation Reached for Christ
(That is, those who are trusting in Christ alone for their salvation)

GENERATION	PERCENTAGE REACHED FOR CHRIST
Builders	65%
Boomers	35%
Busters	15%
Bridgers	4% *

*based on current trends (Rainer, *The Bridger Generation*, Chart 25, p. 169; reprinted and used by permission).

Just look at the loss of people to the faith from the Builders to the Boomers—my generation. The transfer of faith has not been working for a long time, and that is evidenced by the fact that the church has been in decline in America for quite some time. Research is not the only indicator of this reality; it has been a tangible and observable phenomenon in our culture for many years. If we could at least retain the children who grew up in our churches, the church in America would at least remain stable instead of continuing to decline.

In George Barna's research on Christian parents, he says,

> Our national surveys have shown that while more than 4 out of 5 parents (85%) believe they have the primary responsibility for the moral and spiritual development of their children, more than two out of three of them abdicate that responsibility to their church… We discovered in a typical week fewer than 10 percent of parents who regularly attend church with their kids, read the Bible together, pray together (other than meals) or participate in

an act of service as a family unit. (*Transforming Children Into Spiritual Champions,* pp. 77-78)

When this research and others like it first came out, I was reluctant to believe that my church would reflect these findings. So I did a few tests on my own to see if parents were connecting, even on a very basic level, with our teaching in Sunday School via the take-home paper we sent with their children.

At that time, I had a teacher who worked at Starbucks. Cindy and Kathy were teaching a Kindergarten class with 12 children representing 12 families. We put a discrete note in the take-home paper that said, "If you read this, call Cindy and she will get you a $5.00 Starbuck gift card." Out of 12 families, one mom called and happily took the card. Just to give it a fair chance, we did this the next two Sundays. The same mom called and ended up with three free coffee drinks. It became clear to our team that our parents were not connecting with our take-home material at the most basic level: opening the paper and reading it.

An additional motivation to change our current model is an obstacle that is well known to anyone who has served as a children's pastor or children's director in a church with high program demands. By far, the biggest challenge in children's ministries is finding enough people to teach the children in our programs.

Early in my ministry, I identified three types of teachers in our children's programs. The first group of volunteers naturally love children and have a passion to teach them God's Word. They spend a lot of time and effort in their preparations, and they are always praying and thinking about each child and how they can impact children in their spiritual development during the time they are teaching them. This group will keep teaching children as long as they have an opportunity to do so.

The second group is made up of parents who want a quality program for their children and are willing to teach while their children are in the program. While these people are a great asset, we lose them when their children move on to youth group.

The third group is made up of people who are reluctant, but willing, mostly because they have the spiritual gift of serving and will do any job that helps the church in a particular area of need. These are wonderful people but they don't necessarily *want* to work with children. After their commitment is up, many of them admit, "I just don't work well with children," so we have to fill their spot with someone else. At that point, if we still don't have enough teachers, we resort to *requiring* parents to teach, which often includes those who definitely would not choose this role. Many of these parents seem desperate for a break from their children and as a result resist being in the classroom.

Typically, we never have enough of the first group—people who are really passionate about teaching children God's Word, see it as a calling in their lives, and want to build significant relationships with the children they teach. Relationships in the church, just like in the home, are the most important factor for influencing a child spiritually. It is difficult to build relationships with the children you teach when you only see them once a week. When you add the fact that the majority of churches use a once-a-month rotational teaching schedule, and families are typically sporadic in attendance, building relationships is challenging at best. The days of teachers committing to teach for nine months or several years is pretty much over, so unless you go to a small church where relationships are being developed outside of church, the chance for relationship-building between teacher and student is small.

We live in very hectic and busy times with people getting busier all the time, so in recent years a lack of time for lesson preparation has also become a big issue in children's ministries programming. While people used to spend a minimum of an hour a week to prepare their lesson, the only way to now find people to work with children is to have a curriculum that is almost free of preparation. The curriculum companies cater to this need in order to sell their products. Many use teaching videos so the teacher's only role is leading a small group discussion at the end of the video. A committed teacher who has built relationships, is consistently present each week, and is well-prepared can still have success with this type of curriculum. However, it has been my experience and observation that the only group of people who have remained committed to thorough preparation are those in the first group mentioned above.

Are you getting the picture of who is the most frequent teacher of our children? In two of the three examples, we are entrusting the spiritual development of the children God has given our churches to people who are not passionate about the opportunity, or in many cases, don't want to teach or have very little time to teach and to prepare to do so. What is the result of these realities? Larry Fowler said it well in his book, *Raising a Modern Day Joseph*, "Today we suffer from declining commitment, unbiblical worldviews and declining Bible knowledge." (2009, pp. 26-31)

So Where Do We Go From Here?

Because the church has become the primary source for teaching and spiritually developing children, and because we now recognize that this model is not working, we have no choice but to reevaluate our existing ministry model. In retrospect, it is now clear that we overlooked critical elements in God's plan for passing faith from one generation to the next when we adopted the Sunday School model. We missed the fact that the transfer of faith and spiritual development is not in the same category as learning a skill, such as sports, music, or dance, and we overlooked the critical role of parents in the process of faith development.

The role of the parents is clearly outlined in God's original design for the family, but we have given it no significant place in our current model. Instead of taking on the responsibility for teaching the children, the church should have been focusing on strengthening the home, discipling parents, training parents, and sharing resources that help parents to be able to effectively pass their faith to their own children. At the same time, we should retain a focus on those children in our families who do not have faith.

As a church's children's director, I had evaluated every program we had while challenging my team to make sure that each year's programs would be better the next year. Ironically, the mission statement in my ministry in Colorado began with, "We are partnering with parents to...," but we were not necessarily impacting the home, and we seemed powerless to make sure parents were using the materials we sent home.

As I look back, I realize we were usually asking the wrong questions or not enough questions. Instead of only asking if our teaching at the church was connecting with the home, we should have also asked the following set of questions:

- As a result of our program, do parents understand *their role* in the spiritual development of their children?
- What are we doing to foster spiritual development in the home?
- What level of partnership do we have with parents/grandparents/guardians?
- How can we strengthen our homes so we are passing faith to our children?
- What things actually contribute to the spiritual maturity of our children?

The home is primary and the main goal of the church should be to partner with parents to help them impact their own children for eternity. Very practically, consider for a moment the influence of the time factor in the life of a child. The church has an average of 40–60 hours per year to teach children, depending on how many programs are available and how many weeks a family comes to church. Parents, on the other hand, have a few thousand hours per year with their children. This means children may have nearly 50 to 100 hours per week under the potential influence of parents (depending on their age), while the church, at best, has only 1-2 hours a week with their children. In addition, the church is an environment where a child has only a one in three chance of having a teacher who is passionate about children and committed to teaching and relationship building.

It is obvious that parents have more time with their children and will naturally have the most influence in their lives. Every research study conducted on this subject draws the same conclusion; parents are the most influential people in the lives of their children. This should not be a surprise because it is God's design. So, it should be the mission of the church to build up strong homes where children can be nurtured spiritually. Then the church will be able to focus more attention and time on children who do not have a Christian influence in their homes. Such a church would, as a strategy, be wise to have *spiritual adoptions* so these children have *spiritual parents*. It is critical that we shift our thinking and acknowledge parents are the key to the spiritual development of children.

The best efforts of the church cannot replace the impact of parents in passing faith to their children.

The relevancy of God and the Bible in our children's lives is a key factor in determining whether our young adults remain in the faith they encountered as children. Who can make the Gospel most relevant in a child's life, the teacher at church or the parent at home? This issue became very clear to me as I listened to a speaker several years ago at a conference I attended. He was working with several first-year college students, many of whom had been in church all their lives. What he heard them saying was, "Going to church and Sunday School is what I did when I was a kid. I don't need it now. It is no longer relevant in my life."

As teachers, we hopefully apply our weekly lessons to daily life with relevancy and personal insight, but what makes it stick after the children leave our classroom? How do the Bible and the message of the Gospel remain relevant from childhood all the way to adulthood? Even the best and most dedicated Sunday School teachers cannot follow their students around all week to make the Gospel relevant to their day-to-day lives. Only parents can do that! So, when parents don't even know what is being taught from week to week, our teaching is not going to impact the life and direction of the children we teach in these formative years. Someone must connect the lessons being taught at church to the child's daily life issues, so God's Word will become a truly integrated part of their lives.

Certainly, God can and does help our children remember things that have been taught at church and home, and He will accomplish His purposes in their lives. But God created parents to be participants in the faith of their children. One important reason is because it also develops the parent's faith. Most teachers know that when they spend time in God's Word and prepare to teach it to others, they are often the ones who grow the most. My lessons may or may not impact my learners, but they certainly impact me and my understanding and knowledge of God. Just think about how much spiritual growth we are taking away from parents by taking from them their responsibility to teach their own children.

If parents do not have an intentional plan to develop their children spiritually and are not connecting with the teaching done at church, our church-grown children are at risk of abandoning the faith journey they began as children. Add to this the fact that many children are swept away by compelling science presentations that, as taught in middle and high school, do NOT include God. The home needs to be a safe place to discuss all important issues and develop a strong understanding of the reasonableness of their faith.

Children need to know what purpose spirituality has in their lives, and we need to cultivate in them a desire to know the God who created them for a relationship with Him for a lifetime. This kind of spiritual relevancy happens over the course of the 18 years we have our children under our roof, starting from the time they are toddlers to their leaving home as young adults. Except in very rare instances, it is impossible for teachers at church to fulfill this role in the lives of their students, and yet we have depended on this Sunday School model as the key spiritual development strategy in the lives of our children.

The Shift Back to God's Original Model

Recognizing that our children will be with their parents for up to 18 years, we must focus on teaching and equipping parents, grandparents, and guardians to use the God-given influence they have in the lives of their children. We must be committed to do what God has asked us to do in His Word and leave the results to Him. For very practical reasons God gave this responsibility to parents, not the church. Based on research, there is no question who is most influential in a child's life. The focus of the church needs to be discipling parents so they can model their faith and have spiritual discussions at home that give solid reasons for their faith.

Faith that is not integrated into the daily life of a child won't be relevant when they get older. Children need to be reminded in specific ways our teaching applies to life situations. The teacher needs to be with them on a daily basis helping to make the Christian life applicable to the challenges they experience. A teacher on Sunday cannot be with each child during the week to continue talking about Sunday's lesson and show them how God's principles should apply to their experiences. Children need to be guided to an understanding of the Gospel and discipled in their faith. For the church, this means we start with helping parents connect the instruction their children are receiving at church to home and *teach parents* how to teach their children at home to nurture them spiritually. If we are to stop young adults from saying, "Church is what I did when I was a kid, but I don't need it now," we *must* be committed to this shift in our ministry thinking.

The Voices of Other Leaders Confirm These Conclusions

Dr. Ben Freudenberg, a former Christian education and youth pastor, has been a pioneer in what has now become known as "the church/home movement." In his book, *The Family Friendly Church*, he says,

> Under the old paradigm (the only one most of us have ever known), the rules and regulations that governed Christian education were based on a church-centered, home-support faith-development model. That model dictated that the home do all it could to provide support and resources for the church to teach the faith. The home helped the church be the best it could be. As a result, the church said, "Come to us for learning about and growing in the faith. We want a strong church."

Under the new paradigm, the rules and regulations that govern Christian education are based on a home-centered, church-supported faith-development model. The new model dictates that the church do all it can to provide support and training for parents in the development of their kids' faith in their homes. The church exists to partner with homes to be the best they can be. The result is this: The church says, "Come to us and learn how to teach the faith in your home. We'll be a resource of ideas, training, and programs, and we'll provide you everything you need to teach the faith at home." Strong homes make strong churches. (1998, p. 98)

Timothy Paul Jones says this:

What these well-intended ministry models spawned in many congregations was a church culture mirroring the generational gap of the broader culture. Rather than healing ruptured connections between the generations, significant numbers of churches unintentionally welcomed, and perhaps even widened, the chasm between children and parents. (2009, p. 34)

And as Dave Sawler declares: "We see the importance of each generation. A church without the wisdom of the aged and the passion of the youth is dysfunctional. A church without mothers and fathers cannot become mature. A church without the young is visionless and lacks passion." (2008, p. 54)

The evidence is overwhelming; the best efforts of the church cannot replace the impact of parents in passing faith to their children. It is clear that those of us in children's ministry need to see our job as helping parents implement an intentional plan for developing their children spiritually. The church must shift to making its primary focus developing strong homes, equipping and training parents to take back their responsibility for the spiritual development of the children in their homes. Join me now as we take a look back in time, back in Scripture, to find and examine God's plan for families and God's plan for passing faith to the next generation.

Resources

Allen, Holly Catterton & Ross, Christine Lawton. *Intergenerational Christian Formation, Bringing the Whole Church Together in Ministry and Worship.* IVP Academic, 2012.

Fowler, Larry. *Raising a Modern Day Joseph.* David C. Cook, 2009.

Freudenburg, Ben & Lawrence, Rick. *The Family Friendly Church.* Group Publishing, Inc., 1998.

Jones, Timothy Paul. *Perspectives on Family Ministry—3 Views.* B&H Publishing Group, 2009.

Rainer, Thom S. *The Bridger Generation,* Broadman & Holman, 2006.

Rienow, Rob. *Limited Church: Unlimited Kingdom, Uniting Church and Family in the Great Commission.* Randall House, 2013.

Sawler, Dave. *Goodbye Generation.* Ponder Publishing, 2008.

Sciarra, Dr. Michael. *Connecting Generations, Loving God and Making Disciples Through Multiple Generations.* Thesis for Talbot Seminary, 2011.

Spurgeon, Charles. *Spiritual Parenting,* Updated Version. Whitaker House. 1995, 2003.

Notes from Julie on current research:

In the years since I started Reconnect Ministry, there has been ongoing discussion as to whether things are as bad as indicated by the original research of George Barna and others. It seems that not a week goes by without us hearing reports of popular Christian figures leaving the faith and I don't know of anyone in ministry who does not have personal stories of young people close to them who have walked away from their faith. So are things better, or have they gotten worse? Aside from our personal experiences and gut instinct, this a difficult question to answer because "genuine faith" is difficult to measure scientifically and accurately. Church involvement is one indicator that has been commonly used to determine ongoing commitment to one's faith, but even here, there are varied definitions of church involvement. This makes it difficult to find a truly accurate unit of measure for gauging retention rates—let alone genuine ongoing commitment to faith.

As I have continued to look for, and review, research on the effectiveness of the church, I've discovered that the LifeWay Research study, and Barna's research in 2007, are still considered to be some of the best and most thorough research projects to date. It seems that one thing almost all experts agree on is Christianity, the church, and the home are still under attack, and continue to face serious challenges to avoiding continuing decline. For the latest research projects and findings by George Barna, follow these links, https://www.barna.com/research/changing-state-of-the-church/ and https://www.arizonachristian.edu/culturalresearchcenter/research/.

For an in-depth discussion of the impact of research on ministry models (as well as the need to equip parents to be disciples), I recommend *Family Ministry Field Guide* by Timothy Paul Jones. After reviewing and dissecting contemporary research he concludes; "The goal is to call people to Jesus. And so the crucial question is not, 'How many participants have we retained?' but 'Who has glimpsed the truth of Jesus and the gospel in what we are doing?' Retention rates aren't the launching pad or the end point of God's plan, Jesus is (Rev 22:13)" (2011, p. 52). Another excellent book that is the product of a great deal of current research is *Faith@Home Revealed: What's Really Happening Outside of Church* by Mark Holmen & Brian Siewert.

Resources for contemporary research mentioned above:

Barna, George. Latest research projects and findings, https://www.barna.com/research/changing-state-of-the-church/ and https://www.arizonachristian.edu/culturalresearchcenter/research/.

Jones, Timothy Paul. *Family Ministry Field Guide,* Wesleyan Publishing House, 2011.

Holmen, Mark, & Siewart, Brian. *Faith@Home Revealed: What's Really Happening Outside of Church*, Lulu Publishing, 2020.

GOD'S BLUEPRINT AND GOD'S STRATEGY
For passing faith from one generation to the next

God's Blueprint

Have you ever thought about how amazing it is that God's story has passed through so many generations, and it is still living and active today? Think about all the generations who have lived and died since the time of God's Covenant to Abraham and David. His plan for salvation was revealed for the whole world through Jesus' life, death, and resurrection, and those events were over two thousand years ago. Then, when we read about the apostolic church and the challenges of the church throughout the Middle Ages, the enlightenment period, the Reformation, modernity, and now in our post-modern world, only the hand of God could have kept His message going. I find this remarkable and it speaks to me about the truth of God and His message of salvation to mankind.

What *was* God's plan? How did He intend for faith to pass from one generation to the next? Psalm 78:1-7 clearly states God's plan—His blueprint for passing faith to the next generation.

> My people, hear my teaching;
> Listen to the words of my mouth.
> I will open my mouth with a parable,
> I will utter hidden things, things from of old—
> things we have heard and known,
> things our ancestors have told us.

We will not hide them from their descendants;
we will tell the next generation
the praiseworthy deeds of the LORD,
his power, and the wonders he has done.
He decreed statutes for Jacob
and established the law in Israel,
which *he commanded our ancestors*
to teach their children,
so the next generation would know them,
even the children yet to be born,
and they in turn would tell their children.
Then they would put their trust in God
and would not forget his deeds
but would keep his commands (NIV, emphasis mine).

Tell of His Praiseworthy Deeds

The message of Psalm 78 is very clear. The passage tells us not to hide God's praiseworthy deeds. We are to tell the children the stories our fathers told us and then teach them God's commandments. Each generation is responsible to tell the next about their great God: "He commanded our ancestors to teach their children, so the next generation would know them, even the children yet to be born, and they in turn would tell their children" (Psalm 78:5b-6, NIV).

The miracles God performed for the children of Israel as he delivered them from slavery through Moses leadership were astounding. The plagues in Egypt, the parting of the Red Sea, the provision of water and food while wandering in the desert waiting for the Promised Land, and finally, the entry into the Promised Land—all of this is absolutely amazing.

But look at Deuteronomy 11:2. "Remember today that your children were not the ones who saw and experienced the discipline of the LORD your God: his majesty, his mighty hand, his outstretched arm" (NIV). This verse refers specifically to the Exodus from Egypt orchestrated by God to save His people from slavery. There were at most only three generations who experienced firsthand this amazing work of God: the grandparents, parents, and their children. The next generation had to rely on the excitement their parents had experienced and the stories of those days, and so it was with every generation that followed. The excitement of each generation is dependent on the excitement and commitment of the prior generation. I am grateful we have the Bible to remind us of the greatness of God's love and care for His people, but we must continue to share God's story with the same excitement of the generation who experienced it firsthand, if the story is to have an impact on the lives of future generations.

How is this possible? How can we have the same excitement as the people who actually experienced God's amazing miracles firsthand? Obviously, it's impossible to go back and be there, but a good storyteller is one who is able to help his audience get closer to the experience of the story. In order for us to be good storytellers, we need to first spend time meditating on the Bible stories, understand them, engage with them, and allow ourselves to really feel them. We need to put ourselves in their shoes so we can sense their emotions, fear, pain, and joy. Our end goal is engaging our children in the story as if we are just one more generation in the line of those who were actually there in person!

But there is more. Sometimes we forget that sharing God's "praiseworthy deeds" should not be limited to sharing God's story from the Bible. We all have had powerful firsthand encounters with God, experiences of His faithfulness, love, and power that we can share with our children. These are also part of our family heritage and should be shared with our children. The Kurz family has heard many times the story of my father-in-law's hayloft conversion. He was reading his Bible to disprove the faith of his young wife, but God's word brought him to his knees and led him into ministry and a life of experiencing God's faithfulness in good times and bad times. I am also thinking of my Swedish heritage and the many stories of God's faithfulness that were passed down to me from previous generations. I need to make sure my children hear these stories and know these were real people I knew firsthand. Stories like these, of God's faithfulness to you and your family members, can have a powerful impact on your children.

Share His Commandments, Which Reveal His Character

Not only does Psalm 78 tell us to share God's "praiseworthy deeds," but it also says we should teach our children God's commandments. We remember that the commandments were given to Moses on Mount Sinai after the Israelites were rescued by God from Egypt. The people needed to get to know the God who rescued them from slavery in Egypt. The commandments were the only written revelation of God the people had up to that point. God wanted His people to get to know Him through keeping His commandments. The commandments would not only instruct them but would bring them blessing and reflect God's character to the world around them. At that time in biblical history, a desire to keep the commandments was a desire to know God and experience everything good that God had for them in their lives.

There was purpose in these commandments to the children of Israel at the time of the Exodus and for today. Understanding what's behind God's commandments helps children (and us for that matter) know God. From the beginning, God wanted to have a relationship with us, and the first way to get to know God is to gain an understanding and appreciation for His commandments, which reveal His character and His holiness. We have an opportunity to help our children understand who God is and embrace His values through teaching them His commandments. Romans 8:1-4 makes this clear:

> There is therefore now no condemnation for those who are in Christ Jesus. For the law of the Spirit of life has set you free in Christ Jesus from the law of sin and death. For God has done what the law, weakened by the flesh, could not do. By sending his own Son in the likeness of sinful flesh and for sin, he condemned sin in the flesh, in order that the righteous requirement of the law might be fulfilled in us, who walk not according to the flesh but according to the Spirit (ESV).

Psalm 119 is devoted to the meditations of the psalmist in delighting in God's law. Psalm 119:47-48 states, "I delight in your commands because I love them. I reach out for your commands, which I love, that I may meditate on your decrees" (NIV). The commandments were meant for good. They were given because, when followed, life would go well for the Israelites. God would bless them. When I teach children, I remind them that our Creator knows what is best for us because He created us. Just as the inventor knows how his invention works the best and what will keep it working right, God's laws are not meant to harm us or keep us from having fun, but to give us success in all we do.

Of course, in the Old Testament the Mosaic Covenant was still in place. When the Israelites obeyed, God blessed; when they disobeyed, there was punishment. It is important for our children to recognize and acknowledge that none of us can live up to God's holiness. That is why we have 1000 years of Israel's history recorded for us in the historical books of the Old Testament. Through the sin cycle of the Old Testament, God wanted the people not to only see His perfect holiness, but also His compassion and perfect love. God wanted them to see He kept His promises, blessings, and punishment, but He also would forgive them if they turned their hearts back to Him. The best part is that God promised a Messiah would come to be our Savior, to save us from the sin that keeps us from our Holy Creator and Father!

All Peoples on Earth Will Be Blessed Through You

Another reason God gave His children commandments to be followed was to set them apart from all the nations. Remember, God called Abraham and said, "I will make you into a great nation, and I will bless you; I will make your name great, and you will be a blessing. I will bless those who bless you, and whoever curses you I will curse; and all peoples on earth will be blessed through you" (Genesis 12:2-3, NIV). God was working on His bigger plan to bless the nations. He wanted His people to live differently so Yahweh could be seen by everyone in the world as the one and only true God, and that He kept His word whether it resulted in good for the people or punishment for their sin. When God exiled His people to Babylon, He told them through the prophet Ezekiel, "I will show the holiness of my great name, which has been profaned among the nations, the name you have profaned among them. Then the nations will know that I am the LORD, declares the Sovereign LORD, when I am proved holy through you before their eyes" (Ezekiel 36:23, NIV).

God's plan for parents to pass faith to their children doesn't change in the New Testament, but I now see it through a different lens. Jesus left us with a mandate to, "Therefore go and make disciples of all nations, baptizing them in the name of the Father and of the Son and of the Holy Spirit, and teaching them to obey everything I have commanded you" (Matthew 28:19-20a, NIV). Before He ascended to Heaven Jesus said in Acts 1:8, "But you will receive power when the Holy Spirit comes on you; and you will be my witnesses in Jerusalem, and in all Judea and Samaria, and to the ends of the earth" (NIV).

What does this have to do with passing faith to my children? Everything! Our children represent Jerusalem, our home territory, the first priority in our world. We have an unprecedented opportunity to lead and disciple our own children to find a meaningful relationship with their Creator and Father so we can all grow together in Christ. Somehow, we have forgotten that our children should be our *first disciples* who can then be sent out to lead others to Christ.

A few years before I launched out into my ministry, I led a small group of young mothers while I was still the children's director at Bethany EFC. I will never forget a discussion we had about sharing Christ with people in our circles of influence. The discussion led to asking the women if they had ever led someone to Christ. I knew all the moms had led at least one of their children to Jesus, but no one mentioned their children as being one of the people they had brought to Christ. So I asked them if they had led any of their children to Jesus and the answer given was, "Yes!" We talked about why we didn't think of our children first. It was such an eye opener to me and I began noticing how our own children were never mentioned in the church's teaching in relationship to discipleship. Why don't we in the church emphasize that our own children are to be our first and primary disciples?

Rob Rienow, founder of Visionary Families, was the first person I heard talk about parents as disciplers of their own children. In his book *Visionary Parenting* he says this:

> What is the purpose for the family? God created the family to be a discipleship center! He created your family to be a spiritual transformation center. It is the primary environment where faith and character are formed and shaped.... You are together so that you might help each other discover Christ together, grow in Him together, and together make a difference in the world for Him.... Many families today are recreation centers, activity centers, wealth-building centers, television centers, and anger centers. What kind of "center" has your family been?
>
> There is a lot of emphasis in the church today on the importance of discipleship within small groups. Pastors are crying out, "Spiritual growth happens in the context of relationships!" We have to live in authentic community with one another! God believes in discipleship small groups too. He just has another name for them. He calls them "families".... The family is the most powerful discipleship "small group"...where you will find "authentic community" every minute of every day. Are you looking for authenticity? Are you looking for people to be "real"? Just go spend some time in your house; you will find authentic community there...for better or for worse. (p. 9)

We know that God is making sure His Church remains because if it were entirely our responsibility for passing God's story to the generations, the Gospel would surely have failed. As fickle as we are, *God still has a role for us to play—it is an opportunity to participate in the faith of the next generation.* When too many families lose their excitement for God's story and stop telling it, the next generation will be without the story. Judges 2:10 sadly reports about such a generation: "After that whole generation had been gathered to their ancestors, another generation grew up who knew neither the LORD nor what he had done for Israel." God's blueprint for passing faith to their children is His plan to have parents share His story and the impact of His story on their own lives with their children. We are a part of His plan, a part of the framework of his redemption of mankind. It is *His blueprint* for passing faith to the next generation!

God's Strategy

As parents, we are responsible for four areas of our children's lives: *physical care, emotional health, mental development,* and *spiritual development.* To give some brief definitions to these terms, I would define *emotional health* as simply encouraging children to blossom into the person God created them to be on a foundation of discipline. *Mental development* is making sure they have the education or skills to successfully launch them into adulthood with a means of employment to provide for their families. This does not necessarily mean a college degree. *Spiritual development* for Christians is giving our children the opportunity to observe and understand God's story along with His loving and relentless pursuit of relationship with us through our Savior Jesus Christ, all with the hope and desire that our children will want to follow Jesus, too. When we truly know God's story of love and redemption and understand that our eventual home will be an eternal home in a restored world (*Wow!* Who could not want that?), of course we want our children to have the gift of salvation and be with us in this glorious place.

As a parent of adult children, I don't ever remember a sermon based on how or what I should have done to pass faith on to my children. Until recently, this has been a topic that has been virtually left out of our teaching and preaching in the church. Preaching that *has* been done in recent years on this subject is a result of the movement from the past decade to connect home and church for the faith of the next generation.

I remember crying out to God to help me really understand how our children were intended to come to faith so I could communicate clearly the passion God had given me for the faith of the next generation. God directed me back to Deuteronomy 6. As I read, prayed, and meditated on this passage for a long time, I began to understand that God has given us a strategy for passing our faith on to our children. The strategy is found in several places, but Deuteronomy 6:4-9 is the most familiar:

> Hear, O Israel: The LORD our God, The LORD is one. Love the LORD your God with all your heart and with all your soul and with all your strength. These commandments that I give you today are to be upon *your* hearts. *Impress* them on your children. *Talk* about them when you *sit at home* and when you *walk along the road,* when you *lie down* and when you *get up.* Tie them as symbols on your hands and bind them on your foreheads. Write them on the doorframes of your houses and on your gates (NIV, emphasis mine).

This passage teaches us that in passing our faith on to our children there are basically only two things we have to do: Love the LORD your God with all your heart and talk about God's Word in your home.

Love the Lord Your God With All Your Heart

This involves, teaching your children God's story and impressing upon them the reality of God *in your life.* Our *first* responsibility to impart faith to our children and grandchildren is to impress them with the reality of *our faith*! Our first priority must be *our own journey and our own walk with God,* making sure we are modeling faith and talking about Him. Our children need to hear God's story and the stories that led us to understand His story. As our children get older, they need to hear what keeps us on our journey to know Him through all the ups and downs of our lives. They need to observe our commitment to God in the choices we make and fully realize their parents are seeking to know and love God. They need authenticity when we are struggling as we share with them how God answers us in challenging times. They should be able to trace God's hand in our lives as we live our lives before them.

When we have an authentic journey with God, modeling our faith just happens naturally. Teaching your children what God is teaching you might take some effort, but it basically involves teaching your children what you know about God's story, the story you have come to understand in your life. Is that a relief to you, or does it cause you to sense a void in your relationship with God? If you don't know very much yet, you can learn together with your children.

As you know, children have amazing faith when they are very young and still in the stage of concrete thinking. Around the ages of 10–12 and above, they begin to think abstractly and they need to see faith in action. One of the best ways to move our kids from the childish faith of a concrete thinker to that of a more mature adult faith is to allow them to join us on our journey to know God. They need to understand how it works to have a relationship with a God whom we can't see when we talk to Him and a God we cannot audibly hear. They need to hear our questions, our doubts, our discouragements, and then hear the answers we have received and see the victories we experience. This is key to helping them know how to walk with God and be securely launched into their own journey and experience with God. In essence, when growing up in our homes seeing faith modeled and communicated, our children are borrowing our faith until theirs becomes fully developed.

God gave me the opportunity to experience this in my own life as I raised my three children. I began motherhood with the belief that my faith had to be bulletproof, showing no signs of weakness or doubt, if I was going to lead my children to God. I thought my best efforts and my perfect performance of faith would have an impact on my children and then be reflected in their faith. When Rachel, my youngest child, was in early elementary school we experienced a major financial reversal in our family. My faith was shattered, and there was nothing I could do to hold it together. I realize now that my faith had to spiral down to ground zero for God to build me back up so I could represent Him accurately. During this time, I decided to read the Bible from cover to cover to try to discover what involvement God really has in our day-to-day lives. I needed to know for myself, firsthand. I was reading like a detective, looking for clues of

God's personal involvement in our lives on a daily basis, and asking myself "What can I really expect from God?" What I learned from this journey into God's Word is another story, but I soon realized that my youngest daughter had joined me on much of this journey. My other two children were older and busy with high school activities, but Rachel was with me a lot, and I was regularly sharing what I was learning. She had joined me on my faith journey without my really realizing it. I see it so clearly now, that this is how God intends for us to pass faith to our children—by modeling authentic, honest, real faith, and then seeing God at work in our lives. This experience changed my faith and relationship with God in a significant way and gave me understanding of how God intended for faith to be passed from one generation to the next.

Talk About God's Word in Your Home

In verse 7 of Deuteronomy 6, God says we are to teach our children diligently, and He mentions four times of the day that we all have in our family life. When we: "get up" (morning), "sit down" (mealtimes), "walk along the road" (drive time), and "lie down" (nighttime). We can be intentional about these four times every day! We don't have to add anything to our schedule, unless motivated to do so, but these four times can be "tweaked" each day to add spiritual significance in your child's life!

One of my colleagues in ministry, Mark Holmen, has written several books including *Faith Begins At Home, Take It Home, Building Faith At Home, Church + Home,* and most recently, *Faith@Home Revealed.* At a conference, Mark relayed a story that his mentor/friend told him about passing faith to his daughter. Every morning upon waking and evening before bedtime, from the time she was very young, this man blessed his daughter with a blessing from the Bible such as: "The LORD bless you and keep you; the LORD make his face shine upon you and be gracious to you; the LORD turn his face toward you and give you peace" (Numbers 6:24-26, NIV). It wasn't long before they both memorized these verses and she started blessing him when he left for business trips. Later in her life, when "mom

& dad" took their daughter to college and got her settled in, they left rather abruptly to avoid all the emotions of leaving her. When the parents got to the car they heard the voice of their daughter calling to them, "Dad, you forgot to bless me!" What a big difference such a little blessing made in the spiritual culture of that home.

Dinner time can be a great time to build relationships with each other and include God at our table. Our busy culture has made family dinner times very difficult and sporadic. I believe we need to intentionally reclaim these times to be together as a family in a setting where spiritual life lessons can be shared. As parents we need to be telling *our* stories to our children and the dinner table is a natural place to do this. There are so many resources available with great ideas on how to encourage spiritual discussions at the dinner table.

One family I know spends a little time reading one verse together at dinner and talks about what it means and how it applies to their lives right now. Another family is reading through the Bible, reading just one paragraph from *The Message* at breakfast every morning before the kids leave for school.

I have worked with Grace Community Church in Peoria, Arizona. Pastor Tim Wright is doing a great job of leading his families in "Faith5," which encourages families to do five things every day or as many as they can: Share (highs & lows), Read (verse of the week), Talk (about how the verse might relate to highs/lows), Pray (highs & lows), Bless (each person).

Don't forget to have some intentional discussions while you are driving your children around in the car. You have a captive audience unless they are texting or playing video games. Sometimes technology is a hindrance and sometimes we need to enforce "technology time outs" to create space for genuine relationship building.

God's strategy for passing faith from one generation to the next is very clear. It starts with *our journey* to seek and know God in our own life, then as our faith grows and matures we *share our journey with our children* teaching them God's story, sharing His goodness, love, and greatness with them.

Great is the LORD and worthy of praise; his greatness no one can fathom. One generation commends your works to another; they tell of your mighty acts. They speak of the glorious splendor of your majesty—and I will meditate on your wonderful works. They tell of the power of your awesome works—and I will proclaim your great deeds. They celebrate your abundant goodness and joyfully sing of your righteousness (Psalm 145:3-7, NIV).

Resources

Holmen, Mark. *Faith Begins at Home*. Regal, 2005.

Holmen, Mark. *Take It Home*. Gospel Light, 2008.

Holmen, Mark. *Building Faith at Home*. Regal Books, 2007.

Holmen, Mark. *Church + Home*. Regal, 2010.

Holmen, Mark & Siewert, Brian. *Faith@Home Revealed*. Lulu Publishing Services, 2020.

Rienow, Rob. *Limited Church: Unlimited Kingdom, Uniting Church & Family in the Great Commission*. Randall House, 2013.

Rienow, Rob. *Visionary Parenting*. Randall House, 2009.

WHOSE RESPONSIBILITY IS THIS ANYWAY?

Attention Parents! The Faith of Your Children Is All About You, but Not About You at All

This was the name of an article I wrote a couple years after I began Reconnect Ministries. It was the result of trying to think through the paradoxical role parents have in the faith of their children. I couldn't help but think about parents I had known who were strong in faith and shared their faith well with their children but had one or more who weren't following Jesus as adults. Then there were the young adults I knew who had a vibrant faith but whose parents were unengaged, half-hearted Christians in our church. These parents didn't even have a plan at home for their children's spiritual development. What's up with that?

I thought I had this clear in my mind when I began my ministry but then I started asking myself and God a number of questions:

1. What IS the realistic role of parents?

2. What is the church and God's role in the faith of our church-grown children?

3. What about the choices of our children? Obviously, parents cannot control their children's choices!

4. What is God's part in all of this?

5. Why is there so much focus on the parents, in the Bible?

I realized I didn't have as good a grasp on this as I thought I did. Finding answers to these questions has been foundational to my ministry!

My Own Journey to Know and Love God

From Deuteronomy 6, we learned that to pass our faith on to our children we have two areas of responsibility: Love the LORD your God with all your heart, and talk about God's Word in your home. To review, our responsibility and the only thing we can do to impart faith to our children and grandchildren, is to impress them with the reality of *our faith*! Our first priority must be *our own journey and our own walk with God,* making sure we are modeling faith and talking about Him. It cannot be overstated that we must have our own sincere, genuine walk with God before we will have anything of value to share with our children in this area. But there is more. While it may seem that shepherding our children to faith is all about us, our faith and our journey—there is more.

My Child's Role

What about our children? What is their part in salvation? They, like us, must choose to follow God through Jesus Christ. We cannot make that decision for them. They must do it themselves. God knows their hearts; we don't. We are all responsible individually for our response to understanding God's redemptive plan.

I have appreciated John Westerhoff's book, *Will Our Children Have Faith?,* in many aspects. Regarding faith he says,

> Faith cannot be taught by any method of instruction; we can only teach religion...we can only expand in faith, act in faith, live in faith. Faith can be inspired...but it cannot be given to one person by another. Faith is expressed, transformed, and made meaningful by persons sharing their faith. (p. 19)

As parents we can live out and inspire faith, but our children must choose to have faith in the powerful and living God. We can teach them God's story, biblical truths, apologetics, communicate His desire for relationship with them through Jesus, and live our faith out before them, but we cannot *make* them have faith. As we all know, there is mystery in the journey of each of us to know and understand God. (Because it is important as parents to understand how a child develops spiritually, I have dedicated a later chapter to this subject. It includes some very practical resources that I think will be very helpful.)

The Church's Role

What is the church's role and responsibility to parents? It is to come alongside and be their best friend—encouraging, training, equipping them, and providing resources for the journey of parenthood. Home Depot has a great motto, "You can do it—We can help." This needs to be our motto in the church. We need to know our families, build relationship with them, find out what their needs are, and start there. We need to ask how we can make parents the primary influence and teachers in everything we do at church.

Rock Harbor, a church in Costa Mesa, shares a lot of stories of their journey to come alongside their parents. As a result of being in workshops lead by their ministry leaders, I learned that they have made many changes in their traditional way of doing things, including their traditional Baby Dedication. Instead of lining up all the parents in front of the church, they ask the parents to invite people who are going to influence their children spiritually to come to a special ceremony at their home. So those people are the only ones who attend the baby dedication, along with appropriate pastors and leaders from the church. Prior to the dedication ceremony, the parents attend training at church where they are taught that they as parents, will be the primary spiritual influencer in their child's life, and that the church will come alongside them but is not to be depended upon as the sole developer of their child's faith. The leaders help the parents prepare to dedicate their children with a pledge and a prayer of dedication at their special service.

The story is told of a father and his wife who had just come to know Christ and wanted to have their son dedicated to God. The father had never prayed in his life, and on the day of the dedication service he asked the pastor, "Could you at least help me pray for my son." The pastor, of course did, but did not take over and do it for him. This same father returned to the pastor several months later and said, "Thank you for helping me pray. I pray for my son every night now. I would have never done that if you hadn't helped me and shown me how I can do this for my son, and how important it is to pray for him."

Last and Best of All—God's Role

God is much more invested in the faith of our children than we have been, or ever will be. After all, He is the one who knew them and thought of them—and every person ever born. Let's take a look at what Scripture has to say.

> For you created my inmost being; you knit me together in my mother's womb... My frame was not hidden from you when I was made in the secret place. When I was woven together in the depths of the earth. Your eyes saw my unformed body; all the days ordained for me were written in your book before one of them came to be (Psalm 139:13, 15-16, NIV).

> "This is what the LORD says—he who made you, who formed you in the womb, and who will help you: do not be afraid" (Isaiah 44:2, NIV).

> God said to Israel, "You whom I have upheld since your birth, and have carried since you were born" (Isaiah 46:3b, NIV).

> God said to Jeremiah, "Before I formed you in the womb I knew you, before you were born I set you apart; I appointed you as a prophet to the nations" (Jeremiah 1:5, NIV).

> David said, "Your hands made me and formed me" (Psalm 119:73a, NIV).

I came across a great devotional in *Devotions for Sacred Parenting*, by Gary Thomas, that goes along with these verses. He challenges parents to think about the following questions when we get fearful about our children's faith or lack of it.

- Who cares more about our children—us or God?
- Who is better able and more equipped to protect our children—us or God?
- Who looks on our children with greater understanding—not just for ten years' time but for all eternity?
- Who has the power to make all things turn out for the good for those who love him and have been called according to his purpose? (p. 37)

We are not alone on this journey of raising children. God has ultimately taken the responsibility. He loves our children beyond our ability to love them. He has a plan for each of their lives and is drawing them to Himself.

The most amazing thing to me is that God invites us as parents to join Him in loving our children. We get to experience some of His love for our children. I believe God assigns each child to his or her parents knowing those parents are the ones that can influence that particular child in the way God has designed. This applies to children who are adopted as well. We are the *best* people to raise the children we have been given so they will know and love God.

When I had my children, my understanding of God's love soared to a different level. When our first child, Beth, was born, I did not know I had the capacity to love her like I did. And then when our son Joshua was born 14 and one half months later, I wasn't sure how I could love another child like I did the first one. But it was just incredible how I loved him just as much, but in a way unique from my love for Beth. And then Rachel was born five years later. The same thing happened—I was overwhelmed with the love I had for her, again unique from the love I had for my other two children. I always wondered how God could love all the people who have ever lived as if they were they were the only one to love. I was only grasping a fraction of God's love for all humanity. What a gift parenting is in our lives!

God's sovereignty over the lives of our children to know and love Him does not negate our responsibility to do the things He has asked us to do in His Word. He gave us the blueprint in Psalm 78 and the strategy in Deuteronomy 6 and many other places in the Bible. Remember, our only responsibility is to be on our own journey to love the Lord our God with all our hearts, souls, minds, and strength, and then to talk about it. We need to wrestle with our faith and then impress our children with our "God sightings." We need to talk about our faith and teach our children what we know to be true from God's Word and His creation.

Remember, God does not need perfect parenting, or perfect life journeys to accomplish His plans and fulfill His purposes in our children's lives. His plan is much bigger than that, and in the end, it is all about Him, not us. We all want the glory and the credit, but it all belongs to God.

I loved reading *Parenting Beyond Your Capacity* by Reggie Joiner. This is such a good read for parents. You will understand and experience God's grace in parenting from this book. God will use it to lift your parenting stresses as you raise your children with all of life's challenges. Listen to what he says:

> God is at work telling us a story of restoration and redemption through your family. No matter what your family looks like or how limited your capacity might be, you can cooperate with whatever God desires to do in your heart so your children will have a front row seat to the grace and goodness of God. (p. 47)

The church has a responsibility to partner with us in passing faith to our children. Children have a responsibility to respond to God's call in their lives, and I have a responsibility to be on my own journey with God and share that journey with my children. And best of all, God cares more about our children than we can ever imagine. I love being reminded of this. Live out your journey with your children and God will do the rest!

Resources

Joiner, Reggie. *Parenting Beyond Your Capacity,* Orange, a division of The ReThink Group, Inc., 2015.

Thomas, Gary. *Devotions for Sacred Parenting.* Zondervan, 2005.

Westerhoff, III, John H. *Will Our Children Have Faith?* Revised Edition. Morehouse Publishing, 2000.

THE IMPORTANCE OF RELATIONSHIP

Building Relationships That Will Have a Lasting Impact on Your Children

Relationship = Influence

Having raised my own children, become a grandmother, and worked in children's ministries for 30 years, I am more convinced than ever that *relationship* is the most important factor in parenting and passing faith to our children. Without relationship, we cannot hope to influence the direction our children decide to go with their lives. As we all know, control only works for so long. As parents, we have an amazing opportunity and potential to influence our children as they blossom right in front of our eyes. God invites us to be a part of developing those little lives and influencing them to love Him and have a relationship with Him. What an awesome opportunity and overwhelming responsibility!

In God's design, He gives parents the life experiences they need to be able to guide their children in their journey to understand wisdom and truth. Each generation helps the next generation navigate life. It wasn't that long ago when we were children, and as adults we are now just a little ahead of our children on the journey through life. Because we love our children, we want them to avoid the pitfalls we and our parents experienced, and hopefully, have a better life than we may have experienced.

The book of Proverbs is dedicated to the subject of wisdom and is a great resource for teaching wisdom to our children. As we know, children don't just automatically listen to their parents; in fact, many times it is quite the opposite. Some children are harder to guide than others, so it is critical that we develop strong relationships with them if we expect to influence them. It is sometimes quite a challenge to lead and guide our children and still maintain a warm and open relationship with them.

I don't think any of us go into parenting realizing how hard it can be at times. As a young mom, I was regularly calling out to God for wisdom and help, claiming the promise of James 1:5, "If any of you lacks wisdom, you should ask God, who gives generously to all without finding fault, and it will be given to you" (NIV).

Children have the same sinful nature as their parents, and sometimes this shows up pretty early in their lives. So, we need wisdom to teach and guide them in ways that will keep our relationship open. When children want their own way they will naturally resist instruction. This is perhaps why Proverbs continually stresses the fact that children should listen to their parents. Here are just a couple of examples:

> Listen, my son, to your father's instruction and do not forsake your mother's teaching. They are a garland to grace your head and a chain to adorn your neck (Proverbs 1:8-9, NIV).

> My son, do not forget my teaching, but keep my commands in your heart, for they will prolong your life many years and bring you peace and prosperity (Proverbs 3:1-2, NIV).

During the formative years of children's lives our role is to be responsible in the area of teaching and guiding their lives. Relationship means that children should feel secure with their parents. Remember that one of the causes of insecurity in children is being unsure that their parents love each other. They cannot articulate it, but they can feel it. We are the only adults they have on earth, and in those early years we are their caregivers and the major influencers in their lives even when they are in their teenage years.

Consistency is a key factor, and they should know they are valued and loved unconditionally. While under our care they should also feel like they are a priority in our lives. We need to understand that our goal in the child-rearing phase is a healthy relationship with our children, not friendship or their approval. Friendship comes later, as they move into adulthood and there is nothing better than having your adult children as friends. In the meantime, security, consistency, and unconditional love are the things our children need.

Let Them Be Themselves

Relationship requires giving our children the freedom to be who they are—who God created them to be. It is easy for us to decide who we want our children to be and try to force them into the box we've visualized for them. The motivation for that approach is not love. Rather, it is attempting to cause my children to be acceptable to me, making me look good to my friends and my circle of influence. This is a recipe for failure in relating to the children God has given us. All people, including our children, are who they are, and they can't be someone else.

If we want relationship with our kids, we need to accept their unique personalities and aptitudes and ask God for wisdom and help in developing them into everything God created them to be. Isn't it amazing that God invites us to join Him in this process? We need to become students of our children and make it our goal to find out what makes each one tick.

What brings out the best in your child? Certain behaviors are never acceptable, but we need to separate behavior from personality and realize that we will sometimes have personality clashes with our children. It's normal!

I have found several resources that are helpful in this area. These are resources that I wish I'd had as a young mom. For understanding your child's personality, the books I recommend are these:

- *Different Children, Different Needs* by Dr. Charles F. Boyd.
- *Understanding Your Child's Personality* by Dr. David Stoop.
- *I May Frustrate You, but I'm a Keeper!* by Ray W. Lincoln.

The first book, *Different Children, Different Needs,* is great because with a simple DISC© personality test, it helps you identify both your personality and your child's. It tells you how your personality will naturally relate to your child's personality and what changes you will need to make to guide that child effectively. It is very helpful. In some instances, a laid back parent may have to step up their strategy to impact a strong-willed child. This type of change in engagement may not be natural for you, but it may be exactly what your child needs.

I May Frustrate You, but I'm a Keeper uses the Meyers Briggs© as the foundation for determining personality types. *Understanding Your Child's Personality* is also based on Meyers Briggs© and provides an in-depth understanding of these personality types in children.

Another helpful resource in understanding your child is *The New Birth Order Book* by Kevin Leman. Studying characteristics of birth order can help you understand your child's specific responses to life situations and can identify typical strengths and weaknesses that will help you know how to guide and nurture them.

Sometimes they just need empathy. For example, an introverted first-born child may be hesitant and sometimes resistant to new situations because he is the one who has to "forge the way" for everyone else. When we know this we can be more understanding and supportive of our firstborn in those areas. The second child comes along, and nothing is new or scary for them. I was a middle child in my home, and looking back it was difficult for me to find my identity in my family. This is typical of the middle-born. I tended to find my identity outside my home. Helping middle children find their identity in the framework of their home is much healthier for them. Most "black sheep" are middle-born children because they are often unable to find their place in their family.

Dave and I have three children, born from 1976 to 1982. The original *Birth Order* book came out in 1985, and I read it right away. It was so helpful and explained a lot to us. Beth was our firstborn, and Josh came 14 months later. Rachel was born five years after Josh. According to Kevin Leman, they will all have some first-born traits because the second child was the first born male and was born so close to the first child. Rachel was born five years after Josh, and because of the distance between births, she also had some firstborn traits. All three share a characteristic of a first-born child in that they were all very driven children. Even though everything might not apply to your children and your situation, an awareness of common birth order traits can be tremendously insightful and helpful. Sometimes, anything that gives us even a nugget of understanding is a valuable resource!

Handling Conflicts

If relationships are to prevail in the long run, we also need to develop good conflict resolution skills. Conflict is a fact of life, and no matter how hard we try, conflicts will never fully disappear. Our goal should be to know how to keep a clean slate which will, in turn, teach our children how to resolve conflict as they grow up. We need to realize that this will always be hard, but it is something that needs to be attended to regularly.

I grew up in Colorado and lived there most of my life. When I was a child, we played outside a lot. We would find shale and sometimes mica, both of which are common in Colorado, in the ground around our house. It was really fun to separate the layers and try to break them apart. Sometimes we could take the rock apart one layer at a time and break it because one layer would break easily, but when there were several layers on top of each other, the rock was hard to break. For me, this is a picture of conflict. One misunderstanding can be resolved quite easily, especially if we can get to the root of it, but layer upon layer of hurt feelings from conflict is hard to break. When this happens, resolution and restoration may eventually require a professional mediator or counselor. Because unresolved conflicts can build up over years, they can be hard to address or break, so it is imperative that we tackle each conflict one layer at a time and not allow unbreakable layers to build up.

Sometimes resolving conflict is more than just preventing the buildup of layers of hurt from unresolved conflict. Have you had the experience of pulling a weed but not getting all the roots? We all know it just comes back up in a matter of time. It works the same way with conflict. If we don't understand what's really happening and work on the root of issues, the conflicts will just keep coming back. Sometimes resolution is only possible when we find out what is really behind repetitive conflicts. Resolution can be so much quicker and easier when we discover the root cause. Occasionally, it may take the full 18 years of your child's life at home to understand and get to the root of those repeated conflicts. Since we want to have healthy relationships with our children, and we desire for them to have good relationships with each other, we shouldn't ever stop trying.

An outstanding resource in the area of family conflict is *Peacemaking For Families, A Biblical Guide to Managing Conflict in Your Home* by Ken Sande. I think Sande has the best explanation for the reason why we have conflict in our lives: he says it is idolatry, and his explanation of idolatry is the best I've ever heard. Understanding the biblical plan and process for conflict resolution is critical to every family and is the central message of the Peacemaker materials. I taught the Peacemaker Ministries' children's curriculum, *The Young Peacemaker,* several years ago and found it to be excellent material. It is a thirteen week class intended to be used in tandem with the adult Peacemaker class. When it comes to conflict, God's way is the best, and it works when we follow His plan and do it. That's not to say that it's easy or that every conflict is resolvable (it takes two willing people to work things out), but conflict must be dealt with so resentment and bitterness do not build up. It is not easy to untangle a life of unresolved issues with an angry teenager. Keep the slate clean! Ken Sande's material can help you work out the inevitable conflicts in the home.

Be Willing to Say You're Sorry!

Have you noticed how being mom or dad requires a lot of humility? I sure did. As parents, we often think we are right and that our children need to just see things our way. They need to obey and cooperate. Right? Sometimes in the process of leading our families, something goes awry. We don't understand what happened, but we can see that something is not right with one or more of our children. We may not clearly see their heart or their motivations but know we've hurt their feelings; we've injured their heart. In order to maintain a relationship, we need to have eyes to see a hurt heart.

The best book I have seen in this area is an older one, but a classic, *The Key to Your Child's Heart,* by Gary Smalley. In the first chapter, he nails it: "How to Overcome the Major Destroyer of Families—A Closed Spirit." This book, even just this chapter alone, is well worth the read. He talks about how to identify a closed spirit, what causes it, and how to open it up again.

He uses the illustration of a sea urchin, that, when poked, closes up its tentacles. Some children are more sensitive than others and will close up more easily. The key to opening up a child's hurt heart requires humility on the part of a parent and the desire to see situations through your child's eyes. Gary Smalley has "Five Steps to Reopen a Child's Spirit." (Chapter 1, *The Key to Your Child's Heart*, pp. 27-34). They are:

1. Become Tender Hearted
2. Increase Understanding
3. Recognize the Offense
4. Attempt to Touch
5. Seek Forgiveness

Don't "triangulate," which means allowing your children to pit you against your spouse. I was determined not to continue in the ways of my family of origin in this area. Triangulation basically cost me relationship with my dad. Every time my dad hurt my feelings, I would go to my mom and tell her what happened. She would just listen and try to help me understand why he might have done what he did that hurt me, but it ended there. I never resolved any issues with my dad, even into adulthood. With God's help I was determined this was not going to happen in my family.

When my children came to me with a problem with their dad, I told them, "You will have to work this out with Daddy." The response was, "No, I don't want to!" But I would take them by the hand and go with them to talk to their dad. I prompted them in starting the conversation, but had them tell Daddy what the offense was they felt he had committed. I would then leave the room. Dave would then take over, and they would talk it through until there was understanding. I am so pleased to say that contrary to my experience as a child, all of my children have a great relationship with their dad. This "sin-cycle" was broken!

Sometimes our children need patient explanations and sometimes they need us to ask for their forgiveness. This takes humility, but the ability to ask forgiveness of your child when you are wrong goes a long way with children, and it will pretty much guarantee a relationship with them. They need to see we will listen to them and seek understanding. Even when we don't see issues the same way, it is best to validate the child's feelings and ask forgiveness. The rest of Gary Smalley's book, *The Key to Your Child's Heart* focuses on, "Parenting for Positive Results, Powerful Ways to Motivate Your Child, and The Secret of a Close-Knit Family." Great book!

Love Me the Way I Feel It!

Is there anyone out there who has not heard that we each have a love language that speaks to us more than others? By now this is a common conversation, but what an amazing contribution Gary Chapman made when he wrote *The Five Love Languages: How to Express Heartfelt Commitment to Your Mate* and *The Five Love Languages of Children,* which followed close after the first book.

I sure wish I'd had these books when my children were young. The first book came out when our children were in high school, so even then it wasn't too late to start applying the wisdom in this book. It was very helpful. Words of affirmation, quality time, receiving gifts, acts of service, physical touch—we all have one or two that are more meaningful to us than the others.

I read *The Five Love Languages* in 1991, but in looking back I realized that I had begun sensing the concept of a love language when our son was in upper elementary school and was giving me a challenging stretch of motherhood. I was speaking my love language of words of affirmation to him very well, but I could tell I wasn't reaching him. It was clear that my words of affirmation didn't mean much to him. He wasn't responding to my love language, and I could sense it. I finally asked him, "What can I do to make you feel my love?" My question was on the right track, but I didn't fully understand what to do until I read this book. It helped me understand a lot about my son's love needs. I discovered that he responded best to quality time and genuine interest in his projects. I backed off of the words of encouragement that rang so hollow in his ears and made an effort to give him the quality time he craved. I asked Dave to read the book, and then we all did the test and discovered each other's love languages and tried to love each other in ways that were meaningful. It made so much sense.

Have you discovered how hard it is to love in another language? I can love very well in mine because it comes natural to me, but it takes a lot of effort to love in another love language. One day during a dispute with my husband, God spoke to me in a gentle voice, "*Sacrificial love is what you need to have! It doesn't come naturally, but if you want to love like Me, it needs to be sacrificial and the way he needs it. It takes effort!*" It would be great to have the same love language as your spouse or children, but the reality is that we are all different and respond best to our own love language. Offering love to our children in ways that are meaningful to them requires focus and sacrificial love. Taking the time and effort to know how our children feel loved will make a difference in our relationship with them and how they respond to our leadership in their lives.

Resources

As we all know, life is hard and can get very complicated. We need God's wisdom and help in creating the atmosphere in our homes that helps our children see God in the midst of daily life. Strong relationships will develop as a result. Below are resources that I've found to be very helpful.

Boyd, Dr. Charles F. *Different Children, Different Needs.* Multnomah Publishers, Inc., 1994.

Chapman, Gary & Campbell, M.D., Ross. *The Five Love Languages of Children.* Moody Press, 1997.

Leman, Kevin. *The New Birth Order Book.* Fleming H. Revell, 1998.

Lincoln, Ray W. *I May Frustrate You, but I'm a Keeper!* Apex Publications, 2009.

Sande, Ken. *Peacemaking for Families: A Biblical Guide to Managing Conflict in Your Home.* Tyndale House Publishers, Inc., 2002.

Smalley, Gary. *The Key to Your Child's Heart.* Word Books Publisher, 1984.

Stoop, Dr. David. *Understanding Your Child's Personality.* Tyndale House Publishers, Inc., 1998.

Turansky, Scott & Miller, RN, BSN, Joanne. *Parenting is Heart Work.* Journey, Cook Communications Ministries, 2006.

MARRIAGE: THE FOUNDATION OF THE HOME

What does marriage have to do with reconnecting the home and the church so the next generation will know Him?

I will never forget the admonishing advice I received from a family pastor the first time I met with him. This was at the beginning of my ministry when I was sharing my ministry philosophy with many churches. I made an appointment to visit a family pastor in southern Colorado. His wife was the children's director. They had a great ministry partnership at the time. After my presentation he said he loved my ministry philosophy, but also said, "We do need to tell parents who claim to be Christians and are defaming each other in front of their kids, that it would be best that the church tell their children about Jesus, not them, at least until they figure out their marriage. The first responsibility the church has to families is to enrich marriages so the children will want to follow in their parent's faith." I was taken aback by his directness but respected his viewpoint and found that I really agreed with him. I needed to hear that in my new ministry because one of the top reasons why our children leave the church is the hypocrisy in the home and in the church.

He went on to tell me his family ministry philosophy, which I continue to share with churches whenever I get the opportunity. It is the best philosophy and strategy I've seen. It's simple and it is working. This pastor has four pillars in his family ministry: marriage, finances, parenting, and small groups. He raised the bar in his church when he just short of *required* the attendance of his people in workshops in all four areas. His goal was that everyone attend a small group for relationship building and accountability.

He also implemented a program called "Marriage Mentors," which gives couples the opportunity to have a trained mentor couple. These couples come alongside the learning couple by exposing them to their marriage and life journey. The mentors are older couples in his church. He told me that as a result of the program the mentor marriages were also getting stronger. I have never forgotten this meeting because I too believe that marriage is the most important foundation for children. I encourage all the churches I work with to prioritize the marriage ministry in their churches.

The Source of Love and Security for Children

Marriage is inevitably the most challenging yet potentially the most gratifying of all relationships we enter into on our life journey. The home was designed by God to become the source of love and security for the children that follow marriage and the means by which our children would know Him. Children are totally dependent on their parents. That was God's design for humankind.

It all began with the perfect love present in the Trinity and the God's desire to share that love. He created us in His image so He could love us, and we could enter into His love. Without Eve, Adam was not complete. Men and women both represent the image of God in whom we were created. It is the loving environment of a man and a woman that God planned for children to be introduced to Him. Generation after generation would tell their children of God's love and the fact that He is a perfect heavenly Father, and each generation would be committed to following Him.

The natural response to this understanding of God is a desire to honor Him in all His love, glory, majesty, and power. We can sing from our hearts, along with Chris Tomlin, about our good Father.

We know this perfect plan was marred because Adam and Eve made a choice to question God and to doubt His perfect care and plan for them. Their decision impacted every area of life, wreaked havoc on marriage, and made the most sacred and intimate of all human relationships a big challenge. As He always does, God stepped into the middle of our mess with a plan for our redemption and the redemption of the marriage relationship. A redeemed marriage starts with the individual decision of the marriage partners to submit themselves to God and His plans for their lives. As we begin to understand and desire God's original plan and ask Him for help, insight, and wisdom, we can by the grace of God, through Jesus, still come to experience the blessings of marriage as God intended.

Marriage Is Real Work

In all my years of marriage, I have only seen one couple who didn't seem to ever struggle in their relationship and genuinely seemed to have a perfect marriage. I observed that they had the utmost respect for each other, a reality that always has a big influence on the health of a marriage. The other thing I observed was that they recalled all the good times they had had over the years and they laughed together a lot—at each other and with each other. It was such a joy to be with them!

I do not claim to be an expert on marriage, but I have significant experience in this area. Dave and I have been married for fifty years, and we have weathered many storms, disappointments, and significant changes traveling through different stages of life and many phases of personal growth. Our relationship has been challenged time and time again, but by God's grace our relationship has strengthened and deepened. But not without a lot of work. Through it all, we remain committed both to marriage and to our relationship with each other. When people ask Dave how one stays in a marriage for this long, he smiles and says, "The secret to a long marriage is not to get a divorce." But we know there are times when divorce is unavoidable. I'll mention more about this in chapter 6.

Dave and I don't expect every day to be a perfect day, but we still enjoy each other's company, and we're willing to seek God's help on a daily basis to build an ever-growing relationship with each other. We regularly review the history we have created as a couple. This serves to remind us how precious and valuable that history is, and we share a desire to finish well.

Malachi said it so well in chapter 2, verse 15:

> *Has not the one God made you? You belong to him in body and spirit. And what does the one God seek? Godly offspring. So be on your guard, and do not be unfaithful to the wife of your youth* (NIV).

Many years ago, as I was praying an image came to mind that has helped me visualize the goal of our marriage. It was an image of a triangle with God at the top and Dave and me at the two bottom corners. The lines had arrows on both ends, representing a love relationship between each entity. Marriage is a "threesome." I am in a love relationship with God, which allows me to love and forgive my husband like God loves and forgives me. My husband is in a love relationship with God (different from mine). God is at the top of the triangle because He is our Creator. We each, of course, can only control two of those love-lines, but I believe when I focus on what God wants me to do and to be, He will be glorified in my life and will accomplish His purposes in the life of my husband. I just need to be faithful to what I can control; those responsibilities are loving my God and loving my husband. When both husband and wife are loving God and reflecting His love to each other, that is when a good marriage is discovered and experienced.

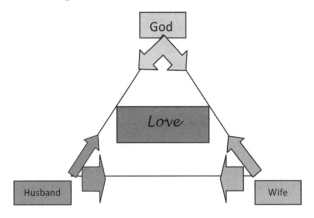

As Dave and I look back over the fifty years we have been married, especially the years when we were raising our children, we are thankful for so many bits of wisdom God gave us that helped us during those challenging days. Here are some principles that we feel are most important:

1. Prioritize your marriage after your children come. That, of course, does not mean you neglect your children's needs, but it does mean you work hard to keep the relationship with your spouse both strong and fresh. It takes a lot of wisdom, work, and maturity when the kids are all sick, work schedules become more demanding, finances are tight, or the kids' activities are driving your life. I'm sure you can add even more challenges to this list!

So how do we prioritize our marriage in the midst of all this? One thing we consistently did was have a short—sometimes very short—time to download our day before dinner. This might seem very trite, but it was amazing what a difference it made for Dave. When he got home from work, we would go to the bedroom and, while he changed clothes, we would talk about our day. Sometimes I had to hold a baby, but our children grew up knowing this was our time and they should wait until we came out of our room for whatever they needed. Squeezing in a little bit of intentional time together can make a big difference in leaving the cares of the day behind and improving the mood of the night. Even though your children may test you and try to interrupt your "alone time," they really do need for you to have these times together. They are testing you to find out how much they can control you.

Date nights are in this same category and are very important. Even though consistency or finances might be a challenge, make sure you create time to nurture your friendship. Date nights don't have to be expensive. Be creative! Sometimes a quiet walk in the park or around a lake is just what your relationship needs. Revisit the things you enjoyed doing before the kids came. Date nights let your kids know that you still love each other and still value quality time together.

2. Learn to communicate well. It's a life-long pursuit. I have long believed that the majority of all conflict is due to a lack of good com-

munication. I still believe it. The best materials I've seen about dealing with conflict are from the non-profit organization, Peacemaker Ministries. Ken Sande has written several books, but the one I recommend for families is *Peacemaking for Families*. The first chapter is "Marriage Means Conflict." I highly recommend you get this book and read it.

3. Avoid unhealthy or unrealistic expectations. I reached a milestone in my life and marriage when I realized I was responsible for my own happiness and that Dave wasn't. He could never meet my needs perfectly, not even close sometimes. I needed to put God in His rightful place in my life and take Dave out of that place. Healthy expectations are good and need to be respected, but unrealistic expectations can kill relationships, especially if the other person is not aware of your expectations. Self-awareness was groundbreaking for me in my marriage as a young woman in my 30s. Facing what was true about me and what was not true was so helpful when we faced inevitable conflicts in our marriage. I remember writing out a list of positive traits and negative traits, things I could change and needed to work on, and things I could not change. It helped me to know myself better, to be more authentic and more transparent. It helped me to no longer pretend I was something that I was not. It gave me peace with myself and the way my Father created me. It gave me the ability to take responsibility for things in our marriage that were mine and to acknowledge and work on them as we encountered conflicts in our marriage.

The resources for building a better marriage are many. Over the years, Dave and I have read many marriage books and we have saved most of them. I have been so thankful all these years that I have a husband who reads a lot. One of the most impactful books for our relationship has been *Love & Respect: The Love She Most Desires, The Respect He Desperately Needs* by Dr. Emerson Eggerichs. I believe the message of this book is fundamental to understanding the way God created men and women. We were created for different roles, but we both reflect the image of God to represent all aspects of God. Understanding that respect is the greatest need of men in a marriage relationship and that love is the greatest need of a woman is the key to a great marriage. I encourage you to read this book and take its message to heart.

For Dave and me, two other favorite books are—*Sacred Marriage: What If God Designed Marriage to Make Us Holy More Than to Make Us Happy?* by Gary Thomas, and *The Five Love Languages: How To Express Heartfelt Commitment to Your Mate* by Gary Chapman. Our most recent read has been, *The Meaning of Marriage: Facing the Complexities of Commitment with the Wisdom of God* by Timothy Keller. Each of these books has proven to be great resources for strengthening and deepening our marriage.

What Happens If the Marriage Fails?

Life does not always work out the way we desire or as we imagined. Sometimes divorce happens for many reasons, even though we never wanted it to enter our lives. Whatever might have happened, the marriage and family shatter when divorce becomes a reality. But Isaiah 59:1a says, "Surely the arm of the LORD is not too short to save" (NIV). As always God stands ready to meet us where we are with a new plan to accomplish His purposes in our lives. That is why I wanted the next chapter by Carri Taylor to be included in my book. Carri has been a friend of mine since 2006 when we served together on the National Association of Family Ministries. I have respected and valued her teaching for couples beginning a second marriage, since I attended one of her workshops. It is the best material I have seen. So if your marriage has not worked out for one reason or another, please read on.

Resources

Chapman, Gary. *The Five Love Languages: The Secret to Love That Lasts.* Northfield Publishing, 2010.

Crabb, Larry. *The Marriage Builder.* Zondervan, 1982.

Eggerichs, Dr. Emerson. *Cracking the Communication Code: Love for Her, Respect for Him.* Thomas Nelson, 2006.

Eggerichs, Dr. Emerson. *Love & Respect: The Love She Most Desires, The Respect He Desperately Needs.* Thomas Nelson, 2004.

Field, David. *Marriage Personalities.* Harvest House, 1986.

Keller, Timothy. *The Meaning of Marriage: Facing the Complexities of Commitment with the Wisdom of God.* Riverhead Books, 2011.

Rienow, Rob & Amy. *Visionary Marriage.* Randall House, 2010.

Thomas, Gary. *Sacred Marriage: What If God Designed Marriage to Make Us Holy More Than to Make Us Happy?* Zondervan, 2000.

Whiteman, PhD., Thomas A. & Bartlett, Ph.D., Thomas G. *The Marriage Mender: A Couple's Guide for Staying Together.* NavPress, 1996.

Yerkovich, Milan & Kay. *How We Love.* WaterBrook Press, 2008.

Divorce! What Now?

BY Carri Taylor

Relationships

When I married, I signed up for life. I had no intentions of ever experiencing divorce. I also had a rather judgmental attitude toward people that did divorce. After all, I was keeping my marriage together, why couldn't they? Not until life's complications and distractions hit my marriage did I understand the complexities involved when a divorce takes place.

The best of intentions don't necessarily protect us from life's realities. Personally, I've never heard anyone divorced say they had planned on it. It usually comes as a huge surprise and forces a re-evaluation of our entire life such as: beliefs, expectations, dreams, etc. Also impacting finances, housing, parenting, custody, jobs, extended family, etc. Now, life takes a paradigm shift that's important to understand when we enter a subsequent marriage with children.

First marriages begin all about "us." The children come along one by one and we grow to know one another. Second marriages in reality began all about "them." "Them" meaning the kids, the ex-spouses, the new in-laws and the "out-laws" (former in-laws). Unfortunately, most step-couples impose the fantasy on their new union that it will be all about "us." Those that treat the remarried couple like a first married couple encourage this concept.

First marriages are "apples" and remarriages are "oranges." It's surprising when we bite into something we thought would be hard, crunchy, and familiar and instead we end up with something soft, squishy, and squirts all over our face.

In my own joy of loving, being loved, and wanting my youngest daughter to have a positive male role model to make up for all her losses, I was oblivious to her pain. She was actually positive about my remarriage and "approved," yet on our wedding day, I started to see her pain. That pain caused her to "act out" within the first month of our marriage.

Later when talking with her, she explained to me that her Dad had his new wife (he married shortly after the divorce five years previous and hadn't been around consistently since); that her grandparents (my parents, who had functioned in a very supportive role after the divorce) had pulled away since the remarriage; and now I had my new husband. So, her friends were her family now. I don't think I need to describe the friends she turned to. Any thoughts of the "us" were gone and focused on "her."

After my husband, Gordon's, divorce, he stayed at the family home for nine years and finished raising his three teenage sons. When we decided to marry, two of the three boys were already "launched" and on their own. The third "launching" was motivated by the sale of his home so he could join me in my condo until we purchased an "ours" home. The boys couldn't believe their father sold their home of 22 years. It looked to them like I was the cause, even though they all acknowledged later that he had discussed plans with them to sell the home before I was even in the picture. This home represented the stability they had lost. Like my daughter, they formed their own "family" outside of "us" for emotional support. Now the focus was on "all of them."

Any remarriage will "shake" the entire family system effecting children, ex-spouses, friends, new in-laws, and "out-laws" from the former spouse. They are still grandparents. Everyone is wondering how things will change and their guard is up. The stepparent is usually the "lightning rod" and blamed for the changes that take place, deserved or not.

Focusing solely on my marriage relationship, as most typical marriage programs emphasize, would *not* have helped us end up with one. Our relationship became one of strategizing, educating ourselves, and momentous efforts to understand and save relationships with our children. This has been a continuing process. We did grow together, but through adversity and the commitment to work on solutions to the problems that were confronting us. I don't think I had a clue about the depth of pain children suffer in divorce and remarriage.

The children have no choice in the decision to divorce and/or to remarry. This decision is made by their parents. The new spouse is, in essence, a stranger and intruder into the biological system that previously existed and still exists in the children's mind. After all, their fantasy is that their parents will get back together.

The boys, even as adults, thought that Gordon had pulled away from them to take care of his "new family" and was investing in his stepdaughter's life more than theirs. Any age child can think they're ignored when a remarriage takes place. Two of Gordon's sons admitted their jealousy and resentment. Sometimes this can result in anger and even aggressive behavior toward the stepparent. This will particularly be the case if the parent does not stay invested in his or her biological children. It is particularly easy for men to turn toward their new wife and her children. This can have a devastating impact.

We've come into this new marriage by the backdoor with a lot of losses and pre-existing relationships that need nurturing and stabilizing. Yes, we have to also nurture our marriage, take time for it and be skillful in it. It can definitely work, but not overnight. Time is crucial!

It took approximately five years for Gordon and my daughter to experience and begin understanding (trusting) each other enough for their relationship to solidify and start to bloom. My daughter was Gordon's "living laboratory" in which their experiments taught him about personality styles (they were opposites), gender differences (again opposites), and most of all communication and conflict resolution skills—which now have become our lifestyle.

If the child is young, approximately six and under, there may be a chance for the stepparent to become the psychological (i.e. invested) parent. However, the stepparent will never be the biological parent. The psychological parent relationship can develop if the stepparent is willing to put in the time, energy, money, etc., to encourage it. This will still depend on the stepchild's ability and willingness to attach to another adult parent-figure.

If you are forming a stepfamily with teens, don't even try to be a parent. The priority is to develop the new relationships. Come in as a friend and support for a lost, hurting child (no matter what age). The most productive role for a stepdad or stepmom is that of a "servant leader." As Stephen Covey said, "Seek first to understand and then be understood." It's important to educate yourself and be willing to seek counsel.

If the children are older, relationship development will take longer. The stepparent will probably be a friend, confidant, or even just an acquaintance. The ultimate challenge for the stepparent is letting the child set the pace for the growing relationship. To be productive, the stepparent must accept this principle. If you've ever tried to push a piece of string to get it to go where you want it to go, you will understand my point.

We did not find out until 12 years into our marriage that Gordon's sons had a wall of reserve toward me, wondering if this union would last. After all, what have we taught our children? That marriage will last? No. We've modeled fragility and taken away their ability to trust something that was and should be foundational in their lives—marriage. After 12 years they believed it was safe to move toward me.

Living in any family brings surprise—that's life. Living in a stepfamily guarantees *lots* of surprises because of the "open" and expanded system it creates. Even in first marriages, we "marry" more than just our spouse. Along with our spouse comes their family. In a stepfamily, we not only marry a spouse and their extended family (parents, siblings, nieces, and nephews), we "marry" their children, ex-spouse, ex-spouse's extended family, any new spouse their ex-spouse may have, etc., etc., etc.

Living in a stepfamily can be like opening package after package after package. When we first join we know how many packages there are. In our case, our package included my two daughters, his three sons, his ex-spouse (not married at the time), and my ex-spouse with his wife and their two sons. Then the packages start bringing more packages and creating more packages.

Over the past 31+ years our stepfamily has had a lot to negotiate and collaborate on, to keep this situation a win-win. Graduations, weddings, grandchildren, divorces, remarriages, and deaths. We've had many painful valleys as well as mountaintop experiences to find our way through.

Right now our total package count is five adult children who brought six spouses and ten grandchildren to our life. Our ex-spouses' count has stayed the same and we've lost through death, five of the biological and step-great grandparents. I know the packages will continue to unfold.

Finances

Underlying everything are our money and possessions. First marriages are usually starting fresh with not a lot of assets, debts, and stuff (belongings). Subsequent marriages have accumulated homes, vehicles, assets, debts, and stuff. How are you going to merge all those together? The standard answer is to put them all in one pot. We never recommend that.

I had a home and vehicles; he had the same. I had my assets and house payment, so did he. I had a film company, was general partner of five limited partnerships, my treasured possessions, and two daughters (one still 14). He had a retirement, investments, and three adult sons.

In our case, we went to an attorney and came up with an eight-year plan for our money to come together. The plan develops trust. We knew what was expected of both of us and watched our behavior as we worked the plan and built trust. Our finances actually came together in two years, not eight. That's when we moved into "our" home. At first, my daughter was excited but on moving day she told me this home was Gordon's and mine and she didn't belong here at all. This is not unusual.

This is a no-win situation. The couple wins by starting an "ours" and the kids lose by being re-located. Or the children win by stability (although strangers are moving in) and the couple lives with previous ghosts (ex-spouses).

The biggest problem in all of this is when counselors and pastors lay the apple on the orange. It doesn't work and creates more problems than necessary and the couple is devastated because their apple expectations don't happen.

Points to Consider and Review

- Before marriage and even before you are "in love," get education on stepfamily development stages and issues that stepcouples will address that never enter the sphere of first married couples. This will avoid the shock, disappointment, and desire to bail out.

- The marriage is a *joy* for the couple and *destabilizing* for the kids. They have no choice in any of the decisions to divorce, remarry, where they will live and be very aware that the kids are living between two worlds and doing what they have to survive in each.

- No matter how happy the kids may be before the wedding, be prepared for attitudes to change at the wedding or shortly afterward. That's when fantasy turns into reality and life is drastically changed!

- Biological versus step-relationships are a paramount factor in the stepfamily. Pre-existing relationships have biological, emotional, and legal bonds. New step-relationships are slowly developing an emotional bond—this is a "baby" relationship and "baby" family that forms backward from the biological family. Neither can be ignored.

- In a first marriage (depending on if you do it in God's order), the marriage comes first so the couple has time to get to know one another, then you become parents with the addition of a kid, then another kid, etc. So there is space and time between each additional member (not counting twins). In a subsequent marriage, the kids are there first, so you are a parent from a broken family, then you become a spouse, and then a stepparent. Relationships are developing all at once.

- In remarriage, you are marrying an entire system just as in a first marriage. However, many more people are involved because of the pre-existing relationships. That "ex" will never go away if children are involved. In one way or another, the bio-mom and bio-dad will be connected—shared parenting, graduations, weddings, grandkids, and even possible divorces.

- $$$. Very important before the wedding (or even engagement) for full disclosure regarding salaries, debts, assets, insurance, and prized possessions. Also, discuss each of your histories with and attitudes about money. An attorney is a wise investment to help put together a plan for how and when your money will come together. This plan can develop trust.

- Regarding parenting and who does what; the bio-parent does the discipline. The stepparent supports from the rear (whether there is agreement or not on one another's parenting style.) You've already been parenting and bringing those styles into the marriage. When the stepparent is alone with the stepkids, you have the role of "babysitter." Everyone knows the rules in that relationship. This demands a parenting plan that the bio-parent establishes with the bio-kids so all the stepparent has to do is HONOR and implement the plan already in place. Never get in the stepchild's face!

- Living together lacks the bond of commitment between the couple that is foundational for the security of the children (marriage is more than a piece of paper). Plus, statistics on living together and those that eventually marry are *not* good. Stats are already against subsequent marriages, so why make things worse?

I am pleased to say that since February 8, 1986 (our wedding date), our relationships have solidified throughout our entire stepfamily system. I've watched God do some miraculous things in healing wounds and redeeming the pain.

Resources

Opportunities Unlimited, Oklahoma City, OK. www.Opportunities Unlimited.com

DVDs

- *Stepfamilies Bringing the Pieces to Peace,* Gordon & Carri Taylor
- *Children of Divorce, The Tough Truth,* Carri Taylor
- *Life After Abortion,* Carri Taylor, 2010 New Liberty Videos

Using a Heart-Based Approach for Parenting

Dr. Scott Turansky and Joanne Miller, RN, BSN

I met Scott Turansky and Joanne Miller when I was still in children's ministries in Littleton, Colorado. The occasion was an annual conference I attended known as (INCM), International Network of Children's Ministries. I was always on the hunt for good parenting resources to recommend to the parents in my ministry, so I was excited to hear about a new organization called National Center for Biblical Parenting (NCBP). As time went on, I started going to their workshops, signed up for their "parenting tips" emails and for many years forwarded them to all the families in my ministry. In 2005, they wrote a book that really caught my attention—*Parenting Is Heart Work*. It is among the best, if not the best book, on parenting I've read. I really resonated with the idea that impacting a child's heart should be our ultimate goal if we are to have a lasting impact on the lives of our children. I quickly concluded that NCBP was the best parenting resource I had come across. I was all in…and then after I started Reconnect Ministries, Scott joined the board of Family Time Training, where I was already serving. During this time, I got to know him personally and he also got to know me, my ministry heart, and my passion for families. As a result, he asked me to be on the Transform World Family Challenge—4/14 Window Team, of which he became our leader. Under Scott's leadership, our team developed the Family Challenge, which can be found on his website, www.biblicalparenting.org under Partners/4-14 Window. Because I have been recommending the National Center for Biblical Parenting for so many years and it has been such an integral part of my ministry, it means a lot to me to have Scott Turansky and Joanne Miller contribute this chapter on heart-based parenting to my book.

—Julie Kurz

Using a Heart-Based Approach for Parenting

If you are a parent, grandparent, or a church leader working with children, please pause for a moment and reflect with us on the sacred adventure we are about to take: a journey into the heart of a child. We'll take you there, show you what the Bible says about it, and give you insight to help you work with a child in powerful ways.

When you enter the heart of a child, you are entering a sacred space. After all, God created people to be different than animals. He gave them spiritual hearts. So, before we proceed, please consider the holiness of this moment.

God asked Moses to do something similar when, through the burning bush, he said, "Take off your sandals, for the place where you are standing is holy ground" (Exodus 3:5, NIV).

When Saul saw the blinding light he fell to the ground (Acts 9:4). When Isaiah had the vision of God on his throne, he humbly proclaimed, "Woe to me!" (Isaiah 6:5).

Why compare the heart of a child with those glimpses of God's presence? It's because God made a significant shift in His work with people from the Old Testament to the New. Under the Old Covenant, the law was written on tablets of stone. God's presence was embodied in the ark of the covenant (Exodus 25:22) or in the tabernacle (Exodus 25:8) or in the Holy of Holies in the magnificent temple (Exodus 30:6).

But even in the Old Testament God promised something new and fresh, something very personal about His presence. He promised that someday He would write His law on our hearts (Jeremiah 31:33).

The heart of a person has become the place where Jesus wants to live (Ephesians 3:17) and where the Holy Spirit works (1 Corinthians 3:16).

What Is in the Heart?

Let's take a tour past the behavior of a child into the heart. The potential is endless. In short, the heart is the operating system of a person. It's the wrestling place where desires (Psalm 37:4), emotions (John 14:1), and beliefs (Romans 10:9-10) churn to form passions (2 Chronicles 31:21), attitudes (Hebrews 4:12), and convictions (Matthew 22:37).

Here are just a few examples of heart challenges that reveal themselves in behavior.

- A fourteen-year-old son wants things to go a certain way and when they don't, he mistreats others including his parents. His desires dominate his reactions.

- A three-year-old has a hard time with transitions because she emotionally invests in her activity of the moment. Those dramatic emotions are generated in the heart.

- A seven-year-old has fits of rage when corrected, or a two-year-old has a temper tantrum when you say no. Simply fixing outward behavior rarely helps children address the deeper issues.

- A sixteen-year-old believes that his job description in life is to have fun and therefore resists work of any kind.

- A twelve-year-old believes, "If my brother is annoying I have the right to punch him."

Kids sometimes want things they can't have or need life to go a certain way. Those desires, when not met, become demands and can prompt emotional outbursts. The problems are made worse, of course, when kids invest emotions into their desires so now the emotional investment increases the dramatic episodes, further complicating the issues. Thus, we see the root of the problem is a heart that must be addressed.

Furthermore, this combination of emotions and desires can create in children a rather narrow tolerance level for life challenges. When things don't go a particular way or expectations aren't met, then the child feels overwhelmed with emotion. The anger or sadness then overflows dramatically.

Trying to change behavior is not enough. Lasting and deeper change takes place when we address the heart. In short, the heart is a holy place, and when we start to work in it, as parents or grandparents, we are standing on holy ground.

A Samuel Moment

We all need a "Samuel encounter" to revolutionize our parenting. Samuel, in search of a king, was taught by God that, "Man looks on the outward appearance, but the LORD looks on the heart" (1 Samuel 16:7, ESV).

"But it's their behavior that gets them into trouble," you might say. Yes, that's definitely true. But behavior problems start in the heart. So, addressing them there produces more powerful results. Unfortunately, all too often parents rely on reward and punishment to motivate kids to change. It might look like this.

"Clean up your toys and you can have a snack." "Finish your homework and you can go out and play." "Straighten your room and you can have a friend over." "If you don't clean up that mess, you can't watch TV." "If you treat me with disrespect, I'm taking your iPad."

Reward and punishment often work for the short term, but serious side effects frequently occur. Here's what's happening inside the child's heart. A steady diet of rewards for desired behaviors and punishment for undesired behavior appeals to the selfishness in a child. It teaches kids to do things to get something in return. "I'll give you what you want if you do what I say."

In short, kids start asking the wrong questions about life. "What's in it for me?" "Are you going to pay me for that?" "I did what you asked, so what do I get?" "What's the minimum I need to do to get back to my video game?" "Is the punishment worth the misbehavior?" Reward and punishment always fall short of true and lasting heart change.

As you observe your child you'll see heart issues erupt into behavior problems like bad attitudes, disrespect, meanness, resistance, defiance, blaming, and tantrums.

Although you may get a fast response from a child by giving a reward or punishment, the new behavior is likely just superficial and short-lived. Kids want the rewards and are less focused on doing what's right. It doesn't take long to see that children who are raised with a justice mentality end up mistreating their parents or they try to bargain with them over even the most basic things.

How Do You Get Inside?

Some parents think reaching the heart means to talk more to their kids. Others think it means more physical touch. Still others think a heart-based approach means being compassionate, or praying more with their children. All of those things are helpful, but the heart is a complicated place and true heart-work goes much deeper.

Every child is unique. But each child develops certain patterns of thinking and acting in response to life situations. Many of those patterns need adjusting and parents are in a strategic role to help make that happen. When you work on the heart, then behavior naturally changes.

In reality, most children need a multi-faceted approach to change, but the starting point is usually the same. Choose one of your children and ask this first question to get things started. "What tendency do I see in my child that makes me feel uncomfortable?"

Tendencies are indications of heart problems. If your child is disrespectful once, that may be an accident. If he's disrespectful a second time, that might be a coincidence, but if he's disrespectful a third time, you better start looking at the heart because it appears that a tendency is developing.

Jesus was on a mission to teach us more about the heart. He said it this way. "Make a tree good and its fruit will be good, or make a tree bad and its fruit will be bad, for a tree is recognized by its fruit" (Matthew 12:33, NIV).

God gives parents an intuitive radar that's sensitive to a child's weaknesses. You'll feel uncomfortable because you know this current pattern your child has, if not changed, will hinder the child's success. Or, if this current pattern continues, this child is in for some big problems. That parental sensitivity is important because it gives parents an indication of where to work in a child's life. That uncomfortable feeling might reveal itself in you as confusion, frustration, or even anger.

For example, some parents identify heart issues with these statements. My son has a tendency to pick on his sister. My daughter tends to be self-focused and complains and whines continually. The anger I see in my child is much greater than the situation warrants. Every time I ask my son to do something, I get disrespect in return. My child is failing at school because he won't apply himself. My son is consumed with electronics. Each of those challenges are indications of something significantly wrong going on in the heart.

The Value of Training

Some parents feel so overwhelmed when they see a child's weakness, they want to get the child into therapy. They know this child is in serious trouble and that seeing a counselor might be productive. So, let's confirm your concern right now. Your child DOES need therapy. Every child needs therapy. But you are the best therapist for your child, if you have a plan. We believe the best counselors for a child are the parents. It's God's design. If parents can develop strategies that reach the heart, then their daily interactions become the therapy kids need to overcome those challenges.

Therapy involves practice sessions. If your child couldn't walk, you'd be getting her physical therapy. If your child couldn't talk, you'd be getting him speech therapy. The work you do in the heart involves practice and it strengthens character. It's called character therapy.

To fully address the heart, it's essential that parents move from correction-dominated parenting to training. Many parents make the mistake of focusing their energy on extinguishing negative behaviors and trying to get rid of them. They are hyper-focused on removing the problem and their primary tool is correction. The result is a lot of negative parenting. "Cut it out." "Stop it." "If you keep that up I'm going to…"

In fact, many parents have in their minds a justice mentality that says, "If you do this then you get that" both negatively in the form of punishment, and positively in the form of a reward. Unfortunately they miss the heart. That's back to a behavior modification system that might produce some immediate change but it will hinder long-term growth.

What you want is an adjustment in the child's heart. God uses a term in His Word to describe how this takes place. It's called training.

Training isn't just stopping a negative behavior, but it's a 180-degree turn replacing the wrong actions with the right response or action and practicing them. That's why the Bible encourages parents to "Train up a child…" (Proverbs 22:6, ESV).

Instead of investing your attention on what your child is doing wrong, ask yourself, "Where do we want to go?" or "What heart quality does my child need to develop to overcome this weakness?" The child with anger episodes needs to develop self-control. The child who is mean, needs to develop kindness. The child who reacts poorly during transitions needs to develop flexibility. And so on.

This one thought process alone makes parenting more positive and helpful. Instead of focusing on what you want to get rid of, you are now looking toward the goal. With this approach, you'll now help your child develop life-skills to face those challenges forever.

Before we delve a bit deeper into specific areas of training, let's look at the issue of consequences. Parents often move to consequences too quickly. Firmness is important in a heart-based approach and there are many other firmness tools besides consequences. Furthermore, consequences have a different function in a heart-based approach than they do in a behavior modification approach. It's another example of how a heart-based approach is completely different and why it works so well.

If you take the iPad away for disrespect, for example, in a heart-based approach, you don't set a period of time. Rather, you require some movement toward the goal. You might say, "Son, I'm taking your iPad away because you are being disrespectful to your mom. I want to give it back to you but first you must demonstrate that you are contributing to family life and responding well to your mom's instructions." Using this approach, you are focusing on the positive goal and using the consequence as motivation to help you train more effectively.

Now, instead of focusing on a behavior to extinguish, you are focusing on a life-skill to develop. Drawing attention to the positive heart quality helps you move from punishment to discipline. That distinction is significant in a heart-based approach.

Punishment focuses on past problems. Discipline focuses on future success.

Punishment is often motivated out of anger. Discipline is motivated out of love.

Punishment seeks justice. Discipline means to teach.

Punishment is negative. Discipline is positive.

The parent's positive stance now gives a new perspective to the daily interaction. As a parent or grandparent, you identify the heart quality as a target and then coach, teach, and require your child make progress toward that goal.

Caden is eight years old and has Attention Deficit Hyperactivity Disorder. His mom and dad want to do what's right but they are puzzled, confused, and often frustrated by their son's lack of impulse control and high energy.

As is often the case, the reward-punishment suggestions they received from books and counselors weren't working. Here's why. Using external motivation for kids who are highly internally motivated rarely works. Caden is already internally motivated. He's driven with strong desires. Using reward or punishment might work for the short term, but it usually doesn't bring about long-term change.

Kids with ADHD need a multi-faceted solution because the biological challenges going on in the brain must be met with strong heart qualities to manage those urges. With practice sessions and training, children grow stronger in their hearts and learn to rely on internal messages to increase impulse control.

With a lot of training Caden developed "others thinking" to become more sensitive to how his actions affect those around him. He also developed more self-control using practice sessions. Also, parents helped create more structure in Caden's heart by practicing following instructions and correction. Parents worked on Caden's heart by increasing his character to match the biological urges he experienced.

Caden is still active, but he's much more pleasant to be around. His heart is more sensitive and he is growing in his ability to manage his behavior. In fact, remarkably, his schoolteacher said, "I see you put Caden on medication." The same changes she saw in Caden are typical of other children who used medication to address the issues.

We aren't opposed to medication. But parents often find it helpful to try other solutions. Often when parents use a heart-based approach, kids change so much they get off medication or don't need it. You'll have to make that important decision with your doctor. Don't rush it. Just work on character and see what happens.

The Importance of Obedience

When parents measure their children's cooperation level, most wish things were better. Children sometimes resist instructions, argue about tasks, and are sometimes defiant. In fact, take a moment and consider your child's cooperation level. When families improve in the "Getting Things Done" department of life, then tension decreases and the family enjoys itself more.

Most children would benefit from intentional work in the area of cooperation and parents and grandparents are the best people to provide that guidance. Here's why. Learning to get things done smoothly isn't just about cleaning up the kitchen and putting the clothes away. It's about life-skills and character development. It's about tendencies of the heart.

In a home, children learn how to give up their agenda, stay on task to finish a job, and follow instructions that meet the expectations of the person giving them. When children grow in their ability to cooperate, they become less selfish, develop responsibility, and learn to think about life from another's point of view.

Cooperation teaches essential life lessons to children. In fact, the Bible calls this process obedience (Ephesians 6:1). God has hidden within obedience the secret ingredients kids need to be successful in life. Important life lessons are learned in the home.

As you are reading this, you are likely nodding your head and recognizing that all of this makes perfect sense. But let's take this a step further. All kinds of weaknesses in a child are addressed when parents teach their children how to follow instructions well.

The child who doesn't have integrity to tell the truth begins to develop that internal strength necessary to do the hard work of being honest. The child who has a narrow tolerance level and is easily angered increases flexibility and doesn't get angry as often. Even the child who has a hard time focusing, practices following instructions and develops a greater ability to stay on task and manage attention better.

So many good things happen inside the heart of a child when practicing following instructions, but the practice sessions need to be practical and targeted at patterns or tendencies. The child who has the wait-a-minute disease each time you give an instruction needs to develop the life-skill of responding to others' needs not just her own.

Jack is four years old and ignores parental instructions. Mom has to repeat herself several times and even has to yell before her son gets up and starts moving. Here's the problem inside of Jack's heart. He doesn't feel that internal sense of obligation when given a task to do or when Mom is talking.

Obligation is the basis for responsibility. It's that internal feeling mature people have that gets their bills paid on time, locks the doors at night, or gets the oil changed in the car. Children can begin to develop obligation at age 2. They learn things like, "When I'm done playing I need to put my toys away."

Jack needs some therapy to strengthen that sense of obligation. So, parents practice 20 times a day requiring Jack to come when called. First they explain to him about this new plan and how valuable it is and how it's going to improve their relationship and give him some very important things in his heart. Then they start practicing.

Several times an hour Mom calls Jack by just saying his name. Jack is expected to come. If he does she encourages him by pointing out the heart quality of cooperation he's developing. If he doesn't come the first time, she goes and gets him to increase the discomfort inside because his name was called. This isn't discomfort with the parent. It's the uncomfortable feeling of obligation that responsible people feel when called or given a task to do.

Coming when called is important for young children. One of the challenges of the child with ADHD is the ability to focus. Twenty times a day, Mom could give an instruction and encourage her son to stay on task, coaching him to complete the job without getting off track. The practice becomes therapy for the heart to develop internal qualities needed to address his challenges.

Don't Forget Honor

God has hidden within obedience and honor the secret ingredients for a child's success. That's why he's given them a two-fold job description in the Bible (Ephesians 6:1-3).

Honor adds a completely different dimension to any home. Honor can be defined this way. "Treating people as special, doing more than what's expected, and having a good attitude." The word *honor* is used in nine different commands in the Bible. It's not just for kids. It's a life-skill.

Romans 10:12 says to honor one another above yourselves. It's for everyone and can permeate a family's DNA if they work on it. Honor affects the way people think, the way they act, and the way they treat others around them. Honor motivates parents to treat children differently. It gives children more constructive ways to interact with their parents. It helps siblings develop tolerance and patience. Honor builds incredibly strong bonds that, in turn, benefit all members of the family.

Honor is customer service brought home. In the same way a business treats you as special to show your value as a customer, every person can learn to show honor to others to communicate their value.

It's interesting that God teaches honor is taught in the home first. Children learn to give up their agenda, give someone else the first piece or best seat, and they generally think of others as more important than themselves (Philippians 2:3-4).

Honor, just like obedience, takes practice. You might send your child to do an honor check in the bathroom. The benefit is that the child must see what needs to be done and then do it. Honor teaches children to take initiative. Reporting back uses accountability to strengthen that inner sense of obligation.

You might have a list of chores for a child to do or the list of tasks to complete in the morning before starting the day. You could add one more thing to the list called "The Honor Thing." What is that? It's undefined. "Look around and find one thing you can do to add energy to this family or contribute to this home."

Honor is about contribution. Sometimes children can become self-focused. When parents train children to show honor, it makes a huge difference in their lives both now and in the future. If you want your children to fly straight, teach them obedience. If you want them to fly high, teach them honor.

Conclusion

The heart can be a confusing place for children and their parents. Emotions, desires, and beliefs swirl around creating all kinds of challenges. What children need is direction, guidance, and order, not just for their behavior but also for their hearts. That's why God gave children parents.

Children don't have the self-discipline and wisdom to manage life alone. They need parental discipline that's focused on life-skill development. The heart contains patterns of thinking that can result in more mature behavior. Training is essential. As parents take on the role of coaches for their kids, requiring practice, affirming progress, and pointing them toward the goal, then children experience powerful change.

If you're experiencing significant tension in your home, it's likely that you'll want to adjust some of the ways you train your children. You're likely doing some good things. But maybe your child needs some different good things.

Some parents give up and simply tolerate the frustration looking forward to the day the child moves out of the home. It doesn't have to be that way. If you're stuck, get help. God wants to provide the tools and strategies you need to influence your children both now and for the rest of their lives.

If you'd like help, please reach out to us at biblicalparenting.org. We've made it our life goal to equip parents with a heart-based approach and to empower church leaders to develop parent discipleship programs in their churches. We'd love to support you in the most significant job in the world, preparing children as the next generation of leaders in our world.

Resources

Dr. Scott Turansky and Joanne Miller, RN, BSN head up the National Center for Biblical Parenting. They have trained over 150 presenters and over 200 coaches to work with parents and church leaders. They have written 15 books on parenting and have four video training programs to strengthen families.

HOW DO CHILDREN DEVELOP SPIRITUALLY?

my model for picturing the way faith is developed in children

O ver the 17 years that I was children's director in Littleton, Colorado, I kept asking God, "How exactly do children form spiritually?" and "What are the factors that are important in a child's spiritual development?" As I prayed, contemplated, observed, and studied God's Word over several years, this is the model that eventually developed in my thinking.

Let's go through it one part at time.

Every child is a new thought of God!

I will never forget the message I received on an invitation to a baby shower. I opened the envelope and read, "Every child is a new thought of God!" What a wonderful truth. One I have never forgotten. God knew us before we were born. We were God's idea, created in His image to bring glory to Himself and to fulfill His desire to have relationship with us. We see all these ideas in God's Word:

> He chose us in him before the creation of the world, to be holy and blameless in His sight (Ephesians 1:4, ESV).

> For you created my inmost being; you knit me together in my mother's womb… My frame was not hidden from you when I was made in the secret place, when I was woven together in the depths of the earth. Your eyes saw my unformed body; all the days ordained for me were written in your book before one of them came to be (Psalm 139:13-16, NIV).

> …He who made you, who formed you in the womb, and who will help you: Do not be afraid… (Isaiah 44:2, NIV).

> …I have upheld you since your birth, and have carried you since you were born (Isaiah 46:3, NIV).

Our children are God's idea; He thought of them and wanted them to be born into this world. He has a special plan for each and every one of our children. He will be with them and will help and guide them to accomplish His purposes as they respond to a relationship with Him. Our prayer is that our children will grow to love God, their Creator and Father, and allow Him to guide and direct their lives.

God's Plan Is for the Home to Be a Discipleship Center for the Children

The spiritual formation of children begins with the love of parents who love God with all their hearts. The way God designed life is for a man and woman to love their Creator and love each other the way God loves us.

I remember when Dave and I had been married three or four years, we began longing to share the love we had for each other with someone else. That is when our desire for children began in our marriage. Our daughter, Elizabeth, came about a year and a half later. Our hearts expanded to welcome this addition to our family, and we longed to introduce her to our heavenly Father. God's plan for the home is that a love for God and each other is modeled so the hearts of our children will receive our teaching, open up to the Creator, and also desire to know and love Him. Does it always work out His way? As we discussed in previously, we live in an imperfect world where our choices sometimes negatively impact God's intended plan, but He always stands ready to forge a new plan for those who humbly ask for new direction.

God's plan is that children be led to Jesus and discipled in their own homes. We need to look at our homes as small groups, life groups, or community groups. When we are trying to find a small group at church, we look for a safe place where people are real, authentic, and live life together. Doesn't that describe a family? We need to think of the home as a child's first small group. Dr. Rob Rienow describes this idea in his book, *God's Grand Vision for the Home*:

> Perhaps you are a part of a church that has "small groups" or "growth groups." These are groups of people who gather together regularly to encourage each other spiritually, study the Bible, and pray for one another. Being part of a group like this can make a big difference in a person's spiritual journey. (2007, p. 33)

In his book *Visionary Parenting*, Dr. Rienow shares four principles for a God-filled life that are so valuable to think about in relation to our homes:

1. Who we are at home is who we really are.

2. A child's heart is impressed through his/her parents' character.

3. A child's view of God is formed through his/her parents' character.

4. A child learns what is important through the family schedule. (2009, pp. 35–42)

Parents that view their home as a place of discipleship for children can have a tremendous impact. A few years ago, I attended a conference where the speaker was Michelle Anthony, author of *Spiritual Parenting*. She shared an example from a time she and her husband spent teaching God's Word to their children. One morning, Michelle's husband read the story of the Good Samaritan to their daughter before she went to school. He told his daughter to watch for an opportunity to be a "good Samaritan" that day. When her daughter got home from school, Michelle informed her they were going out for ice cream. Michelle was unaware of the challenge her husband had given until they got to the ice cream shop and found a homeless man leaning up against the wall of the store. Michelle's daughter said, "Mom, I would rather give my ice cream money to the homeless man than have some today." Her mother was very surprised, but she granted her daughter her request. She later found out about the challenge her husband had given to have the eyes of Jesus on that day. This is the kind of impact we can have when we teach our children God's Word and challenge them to make it relevant in their lives. God delights in honoring our faith in action and brings us opportunities to reflect His love. The faith of our children will soar when "God shows up" like He did in this example!

One of the things I have observed over the years is children who regularly pray at home with their families have a much greater comfort level praying at church. There are so many things that are being accomplished in the lives of our children when we see our homes as a discipleship center.

The Community of Faith Also Has a Significant Role in the Spiritual Development of Our Children

A healthy church is like an extended family. The church can also be a safety net around a home when it goes through the difficult times every family will inevitably experience. Children benefit greatly when they experience the love and acceptance of aunts, uncles, grandparents, and cousins. Children need to know there are people other than their parents who also love and serve Jesus in their lives.

I remember having this experience when I was a child. I was always excited to go to church and receive the hugs from the older people and see my friends. I could feel the love of all of these people and could tell they were excited to see me too. I would watch them worship God in the service and would see them sometimes do nice things for my family. It made a real impact on me. I remember an older gentleman in our church we knew as Mr. Monroe. Our family sat in the row behind him each week—back in the days when your pew "had your name on it." He used to slip me Lifesavers in the middle of the sermon. I always looked forward to that on Sundays when I thought the sermon would never end. It was his way of letting us know he had remembered the little children who worshiped with him each week and he cared about us. I would also watch the older kids and had a desire to be like them. They went to the youth group, and I couldn't wait to join them.

Sunday School was also a regular part of my life. I remember two teachers in particular: Mrs. Olson had a way of making me feel so special and Mrs. DeVries really loved God. It was *so important* to her that we memorize ten verses in our sixth-grade year. Those verses became an early foundation for my faith. Mrs. DeVries had a big impact on my life and my spiritual development. She would have class parties at her house (she always had amazing cake ☺) and since I happened to be her daughter's age, I got to go to her house often, throughout my teenage years. This gave me additional opportunities to experience Mrs. DeVries' love and passion for God. I thought she lived what she taught. There was no hypocrisy that I ever detected.

One of the greatest impacts the church can have is the encouragement and love given to our children by the people who teach them. Lifeway Research did some work on the impact of other Christians in the lives of our children at church. They concluded that all of our children need relationships with people outside the family who believe what their parents are teaching them. This is one of the significant factors that keeps our kids in the faith. Here is the conclusion of their research:

> Teens that had at least one adult from church who made a significant time investment in their lives…were more likely to keep attending church. More of those who stayed in church—by a margin of 46% to 28%—said five or more adults at church had invested time with them personally and spiritually. https://www.dallasnews.com/life/faith/2007/08/08/ways-to-keep-young-adults-in-church

The number of quality resources available to the church for teaching children is phenomenal, and when the teaching in the church is connected to teaching in the home, it can be very effective. Teaching in the church needs to be followed up at home, re-taught, and applied to life situations. If a child has a question on something they were taught at church, they will usually process it for a while and most likely the question will come up at home where they feel more comfortable asking questions.

At the beginning of my ministry in Littleton, I was teaching regularly and had some very funny but revealing discussions with parents. During one quarter, I had a series of vivid flannel graph lessons on choosing the "narrow way" versus the "broad way." (Betty Lukins— the best flannel graph of its time!) It was very effective, so much so children were telling their parents they should not drive on Broadway, the street in front of our church, one of the main streets through Littleton. Several parents came to me and asked me what I was teaching. When I told them it was Matthew 7:13-17, the teaching on the narrow way versus the broad way, we just laughed. In retrospect, I realized I failed to have a proper understanding of a couple of things: the importance of a home/church connection and the principles of concrete and abstract thinking in children In this situation, I certainly could have done a better job with my concrete thinkers.

When parents are engaged with what is being taught at church and therefore have some idea of the context of their child's question, they will be much more likely to capitalize on important opportunities for spiritual understanding. When the home and the church are working together as partners, the spiritual development of church-grown children will be at its best.

The Value and Impact of Our Spiritual Heritage

The last thing in our children's spiritual development that God helped me to see as vitally important is to learn their parents' spiritual heritages. I actually became aware of this as I shared my stories of faith with children in my ministry and had amazing "all eyes on me" experiences. I would share how I accepted Jesus as my Savior, when I had doubted my faith, what mistakes I made as a child, why certain verses were my favorite, and sometimes how I wanted to respond to something that made me feel angry during the week. These personal stories seemed to always hold the attention of the children and what I believe God said to me in His still small voice is that our children need stories of faith in three areas: God's story, our stories and the stories of extended family members, and stories of men and women from past generations whose faithfulness to God set the stage for them to do amazing things for the kingdom of God.

First, it is important that our children know God's story, the big picture from before Creation to the restored kingdom we are looking forward to experiencing. Instead of isolated stories from the Bible, it is critical that children understand the big picture of the Bible, the reason God gave us the Bible. When I teach the Bible to children, I always begin with a timeline from Creation to the restored kingdom, showing the children where each Bible story fits into the timeline of the big picture that is God's story. This gives me the opportunity to share the gospel and God's unconditional love for all of us through Jesus Christ every time I teach. As Phil Vischer says in his video series and curriculum *What's In the Bible?*— "Children need to understand God's rescue plan."

Secondly, our children need to hear *our* stories of faith and the faith stories of extended family members who are Christians. The more stories the better. I have never had disengaged children or discipline problems when a story is being told. If parents don't feel like they have many stories because their faith is recent or they are first generation believers, they can still tell their stories of how they began their journeys of following Christ and what significant events led them to where they are today. Life has a way of forcing us to God's Word sometimes. It is during those times that it is important to share what God is telling you through His Word.

As I was reading all the research about kids leaving their faith after spending all of their lives in church, I started doing some of my own research to try to prove the statistics wrong in my church. I discovered that my church was no different from other churches. When I was the director of children's ministries in Littleton, Colorado, I led a discipleship group of fifth and sixth graders. These kids had to want to be in my group, and I could determine if they wanted to be there because they had to fill out an application and be invited by me. I never turned anyone away, but I wanted to see that they, not just their parents, took the initiative to be there. One afternoon I asked eight children in this group if they had heard their parents' stories of the beginning of their journeys to follow Christ and how they had found faith in Jesus. Only one girl raised her hand. She said she had heard her mother's story but not her dad's. The other seven could not recall being told how their parents found faith in Christ. Children need stories of faith to encourage faith in their lives. These stories represent real stories of real people from their family and documented history. Children need stories of faith to aid them in deciding to have their own faith. It is one of the big determining factors in our children's decision to follow Christ. Spiritual development in the lives of our children must be intentional and a priority in family life. The motivations for our faith and our love for God and His story of redemption should be clearly visible to our children.

Thirdly, they need to hear about the men and women from the history of the Church who demonstrated faith that sometimes cost them their lives. William Tyndale is an example. He was King Henry VII's most wanted criminal because he translated the Bible into English. Another example is George Muller who demonstrated amazing faith as he founded orphanages, which impacted over 2,000 children in England. How about Hudson Taylor who left everything he had in England to reach China for Christ and founded the China Inland Mission? There was also Dietrich Bonhoeffer and his struggle against Hitler; Jim Elliot, who lost his life trying to reach the Auca Indians in Ecuador; Martin Luther and his passion for Scripture to be read by all; and Gladys Aylward, who led 100 children to safety in the name of Jesus. The list goes on and on! Our children need to experience these stories of people whose faith meant everything to them, even at the risk of death.

Vision Video has an excellent series of DVD's on men and women who have made significant contributions and sacrifices for their faith. It is called *The Torchlighters: Heroes of the Faith*, produced by the Christian History Institute and Voice of the Martyrs (www.visionvideo.com). *The Torchlighters* is a series of animated programs with strong values and educational content for youth ages 8-12. Each episode presents the story of a true-life hero from Christian history. Kids will see what God can do through a *Torchlighter* and will be challenged to carry their own torch while learning about the history of our faith. I have been showing these videos to children for years and I am currently using them for our family movie night at our church, followed by discussion questions for families at the conclusion of each movie. This promotes great family discussions, which are so important to a child's faith.

After one of my family movie nights, one of the moms thanked me for the movie and the family discussion questions at the end. She commented that she'd had a desire to have these kinds of conversations with her son for so long but hadn't known how to bring them up. She could now continue to talk about the subject at home. This is exactly what I had hoped to accomplish at these family movie nights.

Some of my favorites in this animated series are stories of Samuel Morris, Gladys Aylward, Robert Jermain, Martin Luther, John Wesley, and William Tyndale. These are stories of faith I did not hear as a child. I find this so perplexing. Christian history and the stories of these men and women were virtually left out of my spiritual journey. I am enjoying this series as much as the children, maybe more, as I see the amazing hand of God in the lives of these people. It encourages my faith. I believe we need to include these stories in the spiritual journey of our children and pray that the stories will have an impact on their faith. I hope this inspires you to get this series and watch them with your children or your grandchildren.

Spiritual development in our children's lives has to be intentional in all of these areas and a priority in our family lives. Our love for God, His story of redemption, the free gift of salvation for all who trust Him, and the motivation for our faith should be clear and observable to our children. If we believe and have the gift of salvation, we will want to share it.

I have the privilege of being a part of the 4/14 Window Movement, which is a global missions movement whose aim is to reach, rescue, root, and release young people all over the world to grab hold of their inheritance in Christ and transform their world through His power. As a part of the U.S. team, we developed The Family Challenge because just living in your home doesn't mean your children are catching the faith. The Family Challenge encourages parents to do three things in the home with their children. These actions are taken from Deuteronomy 6:

- Build relationship
- Share Scripture
- Practice faith

You can learn more about the Family Challenge at the following web address, and hopefully you will decide to commit to the challenge: http://414familychallenge.com.

Resources

Christian History Institute and Voice of the Martyrs. *The Torchlighters: Heroes of the Faith* series (www.visionvideo.com).

Family Time Training—www.famtime.com.

Rienow, Rob. *Visionary Parenting.* Randall House, 2009.

Turansky, Scott & Miller, Joanne, RN, BSN. The Family Challenge: Passing the Faith From Your Heart to Theirs, National Center for Biblical Parenting, 2012, http://414familychallenge.com.

Vischer, Phil, *What's in the Bible,* (DVD series and curriculum). www.jellytelly.com; www.whatsinthebible.com.

SHEPHERDING CHILDREN TO FAITH IN CHRIST

Growing Up With Jesus

In the Evangelical tradition where I was raised, from the time I was a young mom, I sensed parents being very anxious for their children to make a decision for Christ. Unfortunately, I too became one of those anxious parents. We love our children so much that we genuinely want them to believe the truth of the Gospel. We want to see them with us in eternity, and we also want them to live in fellowship with God in ways that will spare them from the snares of this world. So as Christian parents, we wanted our children's salvation to be clear and we wanted it to be decisive, something we could assign a date to, remind our children of, and celebrate, so we wouldn't have to *worry* anymore. When our children make a decision to accept Jesus into their heart and life, it is a great relief for us as parents, but I see now that our anxiousness in this area has caused us to make some unwise decisions with potentially negative consequences for our children.

This topic of childhood conversions is one that has frequently come up in my discussions with youth pastors who have been curious about my ministry of connecting home and church. On many occasions a youth pastor would tell me something like this: "Some of our students who have grown up in the church really struggle with whether they are Christians or not, even when their parents think they are."

"They tell me their parents assure them they were saved because they accepted Jesus when they were young or if they grew up in a liturgical tradition because they were baptized into the faith as an infant. But most of the time the teen doesn't remember the event and it has more meaning for their parent than it does for the teen. Some are not even sure if they now want to be Christians." Many youth pastors have shared with me, the way these childhood conversion experiences have really complicated their work in bringing teenagers into the faith.

This information was a real eye opener for me. It caused me to rethink how children who have grown up in the church and have been taught about Jesus all their lives come to a meaningful and lasting faith. I began to ask myself if a lack of understanding as to how children come to faith has contributed to young adults not staying in church and retaining their faith into adulthood. I wondered if some ever really had faith. Is this time of departure from faith just part of their journey to know Jesus in an authentic way? The questions just kept coming.

How *do* we lead our children into an authentic and lasting relationship with Christ? Does conversion really fit into the neat little box we have constructed when we invite children to ask Jesus into their hearts? Is "belief" the same thing as a decision to ask Jesus into my heart? Is it possible we have been inoculating children with just enough of the Bible to assure them of their salvation without allowing them to really *own* their faith? Have we prevented them from experiencing the growth they need to mature as believers? What is our God-given role as parents and children's workers in leading children to Christ? And most importantly, what can we do to be more effective in keeping our church-grown children in their childhood faith and moving to a mature adult faith?

These are questions I have been wrestling with for the last ten years or more, and I believe they are critical questions for those of us who desire to lead the children entrusted to us, into the kingdom of God. We are living in difficult days for the Church. All our efforts need to be founded in God's wisdom with a clear understanding of what we can do to inspire our children to believe. I don't claim to have a full understanding of the mystery of salvation, but I firmly believe God will give us wisdom and understanding as we seek Him because our desire is the same as His—that children would come into His Kingdom for a lifetime.

This has been by far, the hardest chapter for me to write because my thoughts in this area have changed so much over the years, and my thinking is still not completely solidified. So I invite you to wrestle with me for the faith of the next generation and join me in asking the question, "How do we shepherd our children to salvation in the home and in the church in a way that leads them into a meaningful and lasting faith?"

Is Salvation an Event or a Journey?

If I could go back to those anxiety-ridden days of my early motherhood, I would do things differently. I would chill out and let God work more in the lives of my children and the children I worked with at church, knowing that He knows when they will believe and when they have believed. For some children, a definite decision might be important for their personality, but for others, believing and processing throughout their childhood and teen years is exactly what they need. I see now that our anxiety often kept us from allowing children to wrestle with the gospel so they could really take ownership of their faith.

What if we understood salvation in our children's lives to be a journey instead of an event? What would it look like and how would it be different?

For those of us who grew up in an evangelical tradition, I think you will agree that salvation was an event just like I described above. We were taught that salvation was ours when we made a *decision* to accept Jesus. This decision was described as asking Jesus into our heart and would be followed with our teachers assuring us of our salvation with words like this: "If you have accepted Christ as your Savior, you are saved, and God will never leave you."

For those who were brought up in a more liturgical tradition, you would probably say salvation begins in infancy and matures into acknowledging Christ as Lord because of the finished work of Christ for humanity. Whichever tradition you come from, both are struggling to keep their children in faith through the teen years and into adulthood.

My father was raised in the Presbyterian Church where their tradition was and still is to teach the children God's story during childhood and then have a confirmation class for them in their adolescence. In this class, the students are taught the doctrines of the faith, which encourage students to confess Jesus as their Lord and Savior. My understanding of the Presbyterian strategy is to confirm the children into their faith as a culmination of their understanding of making Jesus Lord and Savior of their lives. My father always said he was saved in his confirmation class, but when he married into my mother's evangelical family, his salvation was questioned (for pretty much all of his adult life) because he hadn't gone forward and made a decision to receive Christ into his life. That was the way his evangelical family members understood the salvation experience. What I remember my relatives saying was that confirmation does not save people. They considered going to confirmation as a work, and works don't save us. But many, like my father, do confirm their belief in Christ as Lord and Savior in the confirmation class.

In the evangelical community, our strategy in many churches was and still is to share the gospel in special events with an opportunity for children to come forward and receive Christ. In reality, these special events were necessary because the gospel was rarely the focus of the Bible story. The Bible story was taught each week as a stand-alone story, making the event of Jesus dying on the cross for our sins just another story. The lesson objectives focused on a biblical virtue, and children were encouraged to strive to attain the virtue reflected in the story of the day, to be like the Bible hero they studied that week— have faith like Abraham, obey like Noah, be courageous like David, etc. Therefore, it was necessary to have additional times where the gospel could be shared, so children could understand they needed to accept Jesus as their Savior. In my church, this would be done during

VBS or at church camp each year. (I will share more on the dangers of virtue-based teaching in Chapters 11 and 12.)

For many children who understand God's story at some level, decisions made in these settings can be very meaningful and the beginning of their relationship with Jesus. For others, this invitation caused stress, and they may have felt pressured into making a decision they didn't fully understand. In some instances, children are motivated to go forward to receive a gift or a Bible or simply because we've told them that making this decision means they will go to Heaven. And who wouldn't want to go to Heaven?

As a result of these types of decisions, many children have ended up with a false sense of security we gave them simply because they prayed the prayer. However, many of these children remain unsure of their salvation as they grow older, especially if they are not living a life of faith and obedience. The result is often like this: when children make a decision without really understanding the implications of that decision, they think they need to repeat the process and *really mean it this time* as they pray and accept Christ again. Sometimes this happens every time they hear the message and they question themselves, "Did I really mean it or did I pray it right?" I was one of those children.

Feeling the need to pray to accept Christ over and over may also be a result of not really grasping the significance of the Gospel when they were younger. Or, it may be the result of gaining new understanding of the Bible as they mature from concrete thinking to abstract thinking. There are also children who don't remember accepting Jesus, but relying on their parents' memory. They don't feel compelled to make another decision.

I remember a revered pastor's wife from my young adult years telling us very boldly at a women's retreat that she couldn't recall a decision she made for Christ. She said she didn't remember a time since she was a child that she didn't "believe in Jesus." Now I can tell you very confidently, that if she had not been that revered pastor's wife during that era in the evangelical community, many of us would have questioned her salvation. Even I was really taken aback by what she said, because we were taught that a clear personal decision had to be made for a person to be saved. We understood you needed to be able to remember it, (well, it was probably alright for your parents to remember it), to be able to share it and the more dramatic it was, the better!

But how can you question someone's faith if they believe the Gospel *now*? I remember as a teenager or young adult when I was starting to question my faith again. I remember just crying out to God and asking Him if I was saved. I still remember what seemed to me to be the quiet voice of God asking me, "Do you believe me *now*?" I said "yes," and that ended my battle. After that, every time I had those fearful thoughts, I would say, "Yes, I believe."

What if We Measured Our Salvation Based on *Belief* Rather Than a *Decision* to Receive Christ?

Several years ago, I decided to read the gospels and listen to the words of Jesus to try to understand for myself what Jesus said about salvation. I was overwhelmed by the number of times He said, "Believe in Me," especially in the book of John. Jesus also said, "Follow me," "Count the cost," and "Repent." But I was surprised at how few times Jesus said the word *repent*. To *believe* was what Jesus taught His disciples and anyone that listened to His message.

John 6 says,

> Then they asked him, "What must we do to do the works God requires?" Jesus answered, "The work of God is this: to believe in the one he has sent" (28-29, NIV).

> For my Father's will is that everyone who looks to the Son and believes in him shall have eternal life, and I will raise them up at the last day (40, NIV).

In John 5:24, Jesus says,

> Very truly I tell you, whoever hears my word and believes him who sent me has eternal life and will not be judged but has crossed over from death to life (NIV).

Grasping the fullness of the meaning of the word *believe* is significant and the key to understanding salvation. Jesus teaches that believing is the only thing we do for salvation, and it really isn't doing but responding in agreement to whom Jesus said He was—the Son of God—and what He did to secure our salvation. It brought me back to my Moody Bible Institute days where we studied the book of John and the Greek meaning of the word *believe*.

In Greek, the root word translated "faith" is the noun *pistis*, and "believe" is the verb *pisteuo*.

Pistis means "faith, belief, firm persuasion, assurance, firm conviction, and faithfulness."

Pisteuo means "to trust in and rely upon, commit to the charge of, confide in, have a mental persuasion."

Dictionary.com says that *believe* means "to have confidence in the truth, the existence, or the reliability of something, although without absolute proof that one is right in doing so. Only if one believes in something can one act purposefully."

So, true belief encompasses everything Jesus said about salvation—believe, repent, follow. Acknowledging my sin is synonymous with belief because that was Jesus' mission—to die for the sins of mankind. Following Jesus means to obey Jesus and walk in His ways. When we believe in something our belief inspires us to live in sync with whatever passion that belief creates in us. So, believing in Jesus will compel us to follow Jesus and walk in His ways despite the cost.

Dictionary.com says to follow means to "to go or come after." As a verb (used with an object) it means "to accept as a guide or leader, accept the authority of, or give allegiance to." Following Jesus and choosing to walk in His ways (obedience) is not a work because it comes as a result of believing the message of Jesus. And on top of that, it is the Holy Spirit who makes our transformation even possible. In John 14–17, Jesus promised His disciples that the Holy Spirit was coming to live within them so they could abide in His presence. The Triune God has it all covered. He did it all for us!

As teachers, how do we know if our children are really making a decision that merits our unqualified assurance of their salvation? There is no doubt that a child, even a preschooler, can express belief in Jesus that is a reflection of their level of understanding, and according to the teachings of Jesus this is *belief*! Only God knows their hearts, and He can give them the assurance they need in His own timing.

Many, if not all of our decisions in life, are flawed or incomplete in some way and as a result, many of our significant life decisions need to be periodically revisited, reviewed, and recommitted to. So, is it realistic to expect that a child can really make a lifetime decision at the age of 4, or 7, or even 12, without ever needing to engage in a recommitment process? The doubt that accompanies many, if not most childhood conversions, should not be viewed as unhealthy, but rather as a healthy opportunity to experience significant new growth. We lose a valuable opportunity to help our children in that growth process when we respond to their doubts with assurances that a childhood conversion experience requires no review, reflection, or recommitment.

The questions we really should be asking about our doubting children are these:

- Do these young people believe the gospel message?
- Are they relying on the finished work of Christ for their salvation?
- Do they have a desire to know God better?
- Do they have a lifestyle that increasingly reflects the values of a Christ follower?

These questions mirror the essence of James 2:14-25 and they are questions from which we should not shy away when older children begin to question the salvation experiences of their early childhoods. James challenges our faith when he says,

> What good is it, my brothers and sisters, if someone claims to have faith but has no deeds? (2:14, NIV).

He goes on developing this thought until verse 25.

What If We Understood Salvation in Our Children's Lives to Be a Journey of Belief Instead of a Transactional Event? What Would It Look Like and How Would It Be Different?

Much to my surprise, I am teaching children again! After we moved to Phoenix, Arizona, a pastor's wife with whom I was consulting was leading children's ministries in a small church plant. She asked me if I would just do it for them. I said no for about six months, and finally heard God's voice which seemed to be saying, "This would be a great opportunity to do all the things you are teaching other churches to do and experience for yourself the challenges of this paradigm shift. It could become a laboratory for your ministry!" So, I said yes to a minimal number of hours per week although my acceptance was contingent on finding a willing team of people to work with me.

I have been pleasantly surprised at how much I have enjoyed teaching children after so many years of overseeing children's ministries. Understanding better the process of spiritual development in church-grown children, and the significance of a journey of belief versus event-based decisions, I have made two big changes in my teaching.

First, I teach God's story in context, making God the main character, instead of focusing on the players in the story. I like doing God's story in one year instead of three years, so I don't lose the child in the long story because of their short attention span. In fact, we repeated "What's in the Bible" over two years so they would really know God's story well. Now I am doing a study called "The Life & Ministry of Jesus," a chronological study of the life of Jesus produced by Group Publishing Company.

As a result of this repetition, the children I teach have come to know God's story very well and they understand the gospel. They understand the problem of sin in the Old Testament, the sin in the world, their own sin, and why God promised a Messiah—a Savior who would rescue us and bring us back into relationship with the Creator. When you teach God's story, the gospel is explained each week, so they get it!

The second thing I do differently is to focus on belief instead of decisions. I have refrained from asking for children to make public decisions to ask Jesus into their heart or commit their lives to Jesus, even though I have had many opportunities to do so. During those moments, I ask the child to retreat to a corner of the room to be alone with Jesus and their journal, and write their response to Him via the questions I am asking each week. They usually end up under a table or desk, thinking, and writing God a letter. I do this so they will get comfortable talking to God on their own. I don't read their responses, even though I could, since they turn in their journals to me so they can be referred to later. I think their thoughts should be between them and God. I am just the teacher of God's Word, the sower of the seed. God does the rest.

I don't feel that responsibility to turn in numbers for annual reports like we used to have to do. I know these children are surrounded by God's sovereign love and protection. I know their belief is growing in size and strength each week, and I know He is going to lead and guide them to a level of commitment to Him that will be evidenced by their daily life choices. I don't want children to feel pressure or guilt, or shame for failing to respond to a very public invitation to receive Jesus. I want whatever happens in their hearts to originate from God speaking to them and working in their heart and not from me.

What If I Lost an Opportunity?

At times, I have questioned myself. What if I missed an opportunity to help a child make a decision to follow Christ? The peace I now feel in this area is the result of recognizing God is in control and He will not lose an opportunity when a child is seeking Him. I believe God is sovereign over all of our seeking and leads us to Himself in amazing ways. He knows a child's level of belief and their time of commitment, and I believe He responds to children who are truly seeking Him. This is the direction God has been confirming in my ministry, and I am seeing His life-changing work in the hearts of my students.

Allow me to give you an example of some of the amazing things that happened in my class this year. One week my lesson was about Matthew, the tax collector, leaving his friends and following Jesus. I wasn't aware this was a particularly moving lesson, but one of the boys, a 4th grader named Blake, raised his hand, and said enthusiastically, "I want to follow Jesus!" Another boy also said, "So do I!" Wow! I didn't even initiate this response. This response came from Blake's heart, not something I inspired. He responded out of his heart, not out of pressure to accept Christ! Others joined him in affirming their belief and desire to follow.

Was this his "decision-event?" I really don't know, but I know God is stirring in his heart, and God knows where this child is in his journey with Him! It wasn't a formal invitation. I didn't lead him through a prayer. He was confessing his belief that Jesus was who He said He was, and I believe this child wanted to be a part of God's kingdom!

When is that point of belief in our lives? Does it need to be a formal decision for God to accept us?

Another week, after studying Jesus Feeding the Five Thousand in John 6 and the teaching that Jesus is the Bread of Life, we played a much needed game to release pent up energy. Connor jumped up in the air, gave me a high five and said, "I believe!" Here was a tangible example of how excited he has become about the Bible and his faith!

We planned a baptism service for Easter, and in staff meeting we talked about whether there were any children around 12 years old who were ready to be baptized. I had two boys around that age in my class, so I talked to them. They understood baptism and what it meant, so I asked, "Are you ready to share your belief in Jesus and be baptized?" Both said, "Yes!" I didn't ask them about a decision, I asked them if they *believed* and were ready to follow Jesus in baptism.

I feel so much more comfortable working with children spiritually when I focus on belief rather than making decisions. It is much more natural to focus on belief rather than a formal decision. How do you talk about a "decision" except to measure what people are "doing" as a result of their decision? Certainly deeds are important but too often these discussions cause shame and guilt, rather than assurance, because none of us are reading our Bibles enough, praying, or sharing Christ enough to really say we are doing well with our decision to receive Christ as Savior.

I believe talking about belief is much more productive because the focus is on our hearts, not our works. One of the boys who had expressed belief a few weeks before asked me, "What if I have trouble believing sometimes?" I told him that most people do have times when belief in Jesus is hard, and even I have those times when I question almost everything. It gave me an opportunity to share how I work through unbelief. We looked up Mark 9:23 where Jesus told the father of the boy he had just healed, "Everything is possible for one who believes" (NIV). Immediately the boy's father exclaimed, "I do believe; help me overcome my unbelief" (NIV). We can even ask God to help us believe, and God works in our hearts giving us comfort and peace.

I am firmly convinced this method of shepherding children to faith is healthier than the event-based strategy of our past. Salvation is a mystery that no one completely understands. Every journey is unique and takes a lifetime to develop. We will not fully comprehend it all until we are reunited with our Father and Creator in Heaven. But with this approach, belief conversations lead to heart conversations, and heart conversations lead to decisions, and those decisions are eventually made visible in daily choices and actions.

What Is the God-Given Role as Parents and Teachers in Leading Our Children to Christ?

I like what the Insight authors Sally Michael, Jill Nelson, and Bud Burk give in their book *Helping Children to Understand the Gospel* (see pages 7-15). They use the parable of the sower in Matthew 13:3-9 to help us understand our role in the salvation of the children entrusted to us. Jesus said,

> "A farmer went out to sow his seed. As he was scattering the seed, some fell along the path, and the birds came and ate it up. Some fell on rocky places, where it did not have much soil. It sprang up quickly, because the soil was shallow. But when the sun came up the plants were scorched, and they withered because they had no root. Other seed fell among thorns, which grew up and choked the plants. Still other seed fell on good soil where it produced a crop—a hundred, sixty or thirty times what was sown. Whoever has ears, let them hear" (NIV).

What if we viewed salvation as a gardening experience, sowing and nurturing the seeds and watching them grow, knowing that God created these children of ours and has a plan for them to blossom in their unique faith story? The most important thing for us as parents and children's workers is to know our role and not try to take responsibility for what we cannot control. Our role is to sow the seed of the gospel in the lives of our children in a partnership with the home and the church. We can cultivate the soil with good relationships and live out our faith before our children. But ultimately children have to believe the gospel on their own, and we must allow the Holy Spirit to do His work. When and if the seed comes up, we can nurture it, water it, and give it the proper light by continuing to teach God's story, share our stories of faith, answer questions, and apply principles of the Bible to daily living. This may take time. God's timing is not always the timing we want in the lives of our children, so this is where we must learn to relax with confidence in God's timing and plan for our children.

I love the way Karyn Henley puts it in her book, *Child Sensitive Teaching:*

> Peter wrote about wanting us to "grow up in our salvation" (1 Peter 2:1-3). In a sense, salvation is like the shoes or

shirt we buy a size too large, knowing our child will "grow into it." We are saved. Period. The work has been done. But salvation is much too big for us! Thanks to God's grace, we have the rest of our lives to "grow into it"... At some point, belief in the facts about Jesus must become faith in Jesus. The lifestyle of Christianity must become life in Jesus. Head knowledge must become heart knowledge. Our wills submitted to His will... We must come to know Him as our best friend, our Master, our Lord... Some people accept Jesus' Lordship earlier than others. Young children can be very sensitive to what Jesus has done for them and to how God wants them to respond. Others may not respond until they are teenagers or young adults. In either case, their response can be deep and life-changing. And whether people are young or old when they come into God's kingdom, their faith continues to develop as they grow up in salvation. (p. 30)

In Leslie Leyland Field's book, *Parenting Is Your Highest Calling and 8 Other Myths that Trap Us in Worry and Guilt*, the author takes great comfort in the fact that God, our Father, dealt with stubborn, obstinate people. In her words she shares this...

That day in the forest, I remembered that the Old Testament records God's parental relationship as one of great desire, incomprehensible love, unending compassion— yet Israel's response to this perfect parental love was disobedience. One particular verse leaped out at me: "All day long I have held out my hands to an obstinate people" (Isaiah 65:2). In these words I found an astonishing reversal that quelled my tears and continues to bring amazement, comfort and freedom. (p. 7)

If I could raise my children in faith again, I would try to just chill out and trust God that He wants my children to believe as much as I do. I would focus on my relationship with God, making sure His love was overflowing in my life. And then I would keep sowing the seed of God's story, and continue watching for belief to sprout in their hearts and affirming them in their belief. I would not go on the "make a decision to accept Jesus" path. I would do the same at church and encourage parents to do the same. Instead of looking at salvation as an event, I would view it as a journey of growing up with Jesus.

We need to make wrestling with faith a safe thing to do in our home and in our church. As our kids get older, they need to feel free to think faith through for themselves, to question issues, and to come to conclusions, which can be ever changing with more information. All this means we need to make apologetics for kids a big focus as they enter middle school. Our children need to know there is good reason to believe that the gospel is the truth! I recommend having resources available for the training of parents such as *The 21 Toughest Questions Your Kids Will Ask About Christianity* by Alex McFarland. This is one of the best books available for apologetics. As teachers and parents, we need to be able to answer these questions, and it would be wise to be intentional and read a book like this together before they enter high school. Lee Strobel now has a series of books—*Case for Christ, Case for Faith,* and *Case for a Creator* in books for 3rd—5th graders. Lee & Sean McDowell also have resources for kids. Remember, wrestling strengthens! Our children will be stronger if we deal with the hard areas in the Bible that many people are afraid to tackle.

One of my friends told me her story of understanding salvation and committing her life to Jesus while attending a friend's church in high school. Her parents had brought her up in faith, so when she told them of the experience she had at her friend's church, her mother said, "Oh, you were already a Christian. You accepted Jesus when you were a child." Her mother downplayed the experience she had just had with Jesus, and how she had come to more clearly understand salvation. When children come into a full and mature salvation as a result of struggling and wrestling, their faith really becomes their own! It doesn't help our children's spiritual journey to assure them of a decision they made for Christ when they were young, a decision that they might not even remember, when God is working today in a new way in their lives. We need to allow God to do His unique work of faith in the lives of our children in His way and in His time frame.

Growing Up With Jesus

I love that phrase! That is what church-grown children are doing—they are growing up with Jesus in their homes and in the church. This reminds me of a song I have always loved. When I was a children's director in Littleton, Colorado, I had the children sing this song each year on children's Sunday.

I Came to Love You Early
by Sue Smith, 1989

I felt sometimes I didn't have a story I could share.

I wasn't rescued from a past destroyed by dark despair.

O, but Jesus, I have memories of the times that we've been through.

And I wouldn't trade one moment of *growing up with you.*

Chorus:

I came to love You early, came to know You young.

You touched my heart, dear Jesus, when my life had just begun.

I gave You my tomorrows and a childish heart of sin,

And You've saved me from a lifetime of what I might have been.

You filled some days with laughter; You held me when I cried.

You said, "Child, you can do anything;" You helped me when I tried.

No, I treasure every memory and I'm sure there couldn't be

a child who could have known more love than You have given me.

I remember how You touched me, but I can't explain it all,

How a choice that's so important could be made by one so small,

I just put aside my questions; what you said to do I've done,

And I thank You for the blessings of coming to You young.

There has always been a debate about when children are old enough to understand committing their lives to Christ. One pastor I have talked to extensively about this subject, believes that until young people reach the ability to think abstractly, ages 12–14 and beyond, they are unable to understand the message of the gospel and the implications of true faith and cannot authentically accept Christ. I have met people on both ends of the argument and everywhere in between on this issue. One of my pastor friends draws the line at a child understanding the need to be willing to suffer for Christ. He believes that if a child cannot understand this concept, they are not ready to make a commitment for Christ. Other pastors I know believe a two- or three-year-old can understand enough to accept Jesus. My criterion has always been whether or not they understand sin and can confess it to Jesus and understand that Jesus died for their sin, so they can be forgiven. It's clear that children will understand these concepts at differing ages. I have also heard the testimonies of people who know they began their relationship with God through Jesus at a very young age. I happen to be one of those people and this is how it happened for me:

It was a rainy day, a "stay inside day," a disappointing day for an active girl of five. She did not understand it then, but it was going to be the most important day of her life. This was the day she would begin her journey with God. That day she would meet Jesus and understand and respond to His loving hand, which reached out to her for salvation and begin a relationship that would then sprout like a tree, deepen its roots, and grow tall and strong over the next 60 years. I was that little girl.

Even as a five-year-old, I was goal oriented and needed a plan for a day that had been changed by rain to become an inside day. I decided to listen to my records—a 4-inch stack of 45s and 78s that my parents had bought for my two sisters and me. It was my goal to listen to *all* of the records, both sides! That was my "work/play" for the morning. As I was enjoying my records I remember thinking, "I don't want to listen to the next one." It was the one I had always skipped over because it had too much talking and not enough music! "But not today," I thought, "because today I have to listen to *all* of the records, including this one!"

The record was called "The Gospel Message for Children," by Uncle Earl. I listened to the entire record and amazingly understood clearly a simple message of salvation for the first time. I felt so bad that Jesus had to die for my sins and remember the tears that came to my eyes when I understood that Jesus had to die because I didn't always want to obey my parents and could be really mean to my sisters, too. Oh, and there was that toy I took from my neighbor's yard! I became aware of *my* sin that day and of the punishment Jesus took on Himself for *me*. I realized Jesus died on the cross for those sins for *me*! I wanted Jesus to forgive me so I could live in Heaven with Him some day.

As I listened to the whole record this time, I remember *wanting to listen to it again* so I could pray the prayer with Uncle Earl, inviting Jesus into my heart. So, I started the record over again listening very carefully, and repeated the prayer with the prompting of Uncle Earl at the end of the record.

No one had to tell me that I should tell someone about my decision to follow Jesus and be His child. I was so excited that Jesus had forgiven my sin and that I could live in Heaven with Jesus someday that I ran into the kitchen to tell my mother what I had done. I remember my mother being very happy and telling my father when he got home.

I will always remember that day, and I believe my faith journey began that day, but I also know from experience, that a childhood journey of faith looks much different than a more mature decision to follow Christ. In some ways, it is far more complicated because it goes through many stages and requires a lot of nurturing on the part of parents and teachers. I now believe many of our children have been "inoculated" with the gospel because they have not been properly nurtured in their new faith and really don't understand its significance as they get older. Nor did it make a big difference in their lives because "before Christ" and "after Christ" look much the same in the lives of most children. Every child who accepts Jesus will need to eventually go through a time in their lives where they truly *own* their faith. As I mentioned earlier, most Christians go through times of review, revisiting, and recommitment. Though my journey clearly began on a particular day, I still later questioned the validity of my childhood decision. This process might be nerve-wracking for parents, but it is wise not to interfere and assure them they are saved and shouldn't be thinking that way.

Children are growing into adulthood and at each stage of development they have new understandings of their life experiences. This includes their spiritual life as well. Their belief might waver as they go through a new stage in their journey, but that is just part of the process of coming to a full understanding of salvation. Not all children grow up spiritually sensitive: it may come later on as they begin to experience the realities of life, sometimes harsh realities. Unfortunately we have no guarantee that our children will ever believe as they go through their life journey. Our job is to lay the foundation in all the ways I've described so each child has an opportunity to respond to God's invitation to a relationship with Him.

Finally, Some Encouragement for Those Who Teach Infants, Toddlers, and Preschoolers

Over the past 30 years, I have heard people say that babies and toddlers are too young to teach. I have not experienced that to be the case. In 2 Timothy 3:15, Paul tells Timothy, "From infancy you have known the Holy Scriptures," and we know from the book that Timothy's knowledge came from his mother's and grandmother's teaching when he was very young.

I believe the foundation for God's story in elementary school is laid for children from as young as 18 months to 3 years, through opening up their little minds to God by teaching them simple concepts such as God made everything, God loves me, God made mommy and daddy, mommy and daddy love you, mommy and daddy love God, God cares about you, mommy and daddy care about you, God cares for His creation, we love God's creation and should care for it, too. This foundation prepares children to hear God's Story later when they can understand. Teaching simple virtues is important when they are old enough as well—kindness, obedience, sharing, truthfulness, thankfulness, etc., also prepares them for understanding God's Story. There are many books you can read to children in this area. My favorite is *First Virtues for Toddlers*, by Mary Manz Simon. Any of her books would be very worthwhile to have in your library to read to children often.

Resources

Comfort, Ray. *How to Bring Your Children to Christ & Keep Them There*. Genesis Publishing Group, 2005.

Fields, Leslie Leyland. *Parenting Is Your Highest Calling (and 8 Other Myths That Trap Us Into Worry and Guilt)*. Waterbrook, 2008.

Henley, Karyn. *Child-Sensitive Teaching, Helping Children Grow a Living Faith in a Loving God*. Child Sensitive Communication, LLC., 1994.

McFarland, Alex. *The 21 Toughest Questions Your Kids Will Ask About Christianity*. Tindale House Publishing, Inc., 2013.

Michael, Sally, Nelson, Jill, and Burk, Bud. *Helping Children Understand the Gospel*. Children Desiring God, 2011.

Murphy, Art. *Faith of a Child, A Step-by-Step Guide to Salvation for your Child*. Moody Press, 2000.

Simon, Mary Manz. *First Feelings, 12 Stories for Toddlers*. B&H Publishing Group, 2017.

Simon, Mary Manz. *First Virtues for Toddlers*. Standard Publishing, 2006.

Strobel, Lee. *Case for a Creator for Kids*. Zonderkids, 2010.

Strobel, Lee. *Case for Christ for Kids*. Zonderkids, 2010.

Strobel, Lee. *Case for Faith for Kids*. Zonderkids, 2010.

Strobel, Lee. *Case for Miracles—Student Edition*. Zondervan, 2018.

Strobel, Lee. *Off My Case for Kids*. Zonderkids, 2006.

Family Time

by Kirk Weaver

Family Nights

Family Nights were one of the things Dave and I did to build family unity, family identity, and provide spiritual training in a fun environment. Our family nights took place every other week and consisted of a special meal followed by fun activities that involved every member of the family. This can be a challenge when there are big differences in the age of children, but we always seemed to manage to make it work and get everyone involved in fun and creative ways. We always picked a night when everyone was free from outside activities. This too can be a real challenge and will require flexibility on the part of everyone but over time we found that our kids did not want to miss "family night" and would regularly choose family night over other activities. I can honestly say that everyone loved family night, and no one wanted to miss it!

I need to point out that all of this took place prior to the advent of great family night curriculums like those available from Family Time Training. It required a great deal of creativity and now, we often find ourselves saying how much we wish we'd had this kind of fantastic material when our kids were still at home!

Join me now, and listen in, as my good friend, and founder of Family Time Training, Kirk Weaver, takes us on a journey inside a night he calls *Family Time*.

—Julie Kurz

Family Time

"I'm trying to be like the beans," my nine-year-old daughter Madison cried. Tears were flowing down her cheeks. I was sitting on the floor of her room, and she was recounting her day at school. Apparently, some girls were being mean to another student, and she had tried to stand up for the picked-on student.

The phrase "I'm trying to be like the beans," came from a Family Time lesson on adversity that we taught in our home early that week. (See appendix for "Adversity" lesson.) Starting in 1994 and continuing for 15 years, our family participated in a parent-led, weekly Family Time lesson designed to teach a biblical principle or value. In the lesson on adversity, we put an egg, carrot, and coffee beans into boiling water. The egg becomes hard. We then talked about how Pharaoh in the book of Exodus had a hard heart when he ignored Moses and refused to let the Israelites go. We also talked about Saul in the book of Acts who had a hard heart, but Jesus softened his heart on the road to Damascus and changed his name to Paul.

The carrot gets soft in boiling water. We talked about King Solomon who started his reign strong by building God's temple. During his reign as King he faced challenges that came from possessions, power, and pleasure. At the end of his life, Solomon is funding the construction of idols (1 Kings 11:3-5).

Instead of getting harder or softer, the coffee beans change the color of the water! Under adversity, represented by the boiling water, the beans impact their environment. We then talked about Queen Esther who chose to risk death and approach the King on behalf of the Jewish people. As a result of her brave action, thousands of people are saved.

Madi's comment, "I'm trying to be like the beans," was the result of her applying the adversity lesson to a real-life situation, standing up for a student at school. I was so proud of her! We talked about what happened and what she could do next. We hugged and prayed for the mean girls, the student, Madi, and their future interactions.

Family Time has been a priceless part of our home life. The story of the beans is one of hundreds of stories resulting from a weekly, 20-minute, Family Time lesson. We started when my daughter was two years old, and my son was soon to be born. The goal was to do one lesson each week. A week turned into a month, three months, a year, and eventually 15 years! Doing a weekly Family Time Bible lesson for 15 years added up to more than 750 Bible lessons in our home.

The fear of boring our kids is a hurdle for families seeking to provide spiritual training in the home. Family Time is not boring. Every lesson includes an activity or object lesson. Adults and children enjoy and remember the interactive lessons. A helium balloon is used to send messages to God. A broom and egg are used to teach the Good News of Jesus taking away our sins. A Rubik's cube is used to teach the differences between the four gospels. Chocolate milk is used to show how the Holy Spirit works in our lives.

To be successful in providing intentional spiritual training in the home, the first step is to ask God for the desire to lead the lessons and use the resources that are now available. Willpower isn't enough. Claim the promise in Philippians 2:13, "For God is working in you, giving you the desire and the power to do what pleases him" (NLT). Desire, which will be provided by God, comes before doing. Spiritual training in the home led by parents and grandparents pleases God.

Second, consider using the Family Time format to help structure your time together. Here is a suggested format:

- **Weekly**

  The goal is to provide one, 20-minute intentional Family Time Bible lesson each week. Pick a day and time. Put it on your physical and mental calendar. "Every Tuesday night right after dinner we are going to do a fun Family Time together." If there is a schedule conflict, then move the lesson to the following night. In our home we used Tuesday night whenever possible. Depending on sports, music lessons, or school programs, we might end up moving to a Thursday night for one week or an entire semester. When we first started, we had dinner, Family

Time, and then dessert. The dessert was an incentive for the kids to participate in Family Time. It wasn't long before we realized the kids didn't need a dessert incentive. They loved doing the Family Time lessons and spending time together.

- **No Fuss Dinner**

  If you choose to do your Family Time after dinner, then keep the meal simple. Minimize dinner preparation and clean up by using paper plates, leftovers, or order in pizza. Put the emphasis on being together as a family. The simple set-up communicates to kids that parents value this time together as much as they hope the kids will value the time.

- **Discuss Last Week's Family Time Lesson**

  During dinner talk about what the family learned last week during Family Time. Challenge the children to try and remember the activity and message. Did any situations come up in the last week that reminded you of the lesson or maybe you were even able to apply the lesson?

- **Family Time Theme Song**

  Pick a family theme song. Play this song after dinner and just before the evening lesson and activity. The song signals that Family Time is about to start. Younger children will like creating a dance or hand motions to go with the song. Musical families might want to write and perform their own song each week. The song signals that Family Time is ready to start while building excitement and anticipation.

- **Prayer**

  Open the Family Time lesson with prayer. Children and parents can take turns. Talk to God about what is going on in the family and ask Him to prepare your hearts to learn something new.

- **Message**

  Decide several days in advance what lesson you want to teach during Family Time. For ideas consider going to www.famtime. com where you can sign up to receive a free monthly lesson, buy age-appropriate activity books, or purchase a membership to

Total Access: an online data base of more than 350 Family Time lessons.

- **Object Lesson**

  Except in a few unique cases, Family Time lessons use common household items or materials that can be easily purchased at a local store. Make sure you have the items you need and practice the lesson if you are unsure how it works.

- **Memorize**

  Some lessons come with a short memorization, which is designed to reinforce the main teaching point. Practice the memorization together. These simple memorizations can become part of your family's language: "Just like air, God is there"; "Be content with what God sent"; "Family sticks together."

- **Prayer**

  Close in prayer. Include what you have learned and how you might apply the lesson in the coming week.

There isn't anything sacred about the Family Time format. Feel free to tweak the format to fit your family. Younger kids love the structure. They like knowing what to expect. Older elementary and teenage youth do not need as much structure.

If you have a three-year-old at home and you announce for the first time, "Tonight is Family Time!" Most likely you will get a very positive response, even if your son or daughter doesn't know what you are talking about. Young children want two things more than anything else in the world. They want the attention of their parents, and they want to play. Through Family Time they get both plus the even more important addition of learning Christian values and beliefs.

If your youngest child is thirteen and you announce for the first time, "Tonight is Family Time!" Most likely you will get more of a questioning response from your teen. My son would have said, "I'm not sure what you are talking about. Sounds like you're excited but I'm not sure I want to be included." Older children and teens are not as motivated by the attention or playing with their parents.

In this example of starting Family Time with older children, consider bypassing the Family Time format. They will not need as much structure. Simply say something like, "Hey, I found this lesson that uses an egg and broom (see appendix for Knock Sin Out of Our Lives lesson) to teach about Jesus. I would love to know what you think." Show it to them. Most likely they will want to try it themselves. My son and daughter even wanted to show their friends the Family Time lessons. Repeat the experience the following week with a new lesson.

Some families will do Family Time for a few weeks and then get out of the habit. Others continue a weekly Family Time year after year. In my experience, the difference has been understanding the "why" behind doing Family Time. The "how," which are the lessons and Family Time format, helps us know what to do. The "why" provides the motivation for maintaining the weekly lesson.

Imagine you are on a desert island with only a Bible and the key to getting off the island is to answer the question, "What is God's plan for passing the faith to future generations, to our children and grandchildren?" So you read the Bible from cover to cover to find the answer.

In the Bible, you will not find a plan for children's ministry or youth ministry. From beginning to end, the Bible clearly communicates God's plan for the "family" to be the primary vehicle for passing the faith from one generation to the next.

My friend Rob Rienow, founder of Visionary Family, helped me to see important components of God's plan as presented in Scripture. Rob examines more than 25 key Scriptures but I will highlight just a few.

In Genesis 12:2-3 God tells Abraham, "I will make you into a great nation, and I will bless you; I will make your name great, and you will be a blessing. I will bless those who bless you, and whoever curses you I will curse; and all peoples on earth will be blessed through you" (NIV). God promises to bless all people on earth through this one man, Abraham. How will God accomplish this promise?

In Genesis 18:18-19, God says, "Abraham will surely become a great and powerful nation, and all nations on earth will be blessed through him. For I have chosen him, so that he will direct his children and his household after him to keep the way of the LORD by doing what is right and just, so that the LORD will bring about for Abraham what he has promised him" (NIV). What does Abraham need to do to become a blessing to all nations? Raise children to know what is right, just and to follow the Lord. Abraham's call is to raise a godly family. How will future generations be blessed? God will do it. God will fulfill the promise He made.

Want a godly home? Raise godly children. Want a godly school? Raise godly children. Want a godly community? Raise godly children. Want a godly country and world? Raise godly children. Like Abraham, God calls us to focus on raising our family. God can take our faithful obedience and exponentially impact the world.

In Matthew 28:19-20, we read about the Great Commission, "Therefore go and make disciples of all nations, baptizing them in the name of the Father and of the Son and of the Holy Spirit, and teaching them to obey everything I have commanded you. And surely I am with you always, to the very end of the age" (NIV). In Acts 2:38-39, Peter shares God's plan for accomplishing this Great Commission, "Repent and be baptized, every one of you, in the name of Jesus Christ for the forgiveness of your sins. And you will receive the gift of the Holy Spirit. The promise is for you and your children and for all who are far off—for all whom the Lord our God will call" (NIV).

Did you catch the three spheres presented in Acts 2? You, your children, and all who are far off. To accomplish the Great Commission we must first accept the promise of God's Spirit, then comes our children, and finally the nations—those who are far off. Today, the church talks extensively about the "you"—getting right with God and developing spiritual disciples. The church also talks about those who are far off—encouraging members to get involved in church outreach programs and missions. The missing piece of God's plan for fulfilling the Great Commission in many churches and families today is intentionally passing this promise of the Spirit to the children.

The ministry of Family Time Training was formed in response to a crisis within the church. Two generations ago, with good intentions, church leaders started adding children's ministry and youth ministry programs with the goal of providing age-appropriate Bible lessons *in addition* to what children and youth were learning in Sunday services with their parents. Plus, everything being learned in church programs was above and beyond the regular spiritual training happening in the home. Over the years, families have abdicated their role of primary spiritual teachers to church staff and programs. Little if any intentional spiritual training is happening at home. Plus at church, children and youth programming is often taking place during the regular service time, which means families are no longer worshiping together on Sundays. A family arrives in the church parking lot on Sunday morning. They spread out to different parts of the church building and do not see each other until they meet back in the lobby before heading home.

There is an alignment problem between God's plan for passing the faith to our children and how the institutional church seeks to pass the faith to children. The institutional church often bypasses the parents and grandparents without training, equipping, or supporting them to provide home-centered spiritual training. Children's and youth ministry are not wrong when they support home-centered, family-led spiritual training. The problem arises when church programs replace family and become the primary and sometimes only spiritual training in the lives of our children.

If you are followers of Christ, then it is important to ask yourself two questions. First, is it important that my children have a personal relationship with Jesus? Second, are there eternal consequences to whether or not my child has a personal relationship with Jesus? If you answer "yes" to one or both of these questions, then you need to get back in alignment with God's plan for the family to be the primary source of spiritual training in the lives of children. Family Time is a tool to help you get back in alignment with God's plan.

In 25 years of teaching Family Time lessons and leading the ministry of Family Time Training, we've seen God move and strengthen families. Children want to learn about Jesus and the Bible. Children will incorporate what they learn and begin to make it their own. God uses children who have been spiritually trained to share the gospel with other children. And the Spirit is already working in the lives of parents and grandparents preparing them for the message of family-led, home-based spiritual training.

Not only does God use Family Time to teach my children, but it is also through the teaching that God has deepened and strengthened my own faith! Parents and grandparents growing in their own faith is one of the biggest benefits and blessings of Family Time. I've learned more about God from teaching my children at ages 2, 6, 8, 14 and beyond than in any other way I've been connected to the church. More than the thousands of sermons I've heard through the years. More than attending a Christian Bible college. This is part of God's master plan. As we teach, we also learn, grow, and strengthen our faith.

We cannot understate the importance of parents and grandparents teaching the faith at home. Nor can we understate the importance of using activities and object lessons to help teach biblical truths. This is the way Jesus taught. In Matthew 13:34 we read, "Jesus always used stories and illustrations like these when speaking to the crowds. In fact, he never spoke to them without using such parables" (NLT).

In 2005, Family Time was invited to train and share its resources with families and church leaders in India. Family Time is an excellent tool for first generation Christian parents and grandparents to learn the faith as they teach their children.

Since the initial trip to India in 2005, Family Time has been invited to train pastors and leaders in Thailand, Ecuador, United Emirates, Ethiopia, Malaysia, Singapore, and Indonesia. We have heard from missionaries that our lessons are also being used in Mexico, Cuba, Cambodia, and Switzerland. Family Time lessons have been translated into German, French, Spanish, Hindi, Bahasa, and Mandarin.

More than 110,000 families and church leaders around the world have been trained to use Family Time. For the sake of your children and grandchildren, join the movement. Get back in alignment with God's plan of family first and church support when it comes to teaching children about Jesus.

Resources

For more information go to www.famtime.com where you can sign up to receive a free monthly lesson, buy age-appropriate activity books, or purchase a membership to Total Access: an online data base of more than 350 Family Time lessons.

FAITH: WHAT CHILDREN NEED TO KNOW TO GROW SPIRITUALLY

What Biblical Information Do Children Need to Know and Understand to Be Able to Grow Spiritually?

As we are building solid, loving relationships with our children, authentically modeling our faith before them, and sharing stories of our spiritual heritage, children also need to be taught the truth of God's Word and how it relates to their lives. They need to understand that the Bible is a letter to us from God that tells us everything we need to know about Him. They need to know why we exist on this earth and to learn of God's relentless pursuit of a love relationship with us. Rather than teaching the Bible as a book of virtues or how we can be good for God, we need to focus on helping our children understand who God is and what He wants us to know about Him. (A special chapter (12) is included on what I call "performance driven faith," which many of us were raised to follow.) Our prayer should be that an understanding of God and His story will transform the lives of our children for their lifetime. In this chapter, I hope to be able to communicate the essence of what our children need to understand over the course of the eighteen years we have them in our homes. What is the central message of commonly taught passages, and why is it important for us to understand them? As parents and teachers we need to understand the importance of these things so our teaching doesn't become legalistic or just a rote transference of information.

Part 1: The Bible—One Story!

The most important thing I believe our children need to understand is that the Bible is one story—the story of God's relentless pursuit of relationship with us. Phil Vischer refers to the Bible as "God's Rescue Plan." There has been a healthy shift the past several years to looking at the Bible as one big story, which I believe is the only way to teach kids the Bible! The first resource I found for kids that told the Bible in a story chronologically was the *Day by Day Kid's Bible* by Karyn Henley. I met Karyn at the Children's Pastors' Conference 10 years before she published this Bible in 2002. I got to know Karyn from many years of going to her workshops and talking with her at conferences, and she soon became one of my favorite authors of children's spiritual resources. She is passionate about God's Word and about children knowing God. She radiates the love of God in her own life, and I have always appreciated the fact that she is a deep thinker. The *Day by Day Kid's Bible* is written in chronological order at a reading level children can understand, and by spending as little as seven minutes per day, it can be read in only one year! Karyn is also the author of the *Beginner's Bible,* which is still one of the most read Bibles for preschool children. Both resources are still available at www.karynhenley.com.

In 2005, Zondervan published *The Story,* and shortly afterward, a curriculum for children was available for Sunday School or children's church. It wasn't long after this material was published that several other "one story" curriculums were available from a number of curriculum companies. Here are several I like:

D6 Curriculum, Randall House

The philosophy of D6 Curriculum perfectly matches my ministry of connecting church and home. Their aim is to *cultivate generational disciple makers to live out what they learn.* They believe, as I do, that the church is the primary equipper of parents and parents are the primary disciplers in the home, based on Deuteronomy 6:5-9. One of the major strengths, and something I love about this curriculum is that all ages are studying the same biblical theme (and often the same Scripture text), making it easier to have spiritual conversations at home with all the whole family. In our busy lives, it is virtually impossible to talk to each child about their lesson and keep that conversation going throughout the week with each child, especially if you have three or more children! This approach makes so much sense to me and something churches should consider.

When I looked at this curriculum and saw that one of the resources available is a quarterly devotional magazine designed to *help the student establish the habit of spending time with God in His Word*, it reminded me of when I was in Sunday School as a child. We had a lesson book to do at home each week before the next Sunday, which prepared us for the coming week's lesson (by contrast, the D6 at-home piece reinforces the at-church lesson from the previous Sunday). I have thought a lot about that little book for years, remembering how it elevated the importance of my Sunday School lesson in my mind each week.

I do believe is important for children to be encouraged to continue to read God's Word and talk to Jesus during the week on their own as they get older—but not out of guilt or legalism. They need to "see" our heart of love for Jesus and hear how this discipline has impacted our journey with Jesus as parents and teachers, and how much we want them to know Jesus as their Savior and God. I know that is challenging, because children don't naturally want to do more "assignments," so we need to do it with them and pray our children will have seeking hearts as they get older and eventually want to do it themselves, with a little encouragement from us.

Tru Curriculum, David C Cook, written by Michelle Anthony

Tru Curriculum shares the faith at home philosophy. Its trademark is that the lesson is given to parents the week prior to teaching it at church. In this way, the parent can be the main teacher of their children, and the church supplements the efforts of the parent. What a great way to transfer the responsibility of spiritual development from the church to the home!

What's in the Bible? by Phil Vischer, produced by JellyTelly

I have the utmost respect for Phil Vischer as a follower of Jesus, and a writer of children's curriculum, in addition to the fact that he is an entrepreneur and creative genius. You may know him as the producer of *Veggie Tales,* but I know him most for his most recent curriculum, *What's in the Bible.* After producing *Veggie Tales* and becoming very successful with great plans to build a Disney-like amusement park, he then lost his company in bankruptcy. You can read his amazingly transparent story in his book *Me, Myself, and Bob.* (Sounds like a Phil Vischer title, doesn't it?) I have heard Phil Vischer speak several times over the years, but the most moving time was at our daughter's graduation from Biola University in 2004. This was less than a year after Phil lost his business. I was amazed that he kept this speaking engagement, which had been made six months prior to losing his company. He humbly shared his story at the point in his life when the rest of the story had not yet been written. God used this "pit" in his life to redirect his efforts in an amazing way. When he discovered research that indicated that many church-grown children grow up biblically illiterate, he started writing again. The result of this new direction and effort is his fantastic curriculum and video series, *What's in the Bible.* God uses His humbled servants! I just love this curriculum. This is material that can be used at home and in the church with great benefit for parents and children.

The Gospel Project, by Lifeway

The Gospel Project is a more detailed study of the Bible for children with a scope and sequence of three years instead of one. This is also great curriculum and a good follow-up to a one-year overview of the Bible. It will fill in a lot of stories that were missed in a 52-week study.

Life With God for Children, Renovare, by Lacy Finn Borgo

Life With God for Children is a study of God's story with an emphasis on spiritual formation and the integration of 12 Spiritual Disciplines. It is a 52-week, big picture story in which the children are given opportunities to practice the disciplines within the context of the stories. It is beautifully done and encourages a very personal relationship with God.

God's Big Picture, by Gospel Light

I would be remiss if I didn't mention a great curriculum that was published by Gospel Light before there was a major focus on the Bible as one story. *God's Big Picture* was published in 1999. This was the first in their Kid's Time series, which was their Children's Church curriculum when many churches were teaching both a Sunday School hour and a children's church hour for the same kids. I have recommended this curriculum to many small churches with combined ages in their Children's Church.

I am sure there are other resources, but these are the ones with which I am most familiar and have had success in teaching. If you are leader in children's ministries, I would recommend you check out these for your program. If you are a parent, look for this philosophy in the church you attend, and then get on board with the teaching in your church and teach at home as well. Several of these curriculums could be purchased and used for teaching at home as material for family night or as material for home schooling. The ones that would work best in these applications would be *What's in the Bible, Life With God for Children,* or *God's Big Picture.* The other three are definitely meant for churches but work really well when parents are partnering with the church in teaching their children. There are also some great Bibles that focus on the big picture instead of the virtues of the Bible characters. One of the best for preschoolers and early elementary children is *The Jesus Storybook Bible: Every Story Whispers His Name,* by Sally Lloyd-Jones.

Part 2: God's Character and Attributes

A close second to understanding God's story is the importance of understanding God's attributes and character through the revelation of His Word. The Bible is the main avenue God uses to make Himself known to us. I always tell children, "Everything we need to know about God is in the Bible. It is His letter to us." So many times we focus our teaching to children on virtues and character in the Bible stories instead of using the Bible stories as a way of understanding God and what He wants us to know about Himself. The question we should always ask at the end of a Bible story is, "What does God want us to know about Himself from this story?"

As I look back to curriculums in the '70s, '80s, and '90s, the sole focus of their teaching (with a salvation message inserted once in a while) was character and virtues, how they should respond to life situations, and how they could be good for God like the Bible hero or avoid the pitfalls of the villain in the story. Virtues, character, and right and wrong should be taught to children, but the purpose of the Bible is not to teach virtues. It is learning to understand our Creator, the Father, through the amazing stories, what He is like, and that He wants to have a relationship with us! The reason Jesus had to die for us is because we cannot live up to the virtuous life required for a relationship with God. If we could actually be completely virtuous within our sinful nature, Jesus would not have had to die for us! The motivation for a virtuous life is to be like Jesus, Who gave His life for us.

John H. & Kim E. Walton put it this way in their book, *The Bible Story Handbook:*

> Biblical application cannot be limited to "action points" for the coming week (though if there are some, that is fine). More importantly, we have to think about "belief points." Much biblical teaching involves belief; as we learn stories, our belief should be affected. If our belief is affected, our behavior should change. If our belief has not been affected, then any change in our behavior is likely to be superficial and temporary... We are not learning an ethical

system, though informed belief of God should result in a sound ethical system. The Bible is about God, and we should have as our desire to know him and to be like him. (p. 18)

So, what are the attributes of God children should understand? God is

- the Creator
- the Triune God (three in One) and One God at the same time
- Spirit (does not have a body)
- transcendent (beyond our universe, intelligence, and imagination)
- infinite (beyond limits) and eternal
- omnipresent (present everywhere) and omnipotent (all powerful)
- immutable (He's always the same; He won't change and suddenly become evil or weak)

Even as I am writing this, I am overwhelmed with our God! In addition to these attributes, God's character is:

- loving
- holy
- good
- just
- merciful

- sovereign
- all knowing
- patient
- faithful
- jealous for us in His perfect love.

All the Bible stories illustrate God's attributes and character. It is essential that as a result of the Bible stories they hear, our children have an understanding of the God who wants to be their Savior, Father, and friend through Jesus.

I have often wondered whether we would have lost so many church-grown kids to the faith over the years if they actually knew who their God was instead of thinking they need to strive to be good for Him! How could they leave their Creator and Father who is above all, loves us perfectly, and is perfect in all of His ways? What follows is a brief review of some of the curricula I recommend, which have a focus on who God is.

Children Desiring God

My favorite curriculums that focus on God's attributes are from the Children Desiring God organization. They are *The ABC's of God, A Study for Children on the Greatness and Worth of God* for lower elementary grades and *How Majestic Is Your Name, A Study for Children on the Names and Character of God* for upper elementary grades. In addition, Sally Michael, one of the writers for Children Desiring God, has a book for parents called *God's Names*. Looking at the names of God is an excellent way for parents and churches to study the attributes and character of God. These curriculums include a Scripture or Bible story, questions to discuss, and an activity. These are great materials for elementary students, especially mid to upper elementary.

My Awesome God by Mark Steiner

This is a great Bible storybook for preschoolers to early elementary age children, which focuses on God's character and attributes. It can be read over and over to children 4–8 years old. Mark Steiner is also the founder of a wonderful curriculum called *Discipleland*.

Rose Publishing

I have also found Rose Publishing to have great resources that can be used to give parents a good understanding of the Bible, allowing them to teach their children from their own understanding of different subjects. Rose Publishing has two curriculums that would be helpful in this area: *Attributes of God: Basic Beliefs About Who God Is* and *Names of God: 21 Names of God and Their Meanings*.

Other great books that will help your children understand God are:

What Is God Like?, Kathleen Bostrom, Tyndale House Publishers, 1998 (Preschool—Early Elementary)

Tell Me About God, Karyn Henley, Charisma Kids, 2005 (Older Preschool—Elementary) *Who Made God?*, Larry Libby, ZonderKids, 2002 (Elementary) *Daddy, Is There Really A God?*, John D. Morris, Master Books, 1997 (Elementary) *God Knows My Name*, Debbie Anderson, Crossway, 2003 (Preschool—Early Elementary) *I Can Talk With God*, Debbie Anderson, Crossway, 2003 (Preschool—Early Elementary

Any of these books are great for reading to your children to help them think about what God is like. Some of these books are older but can still be found on Amazon or eBay.

Part 3: Key Passages of Scripture and How to Teach Them
The Ten Commandments (Exodus 20:1-17)

The Ten Commandments are foundational for understanding God's nature, but they also provide guidance for how we can live in peace and freedom with each other and with God. These commandments (and many other Old Testament laws) were given to God's people, a brand-new nation, to guide them and give them direction once they had been freed from slavery in Egypt. After living in slavery for 400 years in Egypt, the Israelites needed to know the God who had delivered them and how to live in their new life of freedom. The commandments not only set them apart from other nations, but when followed, led to God's blessing within the covenant relationship God had designed for His people. Paul provides relevance for the commandments in Romans 15:4 when he reminds us, "Everything that was written in the past was written to teach us, so that through endurance taught in the Scriptures and the encouragement they provide we might have hope" (NIV).

The first four commandments relate to the God of Israel and how His people should treat the one and only God of the universe. These commandments were the foundation for living with God. Nothing was to come before their love for God; worshiping anything or anyone else would lead to the destruction of their lives and their nation. God knew this because He created humankind in His own image and designed life for them. He wanted to protect the children He loved so much. He would reveal Himself and His character as they journeyed with Him. In this journey, they learned that God gave them a perfect balance of righteousness, justice, love, and faithfulness.

As I have gotten older, one of my favorite passages has become Psalm 89:14-16. (Actually, the whole Psalm is great!)

> Righteousness and justice are the foundation of your throne; love and faithfulness go before you. Blessed are those who have learned to acclaim you, who walk in the light of your presence, LORD. They rejoice in your name all day long; they celebrate your righteousness (NIV).

Consider the safety and security of being with someone who is perfectly righteous and just, but who also loves us even while knowing everything that is true about us. He is faithful to us, never leaves us, and His perfect love provides forgiveness in Christ. That is our God! We were created to love our Creator and be loved by Him. Isn't this what we all long for in our lives? I sure do, and I am experiencing this reality more and more in my life.

The next six commandments are all about loving others and living in community with one another. The environment created by living out these commandments is what humanity longs for because we were created by God, in His image, to be loved by others. But, in our world, our selfishness (that is, our sinful nature) gets in the way. Spend just a couple of minutes thinking about living in a world where there is no disrespect, violence, or unfaithfulness in marriage, or where there is no jealousy, lying or deception, no stealing or coveting. We would live in truth and be content with who we are and what we have. These are the things we want to help our children think about. We need to create a longing for God's kingdom in our home and teach our children that "this world is not our home; we're just a-passing through" (from Hebrews 11:13-16).

So many times in the Christian community we turn the commandments into a list of things God doesn't want us to do instead of thinking about them as God's plan for us to experience life in abundance. God is not an ogre with a big stick withholding pleasure from us. He knows that the "pleasures of sin" are enjoyed only for a "short time" (Hebrews 11:25). The way that we love our children and don't want them to suffer the consequences of mistakes is a picture of the love of our Father, but His love is multiplied a hundred times more!

God had an even bigger picture in mind when He gave the Ten Commandments to the Israelites. It was His plan that the whole world would see the glory of God through this new nation and eventually find peace knowing Him.

Another important aspect in teaching children the Ten Commandments is helping them see that no one is able to perfectly keep the Law; that is why God sent Jesus as a sacrifice for our sins. This is so important for each of us to acknowledge so we can understand the significance of Galatians 3:24:

> So the law was our guardian until Christ came that we might be justified by faith (NIV).

Children need to understand the Ten Commandments from both an Old Testament and New Testament perspective and the way in which Jesus summarized the commandments.

> Jesus replied: "Love the Lord your God with all your heart and with all your soul and with all your mind." This is the first and greatest commandment. And the second is like it: "Love your neighbor as yourself." All the Law and the Prophets hang on these two commandments (Matthew 22:37-40, NIV).

Our children need to have an understanding of God's heart in giving us the Ten Commandments. They need to understand it is by keeping the commandments that we can experience life as He intended. At the same time, instead of striving for perfection, which can lead to the pride of the Pharisees, God requires that we admit we cannot keep His commandments and accept His plan to redeem us through Jesus' sacrifice on the cross. Knowing that we would always struggle to keep the commandments, God sent Jesus to fulfill the requirements of the law for us so we can now be in relationship with God through the love of Jesus; His love and sacrifice for us **become our motivation to keep the commandments.** Our children need a good understanding that the love of God is our motivation for keeping the commandments, which are a roadmap for experiencing peace with God, peace with others, and life as God intended.

We need to teach our children to ask God for help. We can't do it unless our desire to please God stems from His love for us! Our prayer should be that our children keep growing in the understanding of God's love. It is only as they experience His love that they will be motivated to keep His commandments.

The Beatitudes (Matthew 5:1-12)

I remember when I was a child, and even into adulthood, reading or hearing the Beatitudes and feeling unsettled. They seemed so mysterious, unattainable, and therefore, sort of depressing. So I had to ask; "What do they really mean?" and "Does God really expect this of me?'"

Blessed are . . .

- the poor in spirit, for theirs is the kingdom of heaven.
- those who mourn, for they will be comforted.
- the meek, for they will inherit the earth.
- those who hunger and thirst for righteousness, for they will be filled.
- *the merciful, for they will be shown mercy.*
- *the pure in heart, for they will see God.*

- *the peacemakers, for they will be called children of God.*
- *those who are persecuted because of righteousness, for theirs is the kingdom of heaven* (NIV).

How could I ever be like this? I wrestled with these for a long time and ended up sort of ignoring them. I really didn't start engaging with the *message* of the Beatitudes until I understood the *reality* of living in God's grace and in His unconditional love, rather than just the *knowledge* of both, which resulted in striving to perform for God. I slowly realized the Beatitudes represent who Jesus is, the character of God, and that they are the path toward keeping Jesus' new commandment to "Love the Lord with all your heart, soul, and mind, and love your neighbor as yourself." As we grow in desire to be like Jesus, the Beatitudes represent an image of what it means to be formed in the image of God. The only way to attain these qualities is to ask Him to help us, which is actually what the first beatitude, to be "poor in spirit" is all about. It is very unnatural for humans with a sinful nature to become like the people the Beatitudes describe. Our nature is actually pretty opposite. Over time, instead of feeling somewhat depressed by the Beatitudes, I started seeing the beauty of the Beatitudes and the beauty of God in them. I began to experience a deep satisfaction that comes from God transforming me through the Beatitudes. I began to see what it feels like to be "blessed." I began to recognize that God is pleased with what He is doing in my life and the way I am responding to the realities of life. That is ultimate happiness and is what "blessed" means.

Our children need to be exposed to these teachings of Jesus and be allowed to wrestle with them just as I did. When God starts working in their hearts, giving them a desire to be like Jesus, the Beatitudes will already be in their minds and will start to come alive in their hearts and actions, and they too, will experience what it means to be "blessed."

In short, the Beatitudes are the attitudes that need to be in my life in order to "Love the Lord with all [my] heart, soul, and mind, and [my] neighbor as myself." What follows is my summary of the Beatitudes; this is what I believe children need to be taught so they will begin to have an understanding of what the Christian life is supposed to look like. Then, when the time is right, God can begin forming His character in their hearts because they have been taught and can see what God's character and the Christian life really look like.

- *Blessed are the poor in spirit:* Being humble and recognizing my need to rely on God for help in my life and giving Him the credit He deserves for everything in my life.

- *Blessed are those who mourn:* Being able to feel my pain and the pain of others as we live in the consequences of our fallen world while humbly asking God for help.

- *Blessed are the meek:* Being humble and confident in God; at peace with myself and God, who knows the truth about everything. I also like the way George O. Wood defines meek in his book *Beatitude*—"strong but easy to live with."

- *Blessed are those who hunger and thirst for righteousness:* Longing for the Kingdom of God and His righteousness in my life and on earth and doing what I can to bring about His righteousness in my circle of influence and around the world.

- *Blessed are the merciful:* Forgiving others and being compassionate when it is not deserved (just like God's mercy toward me).

- *Blessed are the pure in heart:* Being selfless and pure in my motives before God in everything I do.

- *Blessed are the peacemakers:* Being a lover of peace and justice around me and taking action when needed to help bring about peace.

- *Blessed are those who are persecuted because of righteousness:* Being passionate about the truth and standing up for it; having a firm trust in God for people's responses and the outcome because of my faithfulness to His Word and His righteousness.

Did you notice how many times the word *humble* was used to describe the attitude Jesus encourages us to have? I will never forget when it occurred to me that the God I serve, the Creator of the universe, who cannot be compared with any other, is amazingly humble! He doesn't have to be humble; He chooses to be humble! I had never really thought of it this way until one day when I was meditating on Philippians 2:6-8 (NIV):

> Who, being in very nature God,
> did not consider equality with God something
> to be used to his own advantage;
> rather, he made himself nothing,
> by taking the very nature of a servant,
> being made in human likeness.
> And being found in appearance as a man,
> he humbled himself and became obedient to death—
> even death on a cross!

I pray that our lives as parents would *show* our children the Beatitudes and that God would be glorified through us!

The Deity of Jesus—His Teachings, Miracles, Healing, and Ministry

Children need to be taught Jesus is God, He came down to earth in human form to rescue us from our destiny of life without God, and He is our Creator. He is the Promise of the Old Testament fulfilled! We need to read children the stories in the Gospels so they can understand and believe for themselves that Jesus is God. They need to hear His teachings, ponder His miracles, and feel His compassion for people as He interacted with them, met their needs, and many times healed them.

Our children need to see how Jesus responded to people who were sick, crippled, or broken. We need to help our children understand that we are all broken and in a state of poverty and that Jesus will respond to us in the same way when we see our need for God. Jesus did not come for the proud, self-sufficient, righteous people, but to the broken, the seekers, and the humble. Jesus came to show that He was Savior, Messiah, and God for people who were open and humble enough to listen and hear the Good News. These are the people who could believe that He was God Incarnate, born of a virgin. When we read the Gospels to our children, they will see the consistency of this message.

I remember first grasping the significance of the virgin birth when I was in my adolescent years. I had heard the Christmas story many times, but one day the significance of the virgin birth unfolded in my mind, and it was a beautiful moment; I realize now that it was a worshipful moment. I remember thinking, "Wow! That's why the virgin birth is so important! Jesus *is* God because He does not have a human father. God is His father! This is a miracle!" I was so amazed, and it affirmed my childhood faith and belief that Jesus is God.

Our children also need to understand the upside-down kingdom Jesus represented. His way of living goes against our nature, but down deep it is the desire of our hearts and the only way of life that will truly bring contentment and internal peace. Children can begin to understand this kingdom through listening to the parables, stories, and teachings of Jesus. As we read these stories over and over, children will grow into the significance of the Bible and its hope for mankind. We are giving them a foundation of knowledge for the time when they will understand how amazing the message of the Bible is to them personally and why it is the hope of the world.

I have found the Nest Entertainment DVDs to be very effective tools for helping children understand the teachings of Jesus. Sometimes I integrate clips into my lessons. Nest has taken the liberty of enhancing the stories without deviating from the focus of the text, making them true to life in ways to which kids can relate.

Another resource and curriculum that I like in the area of Jesus and the gospels is Karyn Henley's *JESUS—His Life, His Times, His Message,* a one-year curriculum.

The Lord's Prayer (Matthew 6:9-13)

Teaching our children how to pray is very important. The best way to teach them how to pray is by example; your children will learn how to pray by listening to you pray. Our prayers can teach children a lot about God and also show them how much we love God. Children need to hear our hearts when we pray—our acknowledgement of God, His love, His sovereignty, and our desire to know and follow Him.

The Lord's Prayer is the result of Jesus' disciples asking Him to teach them how to pray. He gave them a beautiful model prayer to guide and instruct them.

Our Father in heaven, hallowed be your name,

The prayer first acknowledges who God is—our Father in Heaven—and exalts His name as holy, loving, and set apart from all others. This is the posture we need to have when we come before God and the reverence our children need to see in us.

There is a desire for God's Kingdom and a surrendering to it reflected in the next part of the prayer.

Your kingdom come, your will be done, on earth as it is in heaven.

When it comes right down to it, do we actually want God's Kingdom? Or is establishing life in America good enough for us? Do our children see in us a desire for the upside-down Kingdom of God? Do we talk about it? Or are we still striving on our own to make this life work for us? Our children will instinctively know our values by what they see in our lives.

The reality of God's kingdom in the future is sure, but for many it is an intangible reality which causes us to focus only on increasing our personal security and making our slice of the world a better place. As long as we have imperfect people in leadership and imperfect people following, there will be selfishness and corruption. I cannot wait for Jesus to be our ruler, but in the meantime, Jesus taught that the Kingdom of God is also within us—here and now! In God's kingdom, Christians should recognize that they are to be stewards of their many blessings and use those blessings to bless others and make life better for everyone in the world. This message is repeated throughout the Bible, but it is perhaps most clearly described in Acts 2:42-47 where it says, "All the believers were together and had everything in common. They sold property and possessions to give to anyone who had need" (verse 44-45), and in Acts 4:34-35 where it says, "There were no needy persons among them. For from time to time those who owned lands or houses sold them, brought the money from the sales and put it at the apostles' feet, and it was distributed to anyone who had need" (NIV). That's the upside-down kingdom of God! It is this unlikely behavior that caused unbelievers to investigate the claims of Christianity in the early church. For more on this subject, I recommend *Generous Justice* by Timothy Keller. Here is a quote from page 51: "Like Isaiah, Jesus taught that a lack of concern for the poor is not a minor lapse, but reveals that something is seriously wrong with one's spiritual compass, the heart."

In Luke 17:20-21, Jesus said, "…The coming of the kingdom of God is not something that can be observed, nor will people say, 'Here it is' or 'There it is,' because the kingdom of God is in your midst" (NIV).

Our prayers need to reflect our desire for not only the kingdom of God in the future, but also a desire to be God's kingdom in our spheres of influence—to be like Jesus and bring His Kingdom into being. This can be summarized by Jesus' command to "love our neighbor as ourselves," which involves caring for the poor, the sick, and "the least of these," and "to do good works, which God prepared in advance for us to do" (Ephesians 2:10). There has been a "sweet place" in my relationship with God as I have learned to desire God's will and His kingdom above my own. Our children need to see us moving in that direction through our actions and the prayers they hear us pray.

After we have acknowledged God for Who He is and surrendered to Him and His perfect will, we can then ask for the things we need.

Give us today our daily bread.

I believe this request for our "daily bread" includes everything that sustains us in life—the physical, emotional, spiritual, and mental needs we have every day. I have found that, for some, it is hard to acknowledge that everything they have comes from God. Our self-sufficiency and work ethic are very strong in America, and sometimes we focus on what we have acquired instead of acknowledging God's sovereignty in our lives over everything, including our gifts and aptitudes, where we were born, and what opportunities we have been given. It requires humility to ask God for what we need—our "daily bread"—and to give Him praise and honor for Who He Is if we have become so self-sufficient we have no real need of Him. We need to give God the glory for everything we have and everything we are. For others, praying for what they need is not hard because life has not come easy for them. It is a way of life for them, and God has become very real in their life journey as they have seen God's care for them in His faithfulness.

Whether in need or in plenty, God wants us to acknowledge He is the source of everything in our lives, and He loves to care for our needs in this life. I love to pray, "Thank you, God, that everything I *have* and all that I *am* is because of you."

Here are a couple of resources I recommend on this subject:

- Intergenerational study—*Lord Teach Us to Pray*, Children Desiring God
- *Kid's Travel Guide to The Lord's Prayer*, Group Publishing

Also see Chapter 17.

The Armor of God (Ephesians 6:10-18)

Why do we need armor to be a follower of Jesus? The Bible teaches that Satan is in an active struggle against God and his goal is to destroy the unity of the Church and the faith of God's followers. The church and the home need to help our children understand the very real battle that exists between good and evil in our world and even in our own hearts. Children need to be able to recognize the lies of the evil one and how those lies can lead us away from the truth of God. The armor of God is our protection against the "devil's schemes." Being aware of this is the first step in being able to resist and remain steadfast in God's way of thinking.

This is not a hard concept for kids to understand, since even at an early age, in every movie or cartoon they see, there are good guys and bad guys. As humans, we always root for the good, although even good and evil are being convoluted these days, and we sometimes find ourselves rooting for the bad guys. Still, in our hearts, we know what is good, and the good is what our hearts truly desire because we were created in the image of God.

One of the simplest and most concise resources for understanding the armor of God is *Put on the Full Armor: The Armor of God,* from Rose Publishing (2005). It has great applications, background information, and a very helpful list of "Devil's Schemes versus God's Plan" with Bible references. I love the personal prayers parents can regularly pray with their families after studying the passage of Scripture with their children:

> **I am ready to take my stand against the powers of darkness.** Please help me to stand against the spiritual forces of evil that want to destroy me, my family, and the church.
>
> **I buckle the belt of truth around my waist.** Help me to be a person of truth and reliability. Please give me the words to say when people ask why I follow Jesus. Help me tell about Jesus' death and resurrection and His promise of eternal life to those who believe in Him.
>
> **I take the breastplate of righteousness.** Thank you for giving me God's righteousness. Because I am not perfect, You graciously protect me with Your own righteousness because I believe in Jesus Christ.
>
> **I stand firmly on feet prepared with the gospel of peace.** Help me to resist temptation and stay away from people, places, and situations that tempt me. Help me live in peace with my family and other believers as much as it depends on me.
>
> **I lift up the shield of faith.** Help me to hold up the shield and stop the arrows of doubt, despair, and hopelessness that the enemy shoots at me.

I place upon my head the helmet of salvation. Help me to know that no matter how tough life is, Jesus has conquered sin, and I live with the assurance that I will one day be with God in Heaven.

I use the sword of the Spirit, the Word of God. Thank you for giving me your Word, the Good News of Jesus Christ. Help me to tell others about Him. (p. 11)

Some other great curriculums that can be used in Children's Church or Sunday School are:

- *Faith Case: Armor of God,* by Gospel Publishing, 2017
- *Kid's Travel Guide to the Armor of God,* Group Publishing, 2004

Remember that these curriculums need to be connected to the home so kids are getting the same teaching there.

The Fruit of the Spirit (Galatians 5:22-23)

What is the fruit that is referred to in this passage? It is the fruit *of the Spirit,* that is, the Spirit of God! Our children need to understand that this is a description of what God is like and what naturally flows from His nature. It is *who* God is! These qualities can also flow through us as we live in God's presence and allow His nature to be reflected in us. This can happen as a result of being reconciled with God through the sacrifice Jesus made for our sin and being in a relationship with Him. The journey to reflect His nature over our self-focused nature is a daily, life-long process for each of us.

Like us, children can recognize their world is a better place when there is an atmosphere of "love, joy, peace, patience, kindness, goodness, faithfulness, gentleness, and self-control." We should first help them understand that our recognition of the fruit of the Spirit as good and desirable is a reflection of the reality that we were created in God's image. It is one of the things that distinguishes us from the animal kingdom. As much as we each possess a sin nature—a desire to put ourselves and our interests above others—most of us know the difference between good and evil, and we all do good and bad at one time or another. Regardless of this truth, that sinful people are capable of reflecting the image of their Creator is a reality that can be seen in many acts of kindness, compassion, and heroism in our world.

So how does this paradox relate to teaching our children Galatians 5:22? When we see acts of kindness, compassion, and heroism in our world, we should help our children see these fruit are markers, or reflections, of God's character and the fact that we were created in His image. Children should also understand that even though we were made in the image of God, these wonderful qualities don't just naturally flow from us. This is what makes true acts of heroism so celebrated by our culture and in the world. Because of the fall and the presence of evil in our world, what is commonly understood as the "fruit of the Spirit" is sometimes defined in an inaccurate way and is sometimes attached to wrong motives where something is expected in return from either God, karma, or others. As parents, it doesn't take long for us to see the sinful nature in our children often spiraling down to a survival-of-the-fittest behavior when not supervised and redirected. We have to teach, train, and expect behavior that resembles the fruit of the Spirit in our children's lives. Here are some ideas for teaching these concepts to children.

As our children mature through the different phases of childhood to adulthood, we can:

1. Teach them how beautiful God's nature is as expressed in the Fruit of the Spirit. God is perfectly balanced in righteousness and justice, lovingkindness, goodness, kindness, patience, faithfulness, and peacefulness. I love thinking about how perfect God is in all His ways.

2. Strive to help them *experience* the fruit of the Spirit through *our* relationship with God. They need us to acknowledge and ask forgiveness for the times we don't display the fruit of the Spirit in our lives, and we should strive to have our homes filled with the all the attributes described in the fruit of the Spirit.

3. Teach them what each part of the fruit can look like in their lives. What does it look like to have patience, show kindness, be

faithful, or exhibit self-control? Watch for teachable moments, opportunities to teach these lessons in the routine events of life. The church and the home can work together to reinforce these life lessons with great curriculums.

4. Teach Bible stories focusing on God and why He put this story in His Big Story and what it tells us about His fruit or His character. We want children to love God's Person as a result of reading them the Bible accounts. So many times Bible stories are taught with a focus on what the Bible hero did right or wrong, promoting a "we should be good for God" mentality. This can develop children who might, to some degree, be good little children but who do not necessarily have a "heart for God."

5. Teach them they will never be able to display the fruit of the Spirit perfectly, nor can they ever be good enough for God. That is why Jesus had to die for our sins. If we could be good enough for God, Jesus would not have had to die on the cross. When we love God with all our hearts, His Spirit will begin to flow out of us, and we will want to be like Him. The focus of any virtue or character-based teaching should be on asking God for help to be like Him, recognizing our inability to ever be good enough for Him.

6. Inspire children by pointing out people who have displayed the fruit of the Spirit in their lives, people who have engaged in acts of kindness, have been faithful, have shown love or self-control, and have highlighted the atmosphere it created for themselves and others.

We can't make children desire relationship with God through Jesus or desire the fruit of the Spirit in their lives. We can only help them understand that all the good we do is tainted by sin, wrong motives, and inconsistencies even in the best of situations, but that being in relationship with God can help us experience His nature and reflect His glory. This is what we all intrinsically desire and living out the fruit of the Spirit is the closest thing we will experience to really living with our Creator this side of heaven.

Psalms

During the 18 years we have our children at home, they need to be able to talk to God comfortably, to worship Him, and to express their honest feelings to Him in prayer. The strength of any relationship is based on the quality of communication we have with the other person, and it is no different in our relationship with God. There is no better place to learn how to do this than to study the Psalms!

Children will first begin to understand how to talk to God by hearing their parents pray. Young children just naturally express their honest feelings without pretention. They pray with such honesty and purity in their hearts! As our children mature and move from concrete thinking to abstract thinking, and as life gets more complicated for them, we must keep encouraging an atmosphere of honesty in their prayers and model our dependence on God in our prayers. Praying out loud with our children and encouraging them to pray with us should be a lifelong habit. It will seem very natural for our children if we start this practice when they are very young and maintain it as they mature.

Reading the Psalms is a great way to experience honest prayers. As we read the Psalms we can sense the Psalmists' joy, praise, worship, sadness, fear, rejection, anger, or frustration. All the emotions are present in the Psalms. The Psalms are great for teaching our children the value of authenticity and for helping them see that God loves us in all our emotions and wants us to be honest with Him. The Psalms also teach us how to worship God, how to express joy, praise, and adoration to God. They teach us to remember what God has done for us when we are feeling down or deserted and to trust Him that He is with us in everything we go through.

In 2010, Kayrn Henley published another one of her *Day by Day Devotions*, but this one was called *A Summer of Psalms*. I bought it even though I don't have children at home to read it with, and as with many other children's devotionals, I read them before I go to bed each night to determine which ones I can recommend to parents. This one blessed me so much, and I learned a lot too!

The Psalms have been a lifeline to God for me over the years, especially since 1990, when I found a little book right after it was published called *31 Days of Wisdom and Praise,* by Zondervan. It is a guide to reading Psalms and Proverbs in one month. It suggests that you read a Psalm that matches the day of the month, and then add 30 to each number so that you read 5 psalms a day, and one chapter of Proverbs, which, of course, already has 31 chapters. On the 31st day, you read the lengthy Psalm 119, since those Psalms were read on the 1st of each month. So over the past 30 years, I have read a lot of Psalms, I suggest that you read them over and over to the children in your world so they will be tucked in their hearts when they really need them later in life.

Resources

31 Days of Wisdom and Praise. Zondervan Publishing House, 1990.

Anderson, Debby. *God Knows My Name.* Crossway, 2003.

Anderson, Debby. *I Can Talk With God.* Crossway, 2003.

Attributes of God: Basic Beliefs About Who God Is. Rose Publishing, Inc., 2012

Borgo, Lacey Finn. *Life With God.* Renovare, Inc., 2013.

Bostrom, Kathleen Long. *What Is God Like?* Tyndale House Publishers, 1998.

D6 Curriculum. Randall House & D6 Family, 2021.

Faith Case: The Armor of God. Gospel Publishing, 2017.

God's Big Picture. Gospel Light, 1999.

Henley, Karyn, *Day by Day Kid's Bible* and *Beginner's Bible.* Tyndale House Publishers, Inc., 2002.

Henley, Karyn. *JESUS: His Life, His Times, His Message, (a one-year curriculum).* Child Sensitive Communication, LLC, 2008.

Henley, Karyn. *Tell Me About God.* Charisma Kids, 2005.

Henley, Kayrn. *A Summer of Psalms.* Child Sensitive Communication, LLC, 2010.

Jones, Timothy Paul. *Put On the Full Armor.* Rose Publishing, 2005.

Keller, Timothy. *Generous Justice, How God's Grace Makes Us Just.* Dutton, 2010.

Kid's Travel Guide to the Armor of God. Group Publishing, 2004.

Kid's Travel Guide to The Lord's Prayer. Group Publishing, 2003.

Libby, Larry. *Who Made God? And Other Things We Wonder About.* ZonderKids, 2002.

Jones-Lloyd, Sally *The Jesus Storybook Bible—Every Story Whispers His Name.* Zonderkids, 2007.

Michael, Sally. *God's Names.* P&R Publishing, 2011.

Michael, Sally. *Lord Teach Us to Pray.* Truth78, 2006.

Morris, John D. *Daddy, Is There Really A God?* John D. Morris, Master Books, 1997.

Names of God: 21 Names of God and Their Meanings. Rose Publishing, Inc., 2003.

Steiner, Th.M. *My Awesome God Bible Storybook.* DiscipleLand, 2011.

The Gospel Project for Kids. LifeWay, 2015.

Tru Curriculum. David C Cook, 2013.

Walton, John H. & Kim E. *The Bible Story Handbook.* Crossway, 2010.

What's in the Bible? Jellyfish One, LLC, 2013.

WATCH OUT FOR PERFORMANCE-DRIVEN FAITH

How to Avoid Using "Let's All Be Good for God" Applications

It wasn't unusual to get a call from our youngest daughter, Rachel, when she was attending Biola University, but the subject of this call took me by surprise. For the most part she loved college and frequently told us how excited she was about her theology class and how much she was learning, but I will never forget this call. "Mom," she said, "I don't think we were ever taught the theology of grace at our church." I was really taken aback and thought, "Really? If she didn't learn the theology of grace at church, well then maybe I don't understand it either because we did attempt to pass on everything we understood about God's Word and the gospel to our children." This conversation launched me into a three-year journey to understand what Rachel was learning about the theology of grace that I had missed. I asked God to guide me and help me see what I had missed; suddenly it seemed like everything I was reading, and hearing was on this topic.

I began to realize that I was not the only one in the Christian community having this "aha moment!" Like many others, I had not been totally living in the freedom of Christ. To make a long story short, I read books and listened to teachings by John Lynch, former pastor for 27 years at Open Door Fellowship in Phoenix, Arizona (www.trueface.org). Then I attended our district conference in my denomination and heard Alan Kraft speak on his then current journey to understand living "in the Gospel." At the time, I was working with a church in Pagosa Springs, Colorado, so I began to listen to a copy of his message each time I made the six-hour drive from Denver to Pagosa Springs. It was a message on grace that I really needed to hear.

So, what exactly is performance-driven faith? From a teaching perspective, it is teaching the Bible as a book of virtues instead of focusing on helping our children understand who God is and what he wants us to know about Him. It fosters thinking that says, "I need to please God by obeying Him and doing the things I know I should so He will be pleased with my behavior and will be free to bless me as a result." It is the belief that I can make God happy because I read my Bible every day, memorize verses, show kindness, obey my parents, make the right choices, and on and on. Now are those things bad? Of course not! Do they make God happy and pleased with us? I'm sure they do, but this way of thinking also produces tremendous guilt when we fail to live up to these standards, and sometimes, a sense of entitlement when we succeed. This is one of the reasons kids leave the faith in their young adult years. When the inevitable trials of life begin to appear, they think, "This Christianity is not working. I've been good for God, and He is not holding up His end of the bargain." These are some of the potential consequences of teaching Bible stories that focus on virtues or character instead of teaching the story in the context of God's story.

I know these things firsthand because I grew up with a performance mentality, and if you grew up in the evangelical community, there is a good chance you did too. I'm a late Baby Boomer, and while I thought I was raising my children without the legalistic bent with which I was raised, I realize now that I moved very little from the performance-driven mentality that was so pervasive in my own childhood. In my generation, we were taught that there were five things that Christians shouldn't do: drink, dance, smoke, go to movies, and gamble or play cards. Those of you who are not of my generation may find this hard to believe, but this was the reality of our lives into adulthood. As young parents, my husband Dave and I realized that we had been raised in a very strict form of legalism. We understood the essence of what our parents had taught us, but we also realized the danger of being Christians who are only known for what they don't do instead of being known for everything we are and everything we do in the name of Jesus. As adults we managed to get past the old way of thinking, but we still missed a great deal in our understanding of God's grace.

Even though a healthy shift from the days of 1950's legalism began to take place in our churches, we still held onto the concept of teaching character in curriculums based on virtues in the Bible. In doing so we failed to teach God as the central figure in the Bible and the main character of His story. We failed to help kids see that Jesus had to die for our sins because we would never *be* good enough for God.

When I went back and looked at the curriculums I remembered teaching and the lesson objectives we were still teaching in some Sunday School programs, this is what I found:

- We should obey God because Adam & Eve disobeyed
- We should have faith like Abraham
- We should obey like Noah
- We should be courageous and trust God like David
- We should be faithful in prayer like Daniel
- We should have a good attitude, unlike Jonah
- We should stand up for our faith like Shadrach, Meshach, and Abednego
- We should share our lunch like the little boy who gave his lunch to Jesus
- (Sampson was sure a hard one to teach! ☺)

I was shocked to see how many times my own children and the children in my ministry had been taught, how to be "good for God."

Listen to what Alan Kraft says in his book, *Good News for Those Trying Harder*:

> Trying to be good doesn't get us any closer to God. In fact, it tends to move us in the opposite direction. (p. 51)

Without even realizing it, my best efforts at being good were actually removing me from living the gospel. I was priding myself for following my list of holy behaviors and yet all the while ignoring the depth of my own sinfulness. (p. 52)

As I studied the New Testament and contemplated a new understanding of living in God's Grace in my own life, I knew I had found the truth. How had I missed this? I felt like one of the people Paul was talking to in Galatians 3:2-3. "Did you receive the Spirit by the works of the law… are you so foolish? After beginning by means of the Spirit, are you now trying to finish by means of the flesh?" (NIV). I began thinking about the ramifications this subtle performance-based teaching had on all of us; by focusing on character virtues we had moved away from the intent of the Bible stories, which was to point to God's story, Jesus, and the gospel. As I began thinking about myself, children in my ministry, and adults who grew up in the church with this teaching, the following diagram began to form in my mind:

In our ministry, we had special events to share the gospel with our children. Vacation Bible School and summer camp were the primary places where children were invited to "ask Jesus into their heart." Typically this would follow a week of teaching Bible stories with a presentation of the gospel story at the end of the week. Kid's who "prayed to accept Jesus" were launched into a spiritual growth plan that included going to Sunday School, children's church, or a mid-week program where, after hearing Bible stories, they would learn what they could do to be "good Christians" and please God. We were happy to see children doing well on the "good for God" plan. Because they were kids, they sometimes messed up, so we made sure we included God's message of forgiveness. Unfortualtely, there were always some that really messed up and then didn't want to be at church or just quit coming altogether. It is my experience that this most often happens with upper elementary age kids and on through the teen years.

What I have observed is that when a child or teenager makes bad choices, one of two things happens. Some kids will have trouble getting back on the "good for God" plan because of the guilt and shame that comes from feeling that everyone else has been so "good." These kids will often leave and not come back. Others actually find God through this time, and with broken hearts, begin to truly seek God.

Even before my new discovery of truly living in God's grace, this was very confusing for me. As a parent and a teacher of children, I didn't want children to find Jesus only as a result of making bad life altering choices. This isn't God's plan for any of us, but isn't our job to protect them and keep them on the "good for God" path? How then do we help a child develop the heart of one who has found real freedom and peace with God?

I found that the kids who stayed on the good for God path went several different directions when they grew up. Some found a genuine relationship with Jesus as they walked with Him and truly grew in faith. Many others became like Pharisees who judged the behavior of Christians who failed to live up to the standards of the day. Still others, after phases of maturity and times of sacrificial service for the kingdom, ended up leaving the faith. These have typically been individuals who felt let down by God when their lives fell apart or they had very hard times. They cry, "Where is God? Is this all I can expect of Him? After all, I have been good for him all of my life! Why is this happening to me? He must not really exist." Many of the kids with these questions have entirely left their faith.

Listen again to what Alan Kraft says:

> We define spiritual growth as us becoming more like Christ, as us becoming less and less sinful, what we are actually pursuing is a spiritual growth path in which we need Jesus less and less. I need him less today than yesterday because the power of sin is not as strong in my life. Is this what spiritual maturity looks like? (p. 28)

About the story of the prodigal son, Alan Kraft says,

> I love the way the father responds to his son's self-rightous indignation: "My son, you are always with me and everything I have is yours" (Luke 15:31). Could I paraphrase that? "Son you don't need to play this, 'I obey you in order to earn my way' game any longer. It's not that kind of relationship. My love for you is never to be dependent upon how good you are or how well you perform. Until you see it that way, you will never know the joy of just being my son." For how many of us are our diligent efforts at being good actually hindering our experience of being loved? (p. 63)

What Have We Been Missing in Our Teaching?

John & Kim Walton, in their book *The Bible Story Handbook, A Resource for Teaching 175 Stories From the Bible,* explain so clearly why and how we should teach the Bible to children.

God tells us his story so that we can understand him... (p. 13)

> . . . our primary concern in teaching any story from the Bible is to explain what the story tells us about God. If the Bible is used only as a jump-off point for one's own educational objectives, the Bible's authority is bypassed. (pp. 14-15)

Bible application cannot be limited to "action points" for the coming week. More importantly, we have to think about "belief points.".... If our belief is affected, our behavior should change. (p. 18)

We want our students to be conformed to the image of Christ and their behavior to have been embraced as a way to imitate God. We accomplish this by helping them know God better, not by telling them that they should obey because Abraham obeyed. The text is relevant because it reveals God to us and thus enables us to understand what he desires from us. (p. 18)

If our children truly understand who God is, His character and heart, will they be less inclined to leave God, their Father and Creator? I believe the answer is "Yes." I believe this represents a significant change we need to make in our teaching and doing so will result in less of our church-grown kids leaving their faith.

The key to spiritual growth in our children starts with us. We are learning, growing, modeling genuine faith, and teaching our children how to live moment by moment in the power of the gospel, knowing God's forgiveness and hope in the midst of brokenness and sin. Spiritual maturity is recognizing one's own sin and brokenness and living with it moment by moment in the power, forgiveness, and hope of the gospel, instead of looking back to my "salvation event" as the beginning of my relationship with God and then trying to please God with my behavior.

Leading children into spiritual maturity requires that we lead them on a journey to know God, His character, His righteousness, and His perfect love for them. We do this by teaching them God's story, with God as the main character.

Galatians 2:20 says, "I have been crucified with Christ and I no longer live, but Christ lives in me. The life I now live in the body, I live by faith in the Son of God, who loved me and gave himself for me" (NIV). I believe this verse is a picture of what living in the message of the gospel is all about, remembering each moment that God loves me, died for my sin, and is helping me to live victoriously in Him.

When we grasp this way of living, we become refreshing and authentic, able to experience gratefulness and joy even in the midst of pain and disappointment because of the eternal goodness of God and the hope of the gospel.

Resources

Anthony, Michelle. *Spiritual Parenting, An Awakening for Today's Families.* David C Cook, 2010.

Kraft, Alan. *Good News for Those Trying Harder.* David C Cook, 2008.

Walton, John H. & Kim E. *The Bible Story Handbook, A Resource for Teaching 175 Stories From the Bible.* Crossway, 2010.

Curriculum:

D6 Curriculum. Randall House, 2020

Borgo, Lacy Finn. *Life With God for Children.* Renovare, Inc., 2013.

God's Big Picture, Gospel Light, 1999.

Phil Vischer. *What's In the Bible.* Jellyfish One, LLC, 2013.

The Gospel Project for Kids. LifeWay, 2015.

Tru Curriculum. David C Cook, 2013.

WHAT IS THE CHURCH TO DO NOW?

New Direction and New Strategies for the Church

On one of my ministry trips, I drove through a beautiful area in central California that appeared to be home to a very large Christmas tree farm. As I got closer, I could see where a whole section of trees had been cut down. As I drove on, I observed numerous sections where the trees were at different maturity levels. Finally, I came upon an expansive area of very small baby trees. Here was a visible example of the fact that the farmer must keep up with planting and nurturing the baby trees if he expects to have mature trees to sell in ten to twenty years. Clearly, he must have a self-sustaining plan for planting new trees, along with patience and funding to secure a future for his business.

As I passed by that tree farm, I could not help but think about the church and its children. We started this book by reviewing the sobering statistics concerning how many church-grown children leave the church and their faith. We all know that these children and young adults are the potential leaders of tomorrow and should be the future of the church. With this in mind we have to ask ourselves if we are spending enough time on program evaluation and making a big enough financial investment to secure the church for the next generation. I was recently talking to a pastor in our area who told me that his denomination was going to have a shortage of approximately 2,000 new pastors next year! As I reflected on the last ten years, I realized the next generation of church leaders would be quite impacted by the trends we have seen in the church this past decade.

The church needs to be radical by making major changes in mission and vision for children's ministries so these ministries reflect the biblical model for passing faith from one generation to the next. We must not allow children's ministry to continue to operate as a spiritual "drop off" ministry in any way. It is imperative that we come alongside parents, teaching and equipping them to take the responsibility of spiritually developing the children God has entrusted to them. It is their biblical role to teach their children, and churches need to make it their mission to come alongside parents to help them in their responsibility.

One Church Takes Action

It was about three or four years ago that I read a blog entitled, "Sunday Schooling Our Kids Out of Church" written by Pastor Tim Wright. I didn't know who Tim Wright was at the time, but after reading this compelling blog, which reflected my ministry passion, my first reaction was, "I've got to find out who this pastor is and meet with him no matter where he is in the country!" As it turned out, his church was in Peoria, Arizona, only 20 minutes from my house. Dave and I went to his church, met him, and we set up a meeting, which resulted in my involvement in the changes he was making at his church. Isn't God just amazing!

Tim and his team decided to cancel Sunday School at his church and develop a family integrated service involving people of all ages. He prepared his congregation for the changes by casting vision and holding training events at his church. He made some minor changes to the service itself to accommodate children, but he also trained the parents so they could have their children participate in the service successfully. He has implemented material known as *Faith5*, and every Sunday he promotes this program which encourages spiritual discussions at home.

I highly respect Tim Wright, the lead pastor of Community of Grace in Peoria, Arizona and count it a privilege to be able to work with him. I highly recommend reading the book he wrote, after his blog received such a big following: *Sunday Schooling Our Kids Out of Church.* He made a bold, strategic move and invited the children into the adult service. He gave his congregation wise and strong leadership *for the faith of the next generation.* Community of Grace is an example of the kind of church that evaluates the effectiveness of its historic programs and recognizes the need for dramatic changes to sustain the faith of the next generation.

Making It Work in Your Church

As I worked with churches in my ministry, I learned that every church is unique and has a culture all its own. No two churches are alike, so it is not enough to have just one strategy; every church will have a plan that works best for its members. The unifying factor is that we all agree on the goals; the parents' role is to pass faith to their children, and the role of the church is to come alongside and equip them to be successful. It doesn't mean that every church should stop programs such as Sunday School, children's church, VBS, or mid-week programs, but honest evaluations need to take place to make sure these programs are truly accomplishing the unifying, overriding goal. If our teaching is to be effective in a child's spiritual journey, every program and everything we teach needs to be *connected* to the home for reinforcement and implementation. In addition, there must be parental accountability to make sure that parents really are involved in their kids' spiritual lives along with constant evaluation to verify that our parent/church partnership is really working. Remember, the role of the church is to come alongside parents, training and equipping them to spiritually develop the children God entrusted to them.

When a church tells me they want to address the faith of the next generation in their church and make necessary changes to refocus their role, my first recommendation is that they put a team together and read the book *Perspectives on Family Ministries—3 Views,* edited by Timothy Paul Jones. In the first four chapters, Timothy Paul Jones summarizes the problem, identifies how we got to this place historically, and provides a definition of family ministry, which is foundational for making changes. "This book defines family ministry as the process of intentionally and persistently realigning a congregation's proclamation and practices so that parents are acknowledged, trained, and held accountable as the persons primarily responsible for the discipleship of their children" (p. 40).

Family ministry is not about hiring a new person or adding more programs to your already full calendar. It is adjusting everything you do in your church to make parents primary in their role of spiritually developing their own children. Family ministry should be at the core of every ministry in the church. Each ministry should be encouraging the spiritual development of families within the programs they represent in the church. Everyone needs to be on the same page; thinking of ways they can *promote spiritual development in the home.*

Perspectives On Family Ministries—3 Views, by Timothy Paul Jones, introduces three approaches or views that will help a church define its philosophy for children's ministry and address changes in their ministry to reach their goals. This is not a "one size fits all" approach, but rather, one that allows for the unique culture of every church to express itself in different ways. The three views represented in the book are: Family Integrated, Family Based, and Family Equipping. The format of the book has each of these views presented and defended by a family pastor who is currently implementing his particular view in his church. The three pastors each agree with the definition established by Timothy Paul Jones in chapter 4 of the book, but they have different strategies for implementing the necessary changes. Each view is explained by the family pastor representing his view and is then challenged by the other family pastors who represent another view. In the end, each pastor is given another opportunity to defend his view based on the challenges from other pastors. This dialog and process makes it is very helpful for readers to think through what their philosophy might be for their church. As a result of reading this book, your team can have very beneficial discussions on the journey to coming up with your own unique strategy for how change can be best implemented in your church. I have found it very interesting to see how each of these views have developed in the churches I helped work through this process.

It is my suggestion that this book be read by the team that will eventually direct the changes within the church. This team will look different in every church; sometimes it is the pastor and his staff, the elder board and the staff, the children's director and a team around them, or lay members or parents in the church with pastor or staff involvement. The important thing about this team is that it includes key leadership (preferably the pastor or pastoral staff) and that it represents every family type in your church. The team should include an intact family parent, a single-family parent, a stepfamily parent, and an empty-nest parent. It should be communicated that God helps all parents in whatever situation they find themselves and that the church is going to come alongside each family type to help them carry out their responsibility of passing faith to their children. As each person on the team gets excited about the truths they are learning and the significance of the changes needed, the hope is that they will influence others in their family type. We also need the buy-in of the empty nesters and older members of the church so they also see their role in this process; many will be excited to get involved and adopt a family to mentor. Seasoned, older parents can be of so much help to struggling families in the church; they just need to be encouraged and sent out into the battle. Those who choose not to be directly involved still need to understand what the church is trying to accomplish and be encouraged to be supportive of the changes.

Developing a New Philosophy of Ministry for Families and Children

After reading *Perspectives on Family Ministry*, I hope you will be convinced that your ministry must crystallize a *philosophy of ministry*. A philosophy of ministry statement provides a clearly articulated mission, vision, values, and strategy statement for the children in your church. Ironically, this will need to be flexible, always changing and evolving with the needs of the children and families in your church.

If you already have such a document in place for the children's ministry program in your church, from my experience, you are a rare church. This process will take time and hard work, but the results will be worth it. Your philosophy of ministry document will be a guide to help you see where you need to go and a measuring stick to see if you are reaching your objectives, or at least moving in the right direction with all the programs and strategies you have decided to put in place. Your philosophy of ministry statement needs to reflect the statement of faith for your church, but it will also be unique to your ministry with children. Very simply, a philosophy of ministry statement should contain the following:

- Vision—our preferred future
- Mission—what we do
- Values—our preferred environment
- Strategies—how we plan to do it

I've included an example of a finished philosophy of ministry statement. This one was put together by my team at True North Church. It reflects the ministry statement of the church and follows the process I describe in this chapter. When completed, policies and procedures for parents and volunteers were also added.

TRUE NORTH NAVIGATORS
Celebrating, Growing, and Serving God

OUR VISION: (preferred future)

As a result of growing up at True North, we envision that our children will be drawn to a relationship with Jesus and choose to be one of His followers. We pray that they will begin their journey during the elementary years. We believe this will happen through the influence of...

- Parents who see themselves as the primary spiritual in-fluencer of their child/children; who are building solid relationships with their children, modeling their faith, and teaching them God's Word at home.

- Teachers and helpers who are building relationships with the children, modeling their faith, and teaching them God's Word with excellence.
- The Community of Faith who are fully invested in the children entrusted by God to True North, by building relationships, encouraging parents and children in a spirit of grace.

OUR MISSION: (what we do)

In **true partnership** with parents and the mission of True North Church, we will strive to help our children Come to Jesus, Connect with Jesus, and Live for Jesus by...

- **Celebrating** God's Love for them as they grow in understanding of God's Story. (Come to Jesus)
- **Growing** in relationship with Jesus with the influence of other followers of Jesus at True North—children, adults, and grandparents. (Connect with Jesus)
- **Serving** God in their homes, schools, and neighborhoods. (Live for Jesus)

STRATEGY: (how we plan to do it)

In true partnership with parents

- Provide activities/resources that encourage teaching at home that connects with teaching at church
- Intergenerational worship—(first part of service together as families)
- Provide resources for teaching at home
- Enrichment classes for parents

In true partnership with the mission of True North Church

- We want to begin fulfilling our churches mission beginning with our children's lives.

- Our mission correlates with the mission of True North Church but uses wording that children can understand better.

Celebrate God

- In Sunday School our goal is for our children to understand who God is, and His Story through the teaching of the Bible with timelines, notebooks, object lessons, games, and crafts.
- Through our corporate and intergenerational worship on Sunday mornings we hope our children will learn how to celebrate God!

Grow in Relationships

- Our intergenerational worship on Sunday mornings will encourage relationships to develop among adults and children as they become more and more familiar with each other.
- Formal and informal church gatherings and activities outside of Sundays will also be opportunities for growth in relationships.
- True North outreach events.

Serve God

True North outreach events.

OUR VALUES: we want an environment of...

- Worship
  ° Sunday worship is all about God, and not about me. We want our children to really understand that God is worthy of our time worshiping Him on Sunday, and we come to give Him honor and glory, asking Him to teach us more about Himself and how we can live more for Him throughout the week.

- Intergenerational relationships
  - ° We desire that our children have relationships with all the generations at True North, so that they will see faith modeled and hear stories of faith. We want our children to be in a congregation that welcomes them and engages with them in their lives.
- Love
  - ° It is so important that our children see God's love reflected in everyone who teaches them and in everything we do.
- Truth and Grace
  - ° We want to live in truth and speak truth but do so with grace.
- Peace
  - ° Conflict in churches is inevitable and we should not be surprised by it. God's Word teaches us how to live peacefully, and we will use principles of the Bible to resolve conflicts between workers, children, and parents.
- Respect
  - ° We will expect children to be respectful of each other and their teachers in the classroom. Teachers are expected to model respect to the children.
- Safety
  - ° We want to be proactive in this area, and do everything possible to protect our children and give them a safe environment at church to worship and to learn about God. We are requiring two adults in every classroom and a background check on every adult who teaches or is in the classroom with our children.

- Teams
  - ° We believe in teams; one person should not have too big of a load to carry in children's ministries. We want 'lots of people to do a little bit. And we want people to work in their giftedness and strengths.
- Fun Engagement
  - ° Fun is not the goal, but we do want our kids to have fun and be engaged with Sunday School and challenged with learning God's Word.
- Relevancy
  - ° We want our teaching to be relevant to the culture our children live in with the goal of helping them see God's perspective in the world today.

How Do You Turn the Ship Around in the Harbor?

I believe there are three components necessary to be able to turn your ship around. Change starts with an *awareness* of the problems and challenges for both parents and the entire congregation. Awareness needs to be followed up by a well-researched *strategy* that is then well communicated. Once your strategy has been decided upon and implemented, it needs to be *evaluated* and regularly adjusted so it will allow you to continue to be effective in reaching your goals.

Awareness: Ideas and Resources for Awareness Campaigns in Your Church

Communication is the key to awareness. There are many ways to help your congregation become aware of what is happening in the church with church-grown kids. Sharing research is often the best way to begin. Make sure to use research from well-respected and reliable sources such as Barna Research, Search Institute, and Lifeway Research. Though the information may not be positive, we need to know the realities of what is happening in the church and how we might be missing the mark. The research definitely jolted me out of my comfort zone and thrust me into Reconnect Ministries almost fourteen years ago. The first *awareness* book I read was *The Family Friendly Church*, by Ben Freudenburg, the "grandfather" of the faith at home movement. The next awareness book I read was George Barna's *Transforming Children into Spiritual Champions*. I recommend both books as excellent resources to prepare you for the task ahead.

Reconnect Ministries has been all about awareness followed by developing strategies to reconnect the home and the church. Whether I present to children's pastors/directors, children's ministries staff, pastoral teams, elder teams, or parents, this is where it all begins. The motivation for change happens when we become aware of needs, and in our area of ministry everyone needs to be aware of the fact that too many of our church-grown kids are leaving the church and their faith.

Following time spent sharing research on this issue, the challenges ahead can be presented in a more positive light by painting a picture of the spiritual role of a parent. A pastor could use a sermon or short sermon series to motivate parents to take the biblical responsibility for their children's spiritual lives more seriously. Research indicates that many parents know this is their responsibility but feel very inadequate because they don't know what they should be attempting to do at home. We need to teach parents what they can do, provide resources, regular trainings, walk alongside them, and help them see they can do this. An awareness campaign might be the first time the parents really understand the spiritual influence they can have in their home and how natural it can be to follow God's blueprint and strategy for passing faith from one generation to the next.

This message of parental responsibility and opportunity does not necessarily need to be followed up with a periodic sermon or sermon series because the message can be successfully included in the context of the messages your pastor preaches each Sunday. At True North, the church I am currently working with in Phoenix, Pastor Thomas (PT) does an excellent job of regularly reminding parents of their responsibility to teach their children and engage with them in spiritual discussions, all within the context of his weekly messages. The reason he can do this well is because he owns the philosophy himself; he firmly believes that spiritual development should take place in the home with the church coming alongside. PT is shepherding his congregation and leading "top down." Having the senior pastor on board and taking the lead is absolutely the most effective way for a church to respond and to create awareness. The process will be much more difficult if the children's pastor is trying to "lead up" and it will take a lot longer to reach the goal. I have seen some churches use written forms of communication to create awareness in their church, but this method is probably the least effective of all awareness campaign efforts. The churches that have been the most successful with this issue are those where the message is delivered from the "top down"; we need more senior pastors to take this issue to heart.

Another pastor who has taken the leadership in his church is Doug Kehr at Cornerstone Church in Johnstown, Colorado. In his small groups, he is using the DVD series, Visionary Parenting, by Rob Rienow to lay a foundation of awareness of the importance of parents teaching and modeling their faith at home. Doug Kehr also encourages parents within the context of his sermons by regularly reminding them they are the most influential people in their children's spiritual lives.

The first four chapters of *Perspectives on Family Ministry—3 Views* could also be made into a great awareness presentation for your congregation that would provide an understanding of this shift in thinking for youth and children's ministries. I use a lot of this material in my own awareness presentations at churches. The last section of the book is philosophical in nature and can be used well in leadership discussions to help determine which model will best fit your church. Once you take a philosophical position for your church, strategies can then be developed.

Another philosophy that provides a great visual awareness strategy for a congregation is found in *Think Orange* developed by Reggie Joiner, founder of the Orange Conference. The basic premise of this visual is that the church is the light of the world (yellow), and the home is the heart of the family (red), so the impact of working together (orange) is greater than two separate influences. As Reggie Joiner says in *Think Orange*, "Two combined influences have a greater impact than two independent influences" (p. 109). Orange can be a great visual reminder of the role of the home and church when everyone knows what it means to be orange.

Strategies to Consider for Your Church

Part 2 of *Perspectives on Family Ministry—3 Views* is very helpful in identifying the direction for your church and how to proceed with a strategy. Here is a brief look at each of the three views or strategies found in the book.

Family-Integrated Model

There are many types of family-integrated churches. Some don't even have a nursery or preschool class. Childcare in the service is accomplished by worshipers assisting each other. This seems a little too loose for me, but some churches do it and love it. I suggest parents or the leadership team decide at what age they want children to come into the worship service. It is important to provide good care for babies and have a quality teaching plan for the preschoolers and early elementary, depending on when you decide to bring them in the service. Typically, a church will decide to have children come into the service once they have been in school a couple of years, usually 1st or 2nd grade. I have also had churches decide to bring the children in at 4th or 5th grade. In a family-integrated service it is important that parents be allowed to bring their children to the service at whatever age they feel comfortable with, but there may need to be some ground rules or guidelines established by your leadership team.

The worship service can also be partially integrated. In our church, the children stay for the worship/singing and are dismissed for their class before the message. This may seem like an old-fashioned way to do it, but from my experience, kids know the worship songs their parents sing (which is great) and more times than not, children do not like "kid worship." Maybe some of the girls do, but for the most part, boys do not. I believe it is so much better for all the children to know they are an important part of their church and can be a part of corporate worship. I just love hearing the children singing, especially young Connor at my church. Parents at True North are free to keep their children of any age in this part of the service. Babies and preschoolers are usually there; toddlers are usually in the nursery from the beginning of the service because parents don't want to run after them when they take off during the service. ☺

The benefits of a family-integrated service are many:

- Everyone is hearing the same thing which can form the basis for family spiritual discussions.

- Teachers for children (increasingly hard to find in most churches) are not needed, so no one has to miss church.

- Children know this is their church because they are a part of it.

These are just a few of the benefits. If there is a concern that children are not getting teaching on their level of understanding, I suggest having a parent-organized Sunday School during the week or a Saturday school. Depending on the size of the church, the children could be divided by ages, or by the maximum number of children a family can host in their home using multiple homes as needed. Teaching could be shared by parents unless teachers are available to teach in host homes. The church could also provide a teaching plan for each home and have a family night to do "Sunday School." This requires a certain level of spiritual maturity in a church, which is definitely part of the goal.

Family-Based Model

The family-based strategy brings parents into the current programming of the church, or the church adds programming to include parents and grandparents. In this strategy the age-segregated programming is maintained and made culturally relevant so new families will feel comfortable coming into the church. Parents are intentionally in-corporated into programming, which includes intergenerational and family-focused events.

These are often fun events that are planned for fathers and sons, fathers and daughters, mothers and sons, or mothers and daughters where spiritual discussions, that would normally not occur at home, can be planned into the event. A couple of years ago I had a moth-er-daughter tea at my home for the girls in my class who were mov-ing into the middle school class at church. In addition to fun activ-ities with moms and their daughters, I had two spiritual questions that daughters were encouraged to ask their moms. This promoted a discussion of information that a daughter didn't know about her mother's relationship with God. These events can be an experiential teaching time for parents without them even knowing it, and it makes it more comfortable for them to begin having spiritual discussions at home.

I have heard of churches using this model by inviting parents to be the special guest in their child's Sunday School class. This gives them an opportunity to experience the class with their child and to know how they can better connect with the lessons at home.

One of things my church in Littleton did that fits into this model was to have older members in the church pray for the teenagers in the church. The program was sponsored by Pastor John, who encouraged the seniors in the church to pick a teenager in the youth group to be their official prayer partner. It encouraged relationships and spiritual discussion between the generations, and everyone loved it.

Family-Equipping Model

The family-equipping model focuses on training and equipping parents for their responsibility to spiritually develop their children. Whether the church chooses to segregate ages or integrate, the goal with this model is to connect parents to every aspect of their minis-try with children and youth. They want parents in their church to be "acknowledged, equipped and held accountable for discipling their children" (p. 144).

Personally, this is the model I like best. If I could design my own program, I would go back to a two-hour Sunday worship experience with an age-segregated teaching hour for children and a family-integrated worship service. Parents would have parent training and fellowship in the Sunday School hour, and, in a perfect world, empty-nest couples would teach Sunday School so parents could take part in their training and equipping hour. The empty nesters could all then go to lunch after church (without kids ☺).

Unfortunately, our culture seems to be dictating a one-hour church experience. With families now only averaging two or less Sundays a month, this is a real challenge for the training and equipping of parents. I believe children at some time still need teaching on their level of understanding, whether it is at home or at church, but it is only valuable at church if it is connected to parents who will reinforce the lessons, engage in spiritual discussions, and take opportunities to apply the teaching objectives to life situations.

There are many strategies and resources for the family-equipping model:

- Mark Holman's *Church + Home* is a must read for churches. I love his *Take It Home* resource that gives inspiration for events to help parents transform their children. He promotes one age-related training per year for parents. So, if you have three children, you will attend three parent trainings a year that are simple and profound. Every parent should hear and apply these trainings to their spiritual parenting. You can find his materials on his website, www.faithathome.com.

- *Spiritual Parenting* DVD series by Michelle Anthony is a must see for all parents.

- *Visionary Parenting* DVD series by Rob Rienow provides a solid biblical foundation for the faith at home movement.

- *Sticky Faith* is a resource by Dr. Kara E Powell and Chap Clark, Fuller Youth Institute.

- *Shift—What it Takes to Finally Reach Families Today* by Brian Haynes highlights a strategic partnership of the church and the home as they walk through the path of seven milestones that every family experiences.

- *Think Orange* is both an awareness campaign and a strategy that was developed by Reggie Joiner for North Point Church in Atlanta (pastored by Andy Stanley). Reggie Joiner spent several years developing this strategy for their church with his team. Because of their passion for the church, they invited others to use it in their churches and homes to work together for the faith of their children. It is a great program, but I have a word of caution; I've worked with many churches that described themselves as "orange," but had no evidence of actually being "orange" at all. I believe there is a danger in using a program that your team hasn't really thought through and custom-designed for your church. It is relatively easy for children's directors to take their pastor to a conference, decide to be an "orange" church, delegate the responsibility to the children's director, and check the "faith at home movement" off their list of things the church should be doing. Just like Reggie Joiner did at North Point, churches need to wrestle with which resource and strategy will really work and custom design it so it will fit in *their* church. Simply using someone else's program without really making it yours will eventually lose its effectiveness. Whatever strategy you choose, it must be managed well if it is to maintain its value.

- The annual *D6 Conference* is, by far, the most helpful resource I've found, for churches that want to implement changes to develop a biblical discipleship strategy and thus reconnect home and church. I remember how excited I was to hear about this conference in 2009 when I was consulting with churches around the country. I went the first year to check it out, and have gone almost every year since. The *D6 Conference* is designed for church leaders, parents, and volunteers. I have recommended it to every church (and the parents) I have worked with because of the teaching, the resources and support available through this awesome conference! Check it out at http://d6family.com/d6conference/.

Evaluation—Guidelines for Your Church

Evaluation needs to be done by the leadership (children's ministry, pastor, elders, ministry leaders) and the parents. We need to listen to what is working and what is not working and brainstorm together for ideas to make our strategy effective. Here are a few questions you can ask yourselves:

- Are we talking to parents regularly through group meetings or questionnaires to ask if they are connecting with the teaching at church or doing other things at home?
- Are we asking them what we can do to help and come alongside?
- How are we training and equipping parents to take the spiritual leadership in their homes?
- Are we hearing stories from families that are encouraging and that indicate there is growth in the home?
- Are we sharing those stories with the congregation or better yet, are we having the families share?
- When do we have the whole family learning or worshipping together? How can we make this more effective? What are the challenges for parents in these settings?
- Are we leading well in this area of ministry?

Without evaluation, our strategies grow stagnant and lose their effectiveness. It is important to revisit our vision, mission, and strategies to make sure we are headed in the right direction and are accomplishing our purpose. It takes regular attention.

I recently went to a memorial service at an established church I had known well. The church had moved into a brand-new facility I had not seen yet. I was able to tour the children's ministry wing. It was amazing! It almost felt like I was in Disneyland. But I kept thinking, "I wonder if they are putting as much effort into connecting with parents to make sure they are leading the spiritual development in their children's lives at home." It is much easier to build great facilities than to equip and train parents to be the spiritual leaders of their children's lives.

++++++++

In all my work with churches in the past 14 years, I have noticed they all have one thing in common; they all desire to see their children understand God's love for them. Their desire is to help children know Jesus and live for Him for a lifetime. We just have to keep working on the home and church connection and make sure we are working together. As I talk to churches and look at websites of churches around the country, I see that much progress has been made in the faith at home movement that began in force around 2005. But I don't sense that we have arrived yet. However, I am encouraged and happy that I followed the call out into the "unknown" and have been able to be a part of a movement that, I believe, is making faith a more meaningful experience for parents and their children. As a result, I believe many more of our children will be in the kingdom of God.

We still have challenges, and we always will. It helps to recognize those challenges so we can identify them as we encounter them. The greatest challenge for children's ministries may be to think in terms of "philosophy of ministry" rather than just "programming for the children." We need to continue to ask ourselves, "Are we accomplishing our mission and vision?" If we aren't, we should ask, "Why not? What needs to change?"

Resources

Barna, George. *Transforming Children Into Spiritual Champions*. Regal, 2003.

Bell, Phil. *The Family Ministry Playbook for Partnering With Parents*. Randall House, 2021

Freudenburg, Ben. *The Family Friendly Church*. Group Publishing, 1998.

Haynes, Brian. *The Legacy Path: Discover Intentional Spiritual Parenting*. Randall House, 2011.

Holmen, Mark. *Faith Begins at Home*. Regal, 2005.

Holmen, Mark. *Take It Home*. Gospel Light, 2008.

Holmen, Mark. *Building Faith at Home*. Regal, 2007.

Holmen, Mark. *Church + Home*. Regal, 2010.

Holmen, Mark & Siewert, Brian. *Faith@Home Revealed*. Lulu Publishing Services, 2020.

Hunter, Ron. *The DNA of D6: Building Blocks of Generational Discipleship*. Randall House, 2015.

Hunter, Ron & co. *Recalibrate: A New Measure for Family Ministry*. Randall House, 2019.

Joiner, Reggie. *Think Orange*. David C Cook, 2009.

Jones, Timothy Paul & Trentham, John David. *Practical Family Ministry: A Collection of Ideas for Your Church*. Randall House, 2015.

Jones, Timothy Paul. *Perspectives On Family Ministries—3 Views*. B & H Publishing Group, 2009.

Kimmel, Tim. *Connecting Church and Home: A Grace-Based Partnership*. Randall House, 2013

Reid, Garnett. *Deuteronomy 6 in 3D: An Ancient Plan for Modern Parents*. Randall House, 2010.

Shirley, Chris. *Family Ministry and the Church*. Randall House, 2018.

Wright, Tim. *Sunday Schooling Our Kids Out of Church, The True Story of How One Congregation Dropped Sunday School to Save its Soul*. E-Book, 2015.

www.D6family.com

www.faith5.com

KEYS TO IMPACTFUL TEACHING WITH ANY CURRICULUM

As I was preparing for a consultation with a church, I was reminded again that parents have 3,000 hours per year to influence their children spiritually compared to an average of 40 hours that the church has per year, depending on how much a family attends church or goes to other activities. This means that to maximize spiritual development in our children's lives, leaders must focus more on training and equipping parents than building bigger and better children's ministries in their churches. As I reflected on this, my mind went on a "bunny trail," and I started thinking about the 40 hours the church *does* have every year in a child's life. How can we maximize the effectiveness of those 40 hours? My mind started putting together a list of the things I have learned and observed over the past 30 years of working in children's ministries. A new workshop was forming in my mind. I've now taught that workshop many times for people who teach children in the church. One thing I have learned about people who have a passion for teaching children the Word of God is that they have a strong desire to impact the lives of children for eternity in the short amount of time they have. Teaching children the Bible is too challenging to "just be doing it." Let's explore six keys to impactful teaching.

⌐▬ Relationship = Influence

Just as it is in parenting, I believe relationship is the most important part of being an effective teacher and impacting the heart of a child. There is a good chance that children will not remember a great deal of what we teach them, but they will remember how much we cared about them. The greater the relationship we have with our children, the more they will listen and value what we teach them. I remember when I was a young mom, I heard a Bible study leader once say that growing spiritually is like growing healthy bodies. We don't necessarily remember what we ate a year ago or even two weeks ago, but it all went to sustaining and building a healthy body. It's the same with our spiritual lives; we don't always remember what we have been taught in Sunday School classes or have heard in sermons, but it has all been forming a spiritual foundation in our lives. The teaching is important for children even if they don't remember specifics because they *will remember* the teachers in their lives who loved them and loved God. I think we all remember the people who genuinely loved us, invested in us, and showed us they loved us by their actions. It was certainly true for me. The teachers I remember and the ones who impacted my faith were the ones who took the time to build a relationship with me. There are others whom I have long forgotten or only remember in a negative light.

Relationship in children's ministries is built by caring, respecting the unique personality of each child, trying to understand the root of their behavior so that we are not always responding to the symptoms of a root problem, and doing things that show that we love them. We won't have a close bond with every child, so we shouldn't be too hard on ourselves. Instead, we need to trust God to show us the students whose hearts are open and the ones that we can open up over time. When there are students that do not relate to you, pray that God will bring someone else into their lives who will be able to influence them. There will inevitably be times when a student tries our patience causing us to react in a way that damages or hinders the relationship. In these instances, apologies and asking forgiveness can go a long way toward getting us back on track to building a relationship that impacts a child's life. None of us is perfect, but we can ask God for wisdom and help and make things right when the situation calls for this humble act of restoration.

The second key to impactful teaching is that we need to...

⊶ Let Them See How Much We Love Jesus

In an earlier chapter, I talked about Mrs. DeVries, an influential teacher who definitely had the biggest impact on my life! She was a little bit stern, but there were three things we all knew in her class. Mrs. DeVries loved Jesus, she loved us, and she was *determined* that we understand Jesus loved us. I wanted to love Jesus because she loved Jesus and because I knew she loved me. I think the other kids in the class felt the same. Her main goal over the course of a year was to have us memorize at least a dozen verses she thought were the most important ones in the Bible. I memorized them even though it was hard and tedious because I knew she thought those verses were the most important thing in my life. She had that influence on me because I knew she loved me and thought it was in my best interest to know them. I still remember all those verses. Mrs. DeVries showed us she loved Jesus and then she demonstrated the love of Jesus to us. She conveyed her concern for us in a strong way. I knew she cared about me and was very concerned about my life and the things I was going through. I knew she was praying for me and she was watching all the choices I made as I grew into my teen years. I knew she was hoping I would make the choices that were best for me and that my relationship with God would remain strong. Mrs. DeVries had more impact on my spiritual journey than she ever knew, and many of us will not know the impact we have had until we get to Heaven and meet all the kids we taught.

It was because of teachers like Mrs. Devries that when I was asked to be the children's director in Littleton, Colorado, back in 1989, I asked God to help me do my ministry in such a way that the children could feel His love flowing out of me to them. I wanted them to recognize through my actions and teaching that I loved God so they would want to love God too. I wanted to have an impact on the children entrusted to me in the same way Mrs. DeVries had had an impact on me.

Just recently I read this dedication by Nancy Guthrie in her book *Jesus Keep Me Near the Cross*.

> I fondly dedicate this book to Estelle Hudgins Teeter, my 6th grade teacher who took an interest in me, invested in me, and is still teaching me with her selfless life. Estelle, I saw in you a radiant joy in knowing Christ, the power of his resurrection and the fellowship of sharing in his sufferings, becoming like him... You made me want to love Jesus like you do. (p. 5)

This should be our number one goal. When it is a teacher's goal to let children see how much we love Jesus, we *can* make a big difference in a child's life with even the few hours we have at church. This is the second key to teaching with impact, regardless of time constraints and regardless of curriculum.

○━ Teach God's Story and a Timeline in Elementary School

The third key to impactful teaching in the few hours we have at church is teaching them God's story instead of a virtue-based curriculum. The Bible is a letter sent to us from God. This is the visual I want children to have when they read the Bible. They need to know the Bible has everything in it that God wants us to know about Him and the relationship He wants to have with us. They need to know this is the reason we treasure the Bible so much and why the stories mean so much to us personally. Our enthusiasm and our reverence for God's story must be contagious, causing children to want to hear more. John Walton says in his book *The Bible Story Handbook*, "The Bible is God's self-revelation to us so that we can get to know who He is, and make sense of this confusing world we find ourselves living in" (p. 27). This self-revelation is how we know God loves us and He wants a relationship with us. This must be our ultimate purpose in teaching the Bible to children: to know God, His nature, His personality, His story of love, and His desire for a relationship with us.

Genesis sets the stage and gives us a Biblical Worldview, which is foundational for understanding God and His purposes for mankind. Through God's covenants with Abraham, Moses, Joshua, and David, God reveals who He is to the Israelites and His expectations for a relationship with them. In the Old Testament, we see the depths of our sin nature as we read and relate to the sins of God's children. We also note that God's promise of a Messiah went all the way back to Genesis 3:15: "I will put enmity between you and the woman and between your offspring and hers; he will crush your head, and you will strike his heel" (NIV). The Old Testament shows us our need for a Savior and promises hope for us. The New Testament reveals the Messiah and God's plan to remedy the issue of sin through the death and resurrection of His Son, Jesus. God then introduces our Helper, the Holy Spirit, who will guide us in truth as we wait for the kingdom God will eventually restore. These are the things our children need to begin to understand as they go through elementary school. It will take repetition for them to understand this fully.

Some great curriculums for teaching God's story are the following:

- D6 Curriculum, Randall House (three years)
- *What's In the Bible*, by Phil Vischer (one year)
- *Tru*, by Michelle Anthony published by David C Cook (one year)
- *Life With God*, Renovare, by Lacy Finn Borgo (one year)
- *The Gospel Project*, Lifeway (three years)
- *God's Big Picture*, Gospel Light (one year)

Once you have finished teaching God's story, Group Publishing has a great curriculum called *The Life and Ministry of Jesus*. This is a one-year in-depth study of Jesus' life, a great follow-up to God's story.

Many of you reading this book do not have input into the curriculum you teach in Sunday School or children's church. The curriculum may not follow an order that flows through the story of the Bible. But the good news is that by using a timeline in your class, you can briefly tell God's story every week and fit the story you are teaching into God's big picture story.

I included a timeline in my teaching many years ago as a result of reflecting back on a Bible survey class I had in my first year at Moody Bible Institute. It was this class that caused God's story to come together for me for the first time. This was after going to Sunday School every week since I was a young child. From my Sunday School lessons I understood salvation and why Jesus needed to die for us, and I knew most of the Bible characters, but I never fully understood how the whole Bible taught the gospel from beginning to end. When I was in Sunday School, the lessons were topical, which required that we skip around the Bible to teach the topic or subject we were studying. If we were studying "Loving God," for example, we might have a lesson on Peter, and then skip to Abraham, then to Zacchaeus, and of course, David. I didn't get how those stories fit into God's story because that was not the teaching objective.

Years later when I was children's director in Littleton, the curriculum was still based on topics and virtues rather than God's story. At the time, I was not aware of any curriculum that were not topical. Realizing from my own life how important it was for children to see the big picture, I started drawing a simple timeline on the board showing where in the Bible each story fit in the bigger story. This allowed me to teach the children that the Old Testament points to Jesus and the New Testament points to God's coming kingdom. The story of the day was either before or after Jesus came as our Savior. I was able to share a shortened version of the gospel every week, instead of waiting for the salvation message to show up on special occasions. Understanding the gospel needs to be our overall objective when teaching the Bible to children; the gospel is not just another story. When we teach a story in the Bible, we need to always ask the question, "Why did God include this account in the Bible, and what does He want us to learn about Him from this Bible account?"

Currently when I am teaching, I start out the year by having the children do a timeline of their lives so they will understand what it means to study the Bible as part of a timeline. I do a basic timeline of starting with "nothing but God," the Old Testament, the New Testament with a cross where Jesus died and an arrow pointing up for the resurrection, a section on the age of the Church and where we are in the timeline and ending with "God's restored kingdom" to come. When I am teaching a "big picture approach" every week, we add the story we are studying that day to the timeline. Sometimes I let them do the timeline as a review before we start the next lesson, leaving out events that they have to find. Soon the children begin to know the books of the Bible, not just by rote memorization, but because they know the story of that book and understand where the book fits in the timeline. I have seen first-hand how much this helps children understand God's message of love and His desire for a relationship with them.

It is so encouraging to see children in my class grow in their understanding. Second grade Connor comes so excited each week asking, "What's next, Mrs. Julie?" As a result of teaching God's big story, he has read the entire Bible several times from his youth Bibles and is now reading through his new "grown-up" Bible. Connor knows God's story and how each story fits into God's message and plan for salvation.

Michelle Anthony summarizes this well in her book, *Dreaming of More.*

> Stories told in isolation don't tell the bigger story where God is central. Instead, baby Moses is the key figure one day, Noah is the key figure one day, and Jesus is merely the key figure on another occasion. But by putting each story in the context of the main story, we can begin to elevate God, the Redeemer, to His rightful place in the storyline— the main character. (p. 128)

○— God-Focused vs. Performance-Focused Teaching

Focusing on God instead of performance is the fourth key to impactful teaching. Chapter 12 has been dedicated to the dangers of teaching children that they can, and should, make God happy by being "good for God" instead of teaching them the theology of grace and how it changes our relationship with Him. When we understand grace, we know we can do nothing to earn salvation because God did it all when Jesus died on the cross. When the stories of the Bible are isolated and not taught in the context of God's big story, the focus of the teaching easily becomes the Bible hero, what he or she did right or wrong, and what we should do as a result of the story we heard. When we teach the Bible with this focus, children miss God's purpose for the Bible account and what it teaches us about HIM!

When I had my revelation in grace, (see chapter 12) I considered the way I was taught the Bible and how we continued to teach the Bible with the curriculums we were using. We taught our children to have faith like Abraham, obey like Noah, trust and do the right thing like Joseph, be courageous, ask forgiveness, and love God like David, pray like Daniel, not be like Sampson, share their lunches like the little boy in the crowd, and so on. The message I got and the one I believe we are giving to every child when performance is the focus is this: "I can make God happy or sad. It's up to me, and with God's help I can be good for God. If I don't fail too badly, God will forgive me. The shame and guilt I feel might keep me away from God for a while, so until I make it right with Him, God goes away from me. Fellowship returns when I admit I was wrong and make it right with Him." (See 1 John 1:9.).

The focus of this kind of teaching is on self and what I am doing for God, instead of a focus on knowing God and what *He did* on the cross for all of mankind. We can't outperform him. We are in Christ, and we cannot please God outside of Jesus. God sees us with the righteousness of Jesus when we believe and make Jesus our Lord and Savior. God does the rest. As we grow in our knowledge and understanding of God, it is our love for Him that changes us to want to reflect His glory in our lives. This does not happen overnight; it takes a lifetime for most of us. Galatians 2:20-21 (NIV) reminds us of this:

I have been crucified with Christ and I no longer live,
but Christ lives in me.

The life I live in the body, I live by faith in the Son of God,
who loved me and gave himself for me.

I do not set aside the grace of God, for if righteousness
could be gained through the law, Christ died for nothing!

We should consider what can happen as a result of performance-based teaching. We might raise Pharisees, or young adults, who when faced with suffering, end up leaving their faith because they conclude that "God must not exist if He would treat me like this since I have been good for Him all of my life."

On the other hand, what is the result of God-focused teaching? Over time as we focus on the character and nature of God through the teaching of God's story, we are able to rest in God's forgiveness. Then our hearts change, and we become grateful for our salvation. We find ourselves wanting to be like Jesus. The Holy Spirit convicts but does not shame us. Only then can He transform us into the image of Christ. Salvation is a mystery, and it begins with believing and confessing Jesus as our Lord and Savior. As we continue to grow in the knowledge of God's glorious Self and want to be like Him, we do start to become like Him.

The Bible Story Handbook by John & Kim Walton is a great resource for teaching children the Bible. It can be a resource for any curriculum you teach. John & Kim Walton state clearly the danger of performance–focused teaching:

> Failure to clearly see the scriptural agenda compromises one's ability to convey this depiction of God through curricula and teaching. Instead, the Bible, particularly the Old Testament, is often treated as merely a tool for developmental and behavioral objectives. (p. 20)
>
> ...If we accept the Bible as God's own account of Himself, we will also understand that He has made us to be

in relationship with Him and to be like Him. If we truly
believe this, God's story will change us. (p14)

○→ Teach Belief Points vs. Action Points

Here is another insightful quote from John & Kim Walton's book *The
Bible Story Handbook.*

> Biblical application cannot be limited to "action points"
> for the coming week (though if there are some, that is
> fine). More importantly, we have to think about "belief
> points." Much biblical teaching involves belief; as we learn
> stories, our belief should be affected. If our belief is affect-
> ed, our behavior should change. If our belief has not been
> affected, then any change in our behavior is likely to be
> superficial and temporary. (p. 18)

The natural result of believing God's Word is transformation in
our lives. This is the goal. This is what should be happening in our
children's lives as they come to a personal belief in the message of
God's Word. Transformation is a very gradual process, but it should
happen as a result of believing God and that His Word is true.

Ideas for Action

Several years ago I was working on a family/children's ministries retreat for a church in California with my friend, Rita Nystrom, who
was the Administrator for the EFCA West district of the Evangelical
Free Church. We combined our passions—Rita's for laying a foundation for teams to create unique action plans based on the culture
and ethos of their church and mine for connecting home and church
for the spiritual development of children. Our objective was to send
each team back to their church with a unique plan the team created
for connecting their children's ministry program to the parents and
homes of their children. Our workshop consisted of four questions:

- What are we doing?
- Why are we doing it?
- How are we doing it?
- When are we successful?

When we got to the end of the workshop, we put together the following chart for the last question. We wanted the leaders and teachers to understand the relationship between Bible knowledge, encouraging behavior that reflects the teaching of the Bible, and transformation. The end goal is always transformation, but Bible knowledge and encouraging a biblical lifestyle are, of course, aspects of transformation. It is natural to focus on Bible knowledge and behavior/performance because knowledge and behavior are more measureable. However, if we end our teaching there, we miss the main goal of teaching, which is transformation.

THE RELATIONSHIP BETWEEN KNOWLEDGE, BEHAVIOR & TRANSFORMATION		
BIBLE KNOWLEDGE	BEHAVIORAL/BIBLE APPLICATION	TRANSFORMATION
Data, Facts	Outward actions	Impacted heart
Principles, Concepts	Performance	Internal motivation
Doctrine	Accountability	The Holy Spirit's work and an authentic response
Theology	Moralism	Biblical Worldview

So how does anyone teach transformation? I believe the answer is that it can't be taught. However, it can be encouraged and stimulated by talking to children about the difference between knowing the Bible and knowing God, and the difference between performing for God and wanting to be like God because there is an understanding of His love. I think the reason we stop short of encouraging transformation is that we know it is a work of the Holy Spirit in their lives, and it doesn't happen overnight. However, we should always be painting a picture for them of what a transformed life looks like and encouraging them to enter into a transforming relationship with their Creator, Father, and God.

The last time I taught this class was at Ignite Tucson in February 2020. I encouraged the class to participate by giving me their thoughts on how we can teach children and impact their lives. One lady raised her hand and shared how she prayed a prayer of blessing each week for each child before they left the classroom. I told her that I had not thought of that one—to pray individually for each child in my class before they left my room. I told her I thought that was a remarkable way to encourage transformation in a child's life, and I would be adding it to my presentation to share with others. And I would be doing it with the little class I teach at my church each week.

⌐ Prayer of Blessing

I was so moved by this thought of a blessing that I want to include it here as my final key to impactful teaching; pray a prayer of blessing over each child each week. Let's pray for the children we teach, not only in our private prayer times. Let's invite the Holy Spirit to work in their hearts as we pray over each child, blessing them in Christ before they leave each week. Sometimes it may be hard to remember to do this in the final minutes of class. Ask God to help you remember to incorporate a timely blessing for each child into the routine. Plan this so children begin to recognize it as a significant moment with God.

My prayer of blessing for you as teachers is that God will impact the lives of the children you teach with His Word, and that He will give you everything you need to be effective in your ministry to children. Remember, when you welcome children in His name, you welcome Jesus (Matthew 18:5). I will leave you with Leslie Pinckney Hill's poem that has meant so much to me over the years.

The Teacher

Lord, who am I to teach the way
To little children day by day,
So prone myself to go astray?
I teach them knowledge, but I know,
How faint the flicker and how low
The candles of my knowledge glow.
I teach them power to will and do,
But only now to learn anew
My own great weakness through and through.
I teach them love for all mankind
And all God's creatures, but I find
My love comes lagging far behind.
Lord, if their guide I still must be
Oh, let the little children see
the teacher leaning hard on Thee.

Resources

Anthony, Michelle. *Dreaming of More for the Next Generation, Lifetime Faith Ignited by Family Ministry.* David C Cook, 2012.

Hill, Leslie Pinckney. *The Teacher.* [emphasis mine] https://poets.org/poem/teacher-0

Walton, John H & Kim E. *The Bible Story Handbook, A Resource for Teaching 175 Stories From the Bible.* Crossway, 2010.

Curriculum:

D6 Curriculum, Randall House, 2020

Borgo, Lacy Finn. *Life With God.* Renovare, Inc., 2013.

God's Big Picture, Gospel Light, 1999.

Phil Vischer. *What's In the Bible.* Jellyfish One, LLC, 2013.

The Gospel Project for Kids. LifeWay, 2015.

Tru Curriculum. David C Cook, 2013.

THE VALUE OF WORSHIPING TOGETHER AS A FAMILY

"Children in the worship service? Really?" "Worship services aren't designed for kids, and they won't get anything out of it!" "They would be such a distraction for the adults who need to be there!" "Aren't we going backwards to the '50s and '60s?" These are the responses I sometimes get when I mention the value of intergenerational worship.

Fuller Youth Institute spent five years researching reasons why young people are leaving the church and their faith, and what we can do about it. *Sticky Faith,* by Kara Powell, is the result of that research. Their research shows that, "High school and college students who experience more intergenerational worship tend to have higher faith maturity" (p. 97, chap. 5).

The first time I experienced an intentional church-wide intergenerational worship service was at Bethlehem Baptist Church in Minneapolis. I was in Minneapolis for a family and children's ministries meeting and had plans to also visit a cousin whom I had not seen in many years. I was excited to learn they were attending Bethlehem Baptist because it meant I would be able to hear John Piper in person for the first time. My cousin, Tim, and his wife, Miriam, have four boys, and when we arrived at the church, I expected them to get the four young boys settled in their classes before going to the worship service. While they did take the baby and their two year old to the nursery, the two older boys, both in early elementary grades, came with us to the church service. I thought this was unusual because I knew that most churches this size have a "cutting edge" children's church program for kids to attend while the parents are in adult church. We sat in the balcony, and the next thing I observed was families—Mom, Dad, and children, coming in and sitting together. The pews were filled with little families. They didn't have children's church.

Instead of a one-hour church experience where adult worship and kids Sunday School take place at the same time, Bethlehem Baptist offers a two-hour program, one hour for families to worship together and the other hour for children to be taught God's Word on their level of understanding. They have an age-graded Sunday School, but families are encouraged, taught, and equipped to have their children in the worship service with them. The purpose of their Sunday School is learning God's Word. The purpose of their service is worshiping together as a family. They offer several options for parents during this Sunday School hour from helping in the children's programs to attending a class of their own.

At the time I was still director of children's ministries at Bethany EFC in Littleton, where, in my circle, we were always striving to have the greatest and best children's church programs so children and their parents would be excited to come back to our church. The closest I had come to intergenerational worship was having the 4th—6th graders stay in the service while using a children's bulletin designed to help kids interact with the worship service each week. While I liked the results I was seeing when I reviewed the bulletins they turned in each week, I still didn't have a vision for a family-integrated worship service like I saw at Bethlehem Baptist.

Twice a year, after my meetings in Minneapolis, I visited Bethlehem with Tim and Miriam and took the opportunity to observe Bethlehem's children's ministry program and talk to their children's pastor and many of their staff. I was fascinated and greatly influenced by this church with its seemingly backward counter-cultural philosophy. This church reflected a determination from its inception to have families worship together in spite of the more common entertainment-based programs found in most large churches. In the years leading up to forming Reconnect Ministries, I continued to spend time with their children's ministry staff and became convinced that their approach had many benefits for families, children, and the church as a whole. I've now worked with many churches that want to develop a family-integrated worship service.

A resource I discovered during my time with the staff at Bethlehem was *Parenting in the Pews,* by Robbie Castleman. I highly recommend this book. It is a very practical resource for parents and church leaders who are considering having a family-integrated service.

What Are the Benefits of Families Worshiping Together?

1. Shared worship experience

An obvious benefit for families who worship together is a shared worship experience. Everyone is singing the same songs, hearing the same message, and participating in the sacraments together. These are things that can form the basis of critical spiritual discussions at home. Even though parts of the message will sometimes seem to be over the kids' heads, there will be surprising things they will understand or can be helped to understand through discussions that take place on the ride home or in planned discussion times at home. Even the songs can be the basis for significant spiritual discussions. A good question to ask children after they have been to church could be, "Is there anything that didn't make sense to you today?" Learning is at its best when kids have questions. I love what John Piper says about this subject in a brochure that he and his wife Noel wrote for their church.

> The content of prayers, songs and sermons gives parents unparalleled opportunities to teach their children the great truths of our faith. If parents would only learn to question their children after the service and then explain things, the children's capacity to participate would soar. (*Family: Together In God's Presence*, by John and Noel Piper, p. 4)

The challenge with sending kids to children's church is that parents don't hear what is being taught, and as a result, lack a logical basis for spiritual discussions on the topic of the day. In most churches the children are whisked off to the children's wing to sing, play games, do crafts, and be taught during the service, and the youth go to their area for their own style of worship. The foundation for follow-up spiritual discussions is greatly diminished because everyone heard something different. When we are reunited with our children, we commonly ask them if they had fun, thereby conveying the message that the church experience is about fun rather than worship and learning about God. When we do remember to ask them what they learned that day, our children often reply, "nothing" or "about God." When parents don't know what songs were sung or what subjects were covered in their classes, the discussion has no basis for continuation. By contrast, when everyone has participated in the worship service together, the discussions can last all week.

I have said for a long time that Sunday School teachers are not able to follow the children around during the week, continuing to teach and apply the lesson to their daily lives. A lesson is not fully taught until it has been, to some degree, lived out in our daily lives. When parents don't know what their children have been taught, how can the implications of the lesson be applied to daily situations and lived out in their lives? Unfortunately, much of the teaching our children receive is going in one ear and out the other because it is not being reinforced at home. God designed parents to be teachers in their children's lives, and the teaching of the church is much more effective when the church and the home are teaching the same thing. This is the beauty of children worshiping with their families; they are all hearing the same thing and working together to put it into practice.

2. Family togetherness and spiritual bonding

With a little effort and a loving atmosphere, there can be a beautiful spiritual bonding that takes place in the life of a family when they worship together each week. This is another benefit of families worshiping together. John Piper emphasizes the spiritual bonding that can occur during shared worship experiences when he says,

> Worship is taught by our example. Cherish the hour as parents! Kids see the difference between duty and delight. It is our responsibility as parents to teach worship to our children…they should catch the spirit of worship by our example. The biggest stumbling block to children in the worship service is parents who do not delight in worship!… The most important job of parents is to fall in love with worshiping God. You cannot impart what you don't possess. (*The Family: Together in God's Presence*, by John and Noel Piper, p. 1)

Piper sums up our need to have families worship together when he states,

> Togetherness counters the fragmentation of families. You can experience 650 worship services together with your family between the ages of 4–17. Worship is the most valuable thing you can do together as a family. (*Family: Together In God's Presence*, by John and Noel Piper, p. 2)

We will inevitably encounter some challenges along the way, but we should try to make this the most loving and gracious hour of our week. Parents need to engage with their children in the service by helping them to stay connected in loving and gracious ways with clear behavioral guidelines, well-defined boundaries, and thoughtful planning throughout the week and prior to Sunday morning. Whew! Yes, parenting is a fulltime commitment, but the results are worth the effort. A commitment to a family worship experience that is followed with planned times of discussion and application is a declaration to children that Christ is the center of the home.

3. Intergenerational community

Another benefit of having children in the worship service is that they thrive in community and need relationships with older generations. These relationships happen naturally in churches where three or four generations worship together. This is especially needed when grand-parents live far away or are not in the picture. Where can you find three or four generations together except in the church?

The early church was a great example of family integrated minis-tries. They began church with all the children present; everyone was together. I'm sure they didn't even think about it. Children were cared for within the church body and grew up hearing all the stories, seeing people care for each other, participating as they could, and having an opportunity to own the faith of their parents.

I will never forget the older gentleman who came to talk to me after I presented my awareness workshop at his church in South Da-kota. He commented that as he was listening to the presentation, he realized that much of his spiritual development happened as a re-sult of going with his father to the farmers' prayer meeting and Bible study in their area once a week. He didn't say a word but just listened to them pray and share how they understood the Bible. He also heard the answers to their prayers and the ways God helped them through hard times. That is where he learned to know Jesus and decided to trust Him. I was so glad he shared his experience with me that night. This type of interaction is sorely missing from our children's lives, and they need it desperately in the church.

In her book *Postmodern Children's Ministries: Ministry to Children in the 21st Century,* Ivy Beckwith emphasizes adults modeling their faith in front of children as one of the processes of a child's spiritual development.

> When the child brushes up against people of faith through this participation in the life of the community, the child sees models of faith. The child sees adults who struggle, who trust God, who make mistakes and are forgiven, who work for mercy and justice, who model kingdom values. As a result, children will remember the people of the faith community and their lives more than Bible facts they learned at a church program. (p. 66)

4. A sense of belonging

A sense of belonging is another important phase of development in a child's life that Holly Catterton Allen and Christine Lawton Ross highlight in their book, *Intergenerational Christian Formation: Bringing the Whole Church Together in Ministry, Community and Worship,*

> Intergenerational faith communities provide experiences that foster this deep sense of belonging in children, teens and adults; all feel welcome and received. Children especially need to feel a deep sense of belonging, and they know if they are welcome or not. (p. 48)

I remember as a little girl how excited the older people were to see me at church each week. They talked to me every week and made me feel very special. They asked me questions and followed up each week with things I had told them. As I got into my teen years, I had opportunities to listen to their stories and this encouraged me to trust God and continue on my own faith journey. I knew I belonged to my community of faith. Children just know!

In *Postmodern Children's Ministry,* Ivy Beckwith also comments on this issue of belonging,

> Children need to know that when they walk through the door of their church building, they are welcome and valued as much as the adults. The soul care of our children depends on their knowing that the church is their church. They need to know the names of the people they see when they walk through the door. And those adults need to know the names of the children. (p. 81)

I remember when information began to circulate in my children's ministries circles that a surprising number of high school and college students were not claiming their parent's church as their church. When asked why, students replied, "We were never a part of our parent's church." How true that was and still is; the youth group was their church, and participation in it ended when they left for college. Because they were not really a part of their parents' church growing up, they did not have the experience or skills to get involved in the larger church body and experience a community of three or four generations working together to accomplish the mission of the church. Thankfully, we are now seeing millennials seeking relationships with older generations and looking for intergenerational ministries for their own young families.

5. Leadership opportunities for children and youth

Part of a sense of belonging is being needed at church. How many times when our children ask if they can help, do we respond, "You're too young." Somehow, we must give our children jobs and the sense of being needed at church. I remember getting a mom's feedback at church where I was consulting. Her son had been helping with the sound on Sunday mornings. He was sick one week, so she didn't want him to go to church that morning. His response to her was, "But they need me!" That is what we want to hear! Children who feel needed will have a sense of belonging and are more likely to stay in church.

I worked with a church plant in Piedmont, South Dakota at the beginning of my ministry that had a wonderful family-integrated service with families sitting around tables on Sunday mornings. As a part of their service each Sunday they had a prayer time. Both adults and kids shared and prayed for each other. I was touched by seeing the comfort level of the children as they prayed for adults. Being welcomed to pray gave these children a sense of belonging in their church.

In his book *Too Small to Ignore: Why the Least of These Matters Most*, Wess Stafford tells the story of his father helping him feel needed in the family's ministry of spreading the gospel in Africa. It still brings tears to my eyes when I read it. Here are some excerpts from his book.

> On certain occasions God uses children instead of adults to accomplish strategic things in his kingdom... Along the way to becoming adults, children pass through stages that at various points made them exactly what God can use. In fact, a walk through Scriptures shows several times when

the perfect tool needed in the hands of almighty God was a child. The task could not be entrusted to adults. They think too much. They know too much...doubt too much, fear too much, are too selfish, too eager for glory... Here are some incidents where God seemed to pause, rub his hands together, smile warmly, and say "I need someone really powerful for this task. I know—I'll use a child." (pp. 211-112)

Wess Stafford grew up in Africa's Ivory Coast. He talks about helping his dad build their house. In talking about that experience he explains,

He had the amazing ability to allow a six-year-old boy to tag along for whatever he was doing and to make me feel he couldn't possibly do his work without me. I used to announce proudly to our rare outside visitors that "me and my dad" built that house. It wasn't until years later that I understood their chuckles and smiles. Our partnership found its way into actual mission work... well, sort of. (p. 39)

He tells about a typical day in their village and other villages they visited. His dad would help in the fields, his mom did the cooking, his sister would care for the babies and toddlers, and he would hunt with the boys using their slingshots. At the end of the day after supper, the people would typically gather under the biggest tree and tell stories, and his father would have the opportunity to tell Bible stories to the villagers.

Only one distraction presented itself: noisy birds! First the cackling of the guinea hens...and then the weaver birds... The noise of the first twenty or so...was distracting but tolerable. However when it got to be hundreds of them, people had to strain to hear Dad's gospel story. From the edge of the gathering, I could sense him struggling to speak louder and louder. And then, without missing a beat, he would turn my direction and give an ever so slight nod. I knew my duty. I would immediately take my trusty slingshot from around my neck and zing a rock into the tree. As it fell from branch to branch, the weaver birds and guinea fowl would fly away—thus giving the missionary another fifteen minutes or so of relative quiet to finish his talk. I would repeat my "ministry" as often as needed... Without someone to control the guinea hens and the weaver birds, how was Africa going to hear the gospel? (pp. 41-42)

If only our children now could feel this needed, how different the church in America would be!

I may be an idealist, but it seems to me that we should start turning some of the leadership of our churches over to our high school students at about 10th or 11th grade with internships in leading music and preaching. We could then let them start to lead in directions that would keep their generation in the church, with the encouragement, wisdom, and direction of the adult staff and the support of the congregation. Older generations could be encouraged to accept the styles of the young with the big picture in mind—we will most likely be going to our home in Heaven a lot sooner than they will. Let them take over the church, and I believe in turn, they will try to meet some of the needs of the older generations. These kids are the next leaders of the church, and we need to encourage and develop their leadership skills now!

Not only do our children need to be needed, but the church needs them, too. Consider these quotes from several well-known authors who are convinced of this

For too long we have assumed that we do good youth or young-adult ministry when we separate kids from the rest of the church. Of course, there are times when 6 and 16 and 66 year-olds need to be on their own with folks in their own life stage, but we have swung the pendulum too far. We have segregated (believe me, this is not a verb I use lightly) students and young adults from the rest of the church—and it is hurting their faith. (David Kinnaman, *You Lost Me*, p. 227)

True community necessitates the presence and interaction of three generations. Too often the church either lacks the third generation or sets the generations apart. Remember that the third generation is the generation of memory, and without its presence the other two generations are locked into the existential present. While the first generation is potentially the generation of vision, it is not possible to have visions without a memory, and memory is supplied by the third generation. The second generation is the generation of the present. When it is combined with the generations of memory and vision, it functions to confront the community with reality, but left to itself and the present, life becomes intolerable and meaningless. Without interaction between and among the generations, each making its own unique contribution, Christian community is difficult to maintain... If our children are to have faith, we need to make sure that the church becomes a significant community of faith. (John H. Westerhoff III, *Will Our Children Have Faith?* p. 52-53)

We see the importance of each generation. A church without the wisdom of the aged and the passion of the youth is dysfunctional. A church without mothers and fathers cannot become mature. A church without the young is visionless and lacks passion. (Dave Sawler, *Goodbye Generation*, p. 54)

Why Have We Been Segregating Ages and Keeping Our Kids Out of Our Worship Services?

In her book, *Formational Children's Ministries: Shaping Children Using Story, Ritual, and Relationship*, Ivy Beckwith poses this question regarding age-segregated worship:

If we agree that worship experiences of an entire faith community are an act of spiritual formation for its participants, why are we so quick to remove children from it? I know all the usual reasons…

> We remove them because they make noise.
>
> We remove them because they are restless.
>
> We remove them because we don't think they will understand what is going on.
>
> We remove them because parents don't want to be bothered with them during worship.
>
> We remove them because the other adults don't want to be bothered with them during worship.
>
> We remove them because the clergy don't want to be bothered with them.
>
> We remove them because they take up valuable seats in our worship space.

By prohibiting children from the worship of their faith community we are, in effect, prohibiting them from an important piece of their spiritual development and denying them the opportunity to learn how to worship God in the tradition of their community. (p. 98)

So what happened? How did we get here? It has only been the last 50 years that we have removed them from the most central activity of the church, which is worship. I believe one reason is the influence that the public school's educational system has had on Christian education. When we moved to age-segregated teaching, we followed the public education model, but in doing so, we have lost our distinctiveness as a church.

Tim Wright (introduced in chapter 12), pastor of Community of Grace in Peoria, Arizona, who wrote *Sunday Schooling Our Kids Out of Church,* has a valuable perspective that helps us understand one other reason why we have separated the children and youth from our worship services for the past forty years.

About 40-50 years ago a profound shift took place in many Christian congregations across the country…for all the right reasons…with one troubling unintended consequence: In the 1960s and 1970s, my generation, Baby Boomers, rebelled against the "institutional church" just as we did with every other institution our parents built and supported. We rebelled by dropping out: two-thirds of my generation dropped out of church. In the late 1970s—early 1980s, innovative pastors and congregations of all sizes and denominations looked for ways to draw Boomers back to church. They began to create worship experiences based on the unique "personality" of the Boomer generation. These churches went "contemporary," "seeker," or "seeker-friendly." Because these were the primary parenting years for Boomers, these congregations recognized the need to not only provide Boomer-friendly worship experiences for adults, but the need to create dynamic experiences for their children as well, knowing that if the kids wanted to come back, the parents were more likely to come back.

So began a shift from kids worshipping with the big people for one hour followed by all ages attending a second hour of Sunday School, to churches creating Sunday School experiences for kids that ran concurrently with their parents' worship service. In other words, kids and parents were separated from each other, having different Sunday experiences.

Again, the reasons were right…or so we thought. Because these new Boomer services had a sense of evangelism about them (trying to win Boomers back to the church) we didn't want anything to interrupt their focus… like squirming or crying or screaming kids… So, dynamic Sunday School programs were created to engage kids at their level, and in their language, while their parents were in worship. In fact, some churches didn't (and don't) allow kids into big people worship at all.

The result: many of these innovative congregations had a positive, significant impact on the lives of disenfranchised Boomers and their kids. Many saw their congregations and their children's ministries grow exponentially. The evangelism imperative to reconnect with Boomers seemed to work but there was (and is) one huge unintended consequence: We have raised the largest *unchurched* generation in the history of our country.

When we shifted kids out of the main worship experience, we enculturated them in their own program, and robbed them of any touch points with the rest of the body of Christ. Another way of saying it: by segregating our kids out of worship, we never assimilated them into the life of the congregation. They had no touch points. They had no experience. They had no connection with the main worship service—its liturgy, its music, its space, its environment, and its adults. It was a foreign place to them. And so...once they finished with the kids/or youth program, they left the church. We've essentially "Sunday-Schooled" them out of church—because we never assimilated them *into* church. (Selected potions from *Sunday Schooling our Kids out of Church*, Tim Wright, Kindle Edition, Loc. 209)

As you can see, this passage reflects and summarizes many of the issues I've tried to address in this book. As David Kinnaman said in his book, *You Lost Me*, "the pendulum has swung too far." So, if keeping our kids in the worship service and giving them a role in it, is one of the keys to reversing this trend, we need to address the question; How do we successfully keep our children in the worship service? The next chapter will answer that question and provide practical tips to help families to be successful at worshiping together.

Resources

Allen, Holly Catterton & Ross, Christine Lawton. *Intergenerational Christian Formation: Bringing the Whole Church Together in Ministry, Community and Worship.* IVP Academic, 2012.

Beckwith, Ivy. *Formational Children's Ministries: Shaping Children Using Story, Ritual, and Relationship.* Baker Books, 2010.

Beckwith, Ivy. *Postmodern Children's Ministries: Ministry to Children in the 21st Century.* Zondervan, 2004.

Kinnaman, David. *You Lost Me.* Baker Books, 2011.

Piper, John & Noel. *The Family: Together in God's Presence.* The Standard, 1986.

Powell, Kara & Clark, Dr. Chap. *Sticky Faith: Everyday Ideas to Build Lasting Faith in Your Kids.* Zondervan, 2011.

Sawler, Dave. *Goodbye Generation: A Conversation About Why Young Adults Leave the Church.* Ponder Publishing, 2008.

Stafford, Dr. Wess. *Too Small to Ignore: Why the Least of These Matters Most.* WaterBrook, 2007.

Westerhoff III, John H. *Will Our Children Have Faith? Revised Edition.* Morehouse Publishing, 2000.

Wright, Tim. *Sunday Schooling Our Kids Out of Church: The True Story of How One Congregation Dropped Sunday School to Save its Soul,* Kindle Edition.

HOW DO WE SUCCESSFULLY KEEP OUR CHILDREN IN THE WORSHIP SERVICE?

We Need to Be Intentional

When I was a child worshiping with my family in my elementary and youth years, many good things were going on. Granted, there were things I did not fully understand, and I was frequently fidgety, but I was listening to bits and pieces of messages, which would gradually come together and make sense. I remember sometimes thinking the sermon would never end, and I was bored, so I would look at all the pictures in my Bible and at the big picture of Jesus praying in the Garden of Gethsemane that hung behind the pulpit. Now I realize I was meditating on Jesus having to go to the cross for my sins.

I think I learned more from singing the hymns over and over again than from anything else. I was looking around and watching people worship, wondering why people went to church. Sometimes I saw people crying as they sang. Some people sang with a lot of enthusiasm while others did not. "Did they really love God?" I wondered. Sometimes I heard stories of how people found Jesus. I always loved hearing people's stories. Sometimes there were missionaries who told stories and showed slides of where they served. Through it all, I felt that people loved to see me each week and that I had a place in the church where my family attended.

Fortunately for me, church as a child was foundational to my spiritual formation. For the children and youth who didn't like going to church, it was a terrible experience, and they didn't want to go back. For both the child who loved church and the one who didn't, the missing piece was intentionality. With more intentionality on the part of parents and the leaders of our church, I believe I could have been guided and taught even more. If adults had been intentional, the children who didn't like coming at least could have understood why they were there. Perhaps many of them would have come to love their God and Creator.

So, what I have learned is that the key to worshiping together as a family is intentionality. Parents as well as the church must be intentional. It takes a lot of effort, thought, and planning, but the rewards are great when we maximize the benefits and are creative with the challenges.

Help Children Understand Why We Worship

What does it mean to be intentional in worship? The first step and the most important key to worshiping begins with knowing *why we worship*. Parents and leaders in the church must be able to articulate this well. It must be repeated again and again. Our children need to know the meaning of worship and be able to repeat back to us why we worship as a family. I believe this is the KEY to meaningful family worship. I really believe this has been the missing piece for generations and is why many children don't want to go to church. It could be a game changer if children actually understood the meaning of worship and why they go to church.

I discovered this missing piece in a book called *Teaching Kids Authentic Worship: How to Keep Them Close to God for Life,* by Kathleen Chapman. The book appealed to me because I was always searching for ways to endear our children to God through the programs we had at church, especially children's church. As I read this book, I realized I had not fully understood the meaning of worship, nor could I tell a child in a clear, concise reason why I went to church. Yes, I go to worship God, but what IS worship? I was stunned that I was not able to communicate these important things in a convincing way after so many years of being in the church.

Being able to articulate why I go to church and understanding what authentic worship is became a spiritual marker in my life. The change for me happened as a result of reading Kathleen Chapman's book. As humbling as it was, I had to admit that I hadn't really been worshiping all my life. There may have been moments of real worship that were spontaneous and unplanned, but since I didn't know what authentic worship was, I couldn't be very consistent or intentional. God has been gracious to me as I continue to learn. I had my whole team read the book, and we discussed it at our team meetings. Now in my workshop on Intentional Family Worship, I always start with the topic of "What is worship?" I see the light bulb turning on for many people, and I have received a lot of positive feedback. We can start worshiping intentionally when we recognize that worship is not just going to church.

I usually begin this section of my presentation by asking these questions and letting people think about their answers:

- Why do you go to church?
- Do you go to church, or do you go to worship?
- What's the difference?

When defining what it means to worship God, I have found it effective to start with what worship is *not*. These were my conclusions. Worship is *not*:

- Going to church and simply participating in a worship service. It is not a "good work" that we perform, thinking it will give us more favor with God. The message of the New Testament is that we cannot be good enough for God, and He doesn't have a scale for the good and bad things we do in our lives. Only through Jesus can we have the righteousness of God.
- A tradition to make us feel good about ourselves. Traditions do make us feel good because they bring structure and security

into a fragmented lifestyle but going to church because this is what our family has always done, does not mean we are worshiping God when we are in church.

- A way to refuel in order to get through another week. Getting refueled at church for the next week is not a bad thing, and hopefully we will get strength and energy from being with the body of Christ and hearing a message from God, but this is not worship.

- A time to unwind, relax, tune out, or take a mental vacation. For many people, just sitting in the presence of God without children for an hour is reason to want to be at church, but this is not worship.

- An hour of Christian entertainment. Worship for many means singing songs of praise to God, and that is a valid part of worship. However, many feel the singing needs to be a certain style. We can find our preferred worship style of music in many other places during the week. Demanding that the music fit my taste means worship is about me, not God.

- Networking for business or developing a social life. This is one of the ways many people choose a church. How will it benefit me? This is not worship! Many years ago when we started a business, a friend told my husband that we really should go to a certain church because it was the largest church in our area and the best place to be able to promote his business and become well-known. While this is the way many people think, it is not worship.

- A place to learn about God. This is what most children say when asked why they go to church because that is what they are expected to do at church. Learning and growing in our faith as a result of going to church should happen, but it is not worship.

If this is what worship is *not*, then exactly what is worship? The word *worship* is taken from its old English root word "woerthship," which means "proclaiming God's infinite worth." Kathleen Chapman notes that "The word worship translates 'God's worth'" (p. 29). She continues by explaining that

> The act of worship is focusing on Almighty God and Him alone. It's the act of assigning to God His true worth...true worship is adoring God alone without ever mentioning yourself... Worship is one-directional. Worship is focusing on God and giving all glory to Him only, alone, singularly, totally—just Him. (p. 31)

While we are focusing on Sunday worship, it is important to note that worship is not just for Sunday. Sunday, the first day of the week, Resurrection Sunday, is the day that the corporate church all over the world worships God. Worshiping as a community on Sunday should thrust us into the week to worship God each day as we go out into the world.

True worship is not about me. Sometimes we feel so low that we don't feel like praising and thanking God. Sometimes we don't like the sermons, the music, or the people because they are ever changing, but God doesn't change. His Person never changes and neither does His message. He always deserves our worship and adoration for being our Creator, for forgiving our sins through Jesus, and because He is restoring His kingdom of peace and love for us. Worship is a commitment to believe God is Who He says He is, in all His glory and majesty. Worship is being able to humbly say, "You are God and I am not!" "You are the Potter, I am the clay" (see Isaiah 64:8).

I missed this subtle, but profound distinction for many years—that worship is only about giving God the honor He deserves, and it is my guess that many others have also missed this distinction. I didn't know how to spend time just worshiping God without bringing myself into my worship. Kathleen Chapman helps us understand how we can do this:

> Please don't misinterpret what I'm saying... Yes, we are to praise God! Yes, we are to thank Him for everything He has done for us. Yes, we are to ask Him about every part of our lives. But we must not confuse praising God

with worshiping God. There is a difference. Praise is about us. Worship is about God—all adoration, adulation, awe, devotion, homage, honor, reverence and wonder for who God is and what He has done. (p. 34)

Have you tried to just worship without praising or thanking God for what he has done for you? I gravitate quickly from focusing on God and Him alone, to what I need and how I need His help. It is not easy at first. What we want to do is focus on God's nature, attributes, and characteristics, spending time thinking about the mystery and wonder of His person. Reading the Psalms and Prophets has been a guide in my worship as well. I now understand better that worship, separates praise and thankfulness from the mystery and goodness of God. This is why it is so important to spend time teaching our children what God is like.

When we worship on Sunday with our families, we are declaring God worthy of the time we give Him; that out of the 168 hours in our week, He is worthy of the one or two hours we spend in church each Sunday. When I teach children the meaning of worship, I often compare tithing with worshiping God. Tithing is giving a portion of our income back to God because we know that everything we have ultimately comes from God. Worship is giving back time to God to tell Him He is worthy of honor and glory. It doesn't matter how good or bad we think the church service is because worship is focusing on God, singing songs about Him, to Him, and getting to know Him better through the message. The worship service is not about me.

Understandably, children have a hard time grasping this concept. Adults have a hard time too, but it's not as noticeable because we are better at hiding our feelings when we don't want to be there. We are born focused on ourselves and spend a lifetime working on being other-centered. On top of that, we live in an age of entertainment and entitlement where children think they deserve to be entertained and not be bored. Adults think they deserve to hear the best sermons and worship with their kind of music. Children think everything should be fun and games. Their attention span has been made shorter and shorter because of games on their phones, movies and television, and the church is expected to keep up with educational trends, video game technology (and Hollywood) so children will want to come back to church and not give their parents a hard time about coming. We have gotten it all wrong. Worship is about God, NOT ME! It doesn't matter what I received from the service. The real question is this: "Did I give God what He deserves and worship Him from my heart with whatever I experienced at church?"

Children can understand the reason we worship God when we take the time to teach them. We need to remind them frequently—every week—why we go to church. Right now, I lead the children's ministry program at my church and teach the elementary students with my team. Our leadership team has decided to keep our children in the first part of worship with the adults so they can sing praises to God along with their parents. The children are then dismissed for a sermon on their level of understanding, which we make every effort to connect to the home. Every week we talk about why we worship, and they listen for attributes of God in the songs we sing. We are training them to listen and worship God in what they are hearing and singing. They are able to tell me why they come to church—to worship God because He is worthy and deserves our worship. Understanding this gives children meaning and a purpose for going to church. They can focus on God and learn about His amazing story and attributes.

It is good to remember, that when the "B" word (*I'm bored*) surfaces, it means we need to step back and remind children of the reason we go to church—to worship God and give God back one hour from all hours He gives us each week. There might be phases our children go through in their lives when they don't want to go to church. They just don't feel like it. This is normal, and we can say to them,

> This is what our family does on Sunday. We worship God because He is worthy of our praise. I understand that sometimes you don't feel like going. Sometimes I don't feel like going either, but God's love for me never changes, so I go to honor Him. We pray you will eventually love God so much that you won't want to stay away from worshiping Him.

Then we should pray that God would draw our children to Himself and give them hearts for God and an excitement to learn more about Him. Most children go through times of not wanting to go to church, but this too shall pass. We need to model faithfulness.

Worshiping Together as a Family—How to Make It Happen

How do we successfully keep our children in the worship service and make it a meaningful time for both our children and us? Keeping our children in the service is hard, especially when we have experienced the service without them. The following suggestions come from several sources: David & Sally Michaels, Bethlehem Baptist Church, John & Noel Piper, *Parenting in the Pews* by Robbie Castleman, and my own personal experience as a parent with my young children in the pew beside me.

The Week Before

Planning for Sunday's worship begins the week before because worship is not something we are supposed to do just on Sundays. Instead, Sunday worship should thrust us into a week of worshiping and reflecting Jesus wherever we find ourselves. Children need to understand this and see it in *our lives*. Having a time to reflect on God each day is very important, so throughout the week look for opportunities to talk about the meaning of worship and why we go to church. Repeating and reinforcing is a part of learning, a teaching method we learn from Jesus Himself.

One way to focus on worshiping God throughout the week is to have an offering project going on at home culminating with the children bringing the money they have earned to give to Jesus. This will give you an opportunity to teach your children to tithe and make it a lifelong habit.

My husband Dave and I found that setting aside Sunday in its entirety as a special day was a great plan for family worship, spiritual discussions, and memory making. Every Sunday morning, Dave took us to the Donut Hut to begin our day. Our three children looked forward to this all week long. It is amazing the excitement they had for their favorite donut and a cup of orange juice each week, and this incentive helped everyone to be ready on time. On the ride to church we would sing our favorite worship songs as a family. Following Sunday School and worship, we had lunch as a family, and many times Dave had something fun planned for the afternoon—usually a hike in the mountains or a bike ride. Sometimes it was just a family walk around a lake near our home. These afternoon activities gave us the chance to reflect on the beauty of God's creation and reinforce the concept of His worthiness for our worship. It also helped us to bond as a family and be thankful for our family. Sunday night was always pizza and a movie. These consistent family activities made Sunday different than any other day. They gave meaning to the concept of a Sabbath and created God-focused memories for each of us.

Sunday Ground Rules (from experience)

1. No overnights on Saturday nights! We let them do it once, and our Sunday was ruined due to tired, grumpy kids. Friday night was the only night we allowed them to spend the night at a friend's house. Summertime was different, but still, no Saturday night overnighters.

2. Make sure your children get to bed on time. It makes a big difference when kids get enough sleep for a big day.

3. Leave the toys at home. Today we are worshiping God; it is not about us.

Sunday Morning Starts on Saturday Night for Dad & Mom Too

There is nothing worse than the Sunday morning get-out-of-the-house rush, but it can be prevented. I learned from my husband to plan ahead. Set out clothes, shoes, and coats. It's amazing how a lost shoe can ruin the morning, isn't it? We can prevent it from happening by planning ahead. The same goes for Bibles, offering, or any supplies you need for the morning. I have found that giving children a "worship bag" helps families get everything in one place.

Plan for breakfast! You will do yourself and your kids' teachers a big favor. Kids don't focus or behave well when they are hungry. When I was director of children's ministries, I learned to keep cheese sticks in the refrigerator at church for kids who said they were hungry.

Sunday morning can go smoothly. It is up to us, the parents! It will make the whole day go a lot better.

In the Car on the Way to Church

When your children are in elementary school, and even earlier in the upper preschool years, the most important thing you can do to make worship intentional is to talk to them about why you are going to church while you are in the car on the way. Part of your discussion should be to remind them that they are going to honor God and to listen for God to tell them something about Himself as they sing songs and listen to the message of the Sunday School teacher. It can be something new or something they already know but were reminded of again. This gives them something to do and a reason to be there. We are teaching them there is a purpose for worship.

Before the Service

Remember to take children to the bathroom and get them a drink. You can *count* on children *needing* these things during the service if you don't remember.

During the Service

Sit together as a family. Your kids will try to convince you to let them sit with their friends or with another family, but you will need to have them close to have influence on their focus and behavior. I truly believe there is a spiritual bonding that can happen when you consistently sit together as a family in church.

Be attentive to them and engage with them in worship. Let them see you worship authentically and be engaged however that looks for you. Some people clap during the songs or raise their hands. Whatever is natural for you, do it.

I have seen parents engage in worship themselves but have no idea what their children are doing. I've seen children under the pews/chairs, sitting and reading a book from home, or playing with toys. This is not intentional worship. This approach accomplishes very little. I know it can be hard, but you **can** be engaged in both your worship and your child's, and it gets better with consistency.

Discipline in the Worship Service

It always helps when children know their boundaries, and we all know they will test the limits, some children more than others. Talk about what you expect from your children and enforce your expectations, if needed, during the service. We need to be firm, but we also need to be very loving and not legalistic.

When I was talking about this subject, my pastor at Bethany in Littleton would always tell his story about growing up in the church. He would want to look around, but his mother would pinch his neck every time he did. As a result of that experience and others, he did not like going to church growing up. This is *not* the environment we want to have in worship. We want to have a gracious environment with loving boundaries. I believe a loving atmosphere encourages good behavior most of the time. Sit close to your kids, let them sit on your lap, be affectionate, smile, whisper instructions directing them back to worship. Sometimes little children just need a little break if they are restless. Take them for a short walk and bring them back to service. We don't want them to feel badly about themselves. They are children, not adults. This type of atmosphere will go a long way in them wanting to go to church each week. Make sure children can see well, even if they have to stand on a chair. Help them follow along with Scripture in their Bible and help them participate in the service. I believe the worship service should be the most loving and gracious hour of the week, but with some boundaries that you have talked about during the week.

Listening to the Sermon

If you and/or your church decides children will stay in the service during the sermon, this will be the most challenging part of the service for you and your children. Parents and church leaders should discuss what age you want to begin to have them stay for the sermon. The age when they begin to stay in the service has been different in every church I have consulted. I recommend that there is always a nursery and preschool unless the leadership wants to have a full-on family integrated service. Churches with nursery and preschool provided usually wait until children have been in school at least one year (six or seven years old) before the children attend the full service. Fourth grade is another marker that is commonly used for bringing kids into the full service. I encourage churches to have children remain in the service before they reach middle school because it is much easier to teach a four-year-old to worship than a 14-year-old who has never been in a worship service.

We need to understand that while children will tune in and out during the sermon, it is still amazing what they are getting out of the sermon. It is much more than we think. During the times that I had kids in the service when I was director of children's ministries, I had a children's bulletin with some standard questions for them to answer, a puzzle which connected with the sermon passage, and a loose piece of paper for them to draw what they heard. They turned in everything to me and I graded them, sent them back in the mail, gave them points toward a Dairy Queen ice cream cone, and saved the best picture for the cover of the bulletin the next week. It worked well. They had the opportunity to ask questions. This was interesting as we wrote back and forth. They often raised issues they did not want to talk about in person. The thing that surprised me the most was how much they really comprehended from the sermon. So, when your kids are fidgeting and not seeming to listen, they probably are getting a whole lot more than you think.

For young children, preschool to second grade, I recommend putting a couple of books about Jesus or a Bible with pictures in their worship bag. The worship bag should be reserved for the sermon and not used during the singing. Kids should participate in whatever everyone else is doing. They should not be allowed to do their own thing.

I think it is fine to have a little surprise in your kid's bags, too. I mention this story again: When I was a child in the service there was an older man who sat in the pew in front of us every week. Every week he brought Life Savers and slipped us a package when we were about halfway through the sermon. I loved it, of course, and began to expect it and was disappointed if he wasn't there. He helped me get through sitting that long.

Robbie Castleman has many suggestions to help younger children in the service. I recommend you read her book if you want to have your children listen to the sermon. She suggests things like having your child squeeze your hand every time they hear Jesus, or some other word. As you listen to the sermon, you can jot down words your kids might not understand for a discussion later. You can do the same with the worship songs. There are numerous conversation starters from the things we hear and sing in the service. You will soon find out how much your kids really understand about what they are hearing.

The children's bulletin that I designed in my children's ministries days worked very well. Church leaders and parents can work together to have one designed and copied each week. If I were doing this now, after everything I have learned, I would recommend that the only thing that gets turned into the children's director is the picture to be considered for the following week's cover. Everything else would then be graded and reviewed by parents with a reward system at home. Perhaps a jar of marbles could be filled up as they answer all the questions in the bulletin. Then when the jar is full, it's time to go out for ice cream as a family. In this way, parents are staying tuned-in to their child's questions and spiritual development. One of the benefits of parents and children all singing the same songs and hearing the same sermon is the foundation it provides for spiritual discussions at home.

Another benefit I observed when we had children in the service during the sermon was the discipline that was developed in a child's life when they were encouraged to listen and sit still for 30—40 minutes. This is a discipline they need to learn. One parent at Bethany even told me that her son was doing better in school, and she wondered if it had anything to do with learning to listen to a sermon in fourth grade and being challenged to get the main point of the sermon. We need to raise the standard for our kids. They are capable of doing this. It takes some effort and patience on our part, but the rewards, I believe, will be great!

My daughter Rachel was in the first group of kids included in the service after fourth grade. The pictures she drew illustrating the sermon were outstanding, as was the case for most of the kids who were creating pictures to illustrate the sermon. I was really blown away! By the time she was in the fifth grade, she was critiquing the messages, telling us if the sermon was "good today," or if the guest speaker did a good job or not. She now has a master's degree in Apologetics and Theology.

After the Service

On the way home, talk about the service, their favorite song, something they liked about the service, and questions they might have. Children should also hear their parents discuss the sermon with each other. I learned so much by listening to my parents talk about the sermon we all had heard. The same thing happened with my own children when Dave and I discussed the sermon.

The Most Important Part of Being Intentional

Remember, you told your children to listen for God. Now is the time for everyone to share what God spoke to them about. You can ask:

- What did you hear God saying?
- What did you learn about God?

- What did He remind you of?
- What is God telling you to do in response?

Remember the words and phrases you jotted down from songs and the sermon? Talk about them. Did you take communion or have baptisms? Talk about what they mean. Mom and Dad, you be the first to share. We are training our children to hear God, and in the process, we are also training ourselves. When we as parents take the responsibility to teach and train our children to worship, we will also experience spiritual growth. When we leave it all to the church, we are the ones missing out.

Consider these reminders by John Piper:

- Worship is taught by our example. Cherish the hour as parents. Kids see the difference between duty and delight.
- It is our responsibility as parents to teach worship to our children…they should catch the spirit of worship by our example.
- The biggest stumbling block to children in the worship service is parents who do not delight in worship. The most important job of parents is to fall in love with worshiping God. You cannot impart what you don't possess.

One Last Story: Intergenerational Worship Put to the Test

At the beginning of Reconnect Ministries, some very good friends of ours moved out of state. Mirjam, my German friend, had been on my children's ministries team for several years, and she felt like they were missing out on the teaching I was doing for families after they moved. When I told her about my Intentional Family Worship workshop, she asked me if I would come to Oregon to have a private presentation for her and her husband Doug. They paid my way to come, and I was thrilled to do it. Their daughter MacKenzie was five at the time and going into kindergarten soon. She was younger than most of the kids of parents I had taught. She didn't want to go to her class, so she stayed in the service with Doug and Mirjam. They didn't think she was getting much benefit from being in the service. After I arrived, we went through my presentation—why we go to church, what worship is, and all the practical suggestions for making the worship service very intentional.

The rest of the week, we talked to MacKenzie at her level of understanding about the meaning of worship and going to church. On the way to church, I reminded everyone that we were going to talk about what we heard and how Jesus talked to us. The first challenge when we arrived was dealing with an outdoor service. Everything was being done on a big grassy area, which meant there was not much structure for children. Singing worship songs went pretty well, but when the sermon started, I thought, "Well, this might not work." MacKenzie was up and down, twirling and doing somersaults on the grass. I was getting nervous. MacKenzie was possibly too young to have the desired outcome of my teaching on intentional family worship.

We made it through the service and off to the car we went. I thought about just not doing the rest, but I courageously proceeded with fear and trembling, praying hard. We started by telling each other our favorite worship song and why. That went well. I thought she might be too young for the "hearing God" concept, so I continued by asking her what she heard the pastor talk about. The pastor's sermon was from Luke 18—"A Blind Beggar Receives Sight."

I asked MacKenzie, "What was the message about?"

She replied, "A blind man that asked Jesus if he could see again."

"What did the blind man call Jesus when he heard Jesus was passing by?" I asked.

She then replied, "Jesus, Son of David!"

I was so surprised she had noticed the "Son of David" part. I continued, "What did the blind man ask Jesus for, MacKenzie?"

"For mercy so he could see again."

Again, I was surprised she picked up the word "mercy." So, I asked, "Did Jesus heal the blind man?" "Yes," she replied, and I then I asked, "What did Jesus say healed the man?"

Her simple answer was, "His faith."

I was completely amazed and relieved. She had been listening very well in the midst of all her movement. We continued to talk about what mercy meant and why it was so important. She seemed to understand it very well for her age. The fact was that she was listening well while I thought she wasn't concentrating at all.

Now MacKenzie had a context for the discussion her parents and I would have. I shared that what spoke to me was the blind man's belief when he called Jesus "Son of David," which meant he already believed Jesus was the Messiah. Her mom and dad also shared what they had learned while MacKenzie was listening carefully. This is spiritual development at its best.

But Doug said something to me that was the most significant thing of all. He said, "I am going to have to engage and listen in a whole different way if I am going to do this every week with my family after the worship service!" Leading our families spiritually is actually developing us spiritually. Whenever someone teaches, the teacher benefits as well. I have found this to be true in my life. I am blessed and grow along with my students as a result of studying and presenting my lessons to children. As a church, we have taken this blessing and responsibility away from parents and stunted their spiritual growth in the process.

Here are some key thoughts for churches that decide to have a family-integrated worship service:

- The philosophy behind family-integrated worship must be repeated often and "dripped" into the messages each week by the pastor.
- Regular parent trainings and enrichment, in person or online, must be incorporated into the program.
- Parents must be asked regularly how they are doing and what help they need.
- New people must be made aware of why the children are in your service. Training should be offered right away. There will be a church just down the street that offers children's church. They must understand as soon as possible *why* you do what you do.

Resources

Allen, Holly Catterton & Ross, Christine Lawton. *Intergenerational Christian Formation: Bringing the Whole Church Together in Ministry, Community and Worship.* IVP Academic, 2012.

Castleman, Robbie. *Parenting In the Pews: Guiding Your Children Into the Joy of Worship.* InterVarsity Press, 1993.

Chapman, Kathleen. *Teaching Kids Authentic Worship: How to Keep Them Close to God For Life.* Baker Books, 2003.

Piper, John & Noel. *The Family: Together in God's Presence.* The Standard, 1986.

WHAT'S THE GOAL?

How Do We Measure Our Progress? How Do We Know We Are on Track?

I was in Pennsylvania for a week of workshops. I had been asked to do a workshop for parents on how to measure our progress in leading our children to a mature faith. I thought I had the presentation ready, but something inside me told me there was a better way to present the material. I found myself awake in the middle of the night thinking about my presentation and wondering what might be missing. Two questions kept coming to my mind, "How do we *know* how we are doing in the midst of this journey of passing faith to our children? Is there really any way to gauge how we are doing?" The answers I had prepared seemed so vague. I had to ask myself, "What is the standard or goal that we can use to gauge our progress?" Unhappy with what I had prepared, I cried out to God for His guidance and wisdom. As I was praying, the Lord's Prayer kept coming to my mind, causing me to ask, "What could the Lord's Prayer have to do with parents evaluating their progress in passing faith to their children?" In my heart I knew this was God's voice speaking to me. I stopped and recited the prayer from memory.

Our Father in heaven,
hallowed be your name,
your kingdom come,
your will be done, on earth as it is in heaven.
Give us this day our daily bread.
And forgive us our debts,
as we also have forgiven our debtors.

And lead us not into temptation,

but deliver us from the evil one.

Matthew 6:9-13 (NIV)

Suddenly it hit me. This was it! This is what God wanted me to share. I began to see that everything I had hoped to say about measuring spiritual progress could be found in the Lord's Prayer. I realized that if the Lord's Prayer was Jesus' response to His disciples when they asked Him to teach them to pray, then what He gave them must be a summary of what He wanted them to be like when God answered this prayer in their lives. Jesus told them how to address God their Father and *what* they should ask for; the result of this prayer being answered would be a transformed life. He wanted them to give God His rightful place in their lives and have the desires of God's heart as they lived on earth. So too, we can ask, "When God answers this prayer in our lives, what will we be like? What will our families be like?" I believe He wants this prayer to truly be the desire of our hearts. If that is true, then this prayer is a good way for families to gauge their progress and see if what they are modeling and teaching is actually leading to transformation in their lives and the lives of their children.

With these thoughts in my mind, my outline came together, and I rewrote my workshop for the next day. Since then, the Lord's Prayer has become the template that I suggest using to evaluate progress during the eighteen years that our children are at home. Here are the questions we need to ask:

- Can I honestly pray this prayer as the desire of my heart?
- Do I understand the concepts in this model prayer that Jesus asked us to pray?
- Are my children beginning to understand these concepts as related to their age level?
- Are we endeavoring to live out this prayer in our home?
- Are we beginning to see our children develop God's heart?
- How is this prayer transforming the hearts of our children and our family?

So let's start breaking this prayer into questions we can ask as a method of evaluation while also developing activities to help our children understand the model prayer that Jesus provided.

Our Father in Heaven

Can your children see that God is *your* ultimate Father? Can they see that *you* have a relationship with your heavenly Father? In what ways do they see you relating to your Father in Heaven? The only way our children are going to understand God as their Father is through us. They need to know that His love is perfect, unconditional, and abundant. Our children must know that God is a perfect Father beyond what we can offer or provide for them.

Do they know that as their Father, He is their Creator, the Creator of the universe, and no one else is like Him? Do they know that their heavenly Father is perfect in righteousness and justice, but also perfect in love and faithfulness, unchangeable, and ever-present? In other words, are they grasping the character of God and beginning to understand that He is their ultimate Father?

Hallowed Be Your Name,

"Hallowed" means "holy, set apart, and like no other." God's name is worthy of being honored, respected, and kept sacred. Do we honor God's name and keep it sacred in our home? God is so awesome, majestic, and unlike anyone else that just one name doesn't work for Him. He has many names that describe Him. God's names help us understand all aspects of His personality and character. Do you talk about God's many names and their various meanings?

Think about doing a family study on the names of God. Sally Michael has a great book for families called *God's Names*. If your children are in elementary school, this would be a great way to teach them the character and attributes of God. Each of the 26 chapters has a short portion to read, and then a section called *Learning to Trust God*. There is a portion of Scripture to look up, along with questions to ponder and a great family activity. I strongly recommend this book. It works best to take a chapter every week instead of trying to do one each day.

Ministry leaders could do a study on the names of God and connect the parents in a creative way. They could combine parents and kids into family small groups or use Sunday School or children's church time to do activities for families. *Children Desiring God* has a wonderful 40-week curriculum called *How Majestic Is His Name,* which would work well.

"Hallowed be your name" can be understood by our children in our prayers as well as through our formal teaching. Do your children hear you pray out loud? In those prayers do they hear you praising God for who He is, setting Him apart, and acknowledging His greatness and majesty?

Teachers of children might pray out loud in this way as well. We have an awesome opportunity at church to let children see that there are people other than their parents who also love Jesus. When I was in upper elementary school, I came to this important realization, and it served to strengthen my faith.

After many years of not directly teaching children, I am enjoying being back in the Sunday School classroom again. One of my strategies for capitalizing on the forty-five minutes to one hour that I have with these children each week is to ask them, "What did you hear about God in the worship songs today?" This question and the discussion that follows can help children focus on what they are singing in worship and give them purpose for their participation with their parents. They seem to actually understand what it means to worship and hallow the name of Jesus. Some of the responses to my question have been: He is holy, He is worthy of praise, He is faithful, He loves us, He is righteous, and He gives grace and mercy. They actually understand what it means to worship and "hallow the name of Jesus." Their answers give me an opportunity to explain words they may not understand. Then I pray, pouring out *my heart* in worship. This is a very intentional prayer. I want the children to see that their teacher loves her Father and Creator with all her heart and that she sets God apart from everything. I don't want them to ever doubt that Mrs. Julie loves Jesus.

We need to remember that the same principles that lead our children to faith in the home apply in the church. As leaders in the church, we must train our teachers to open up their relationship with God to their classroom. Just like in the home, it's not all teaching. Teaching is much more impactful when someone models the relationship. Some of our children may not have the opportunity to see faith modeled at home, so we must take advantage of every opportunity to share our relationships with Jesus with the children in our care. We want every child to know Jesus as Savior and get safely home to Heaven. We don't know how God is using each opportunity we have as part of a child's journey to know Jesus.

Another wonderful way of worshiping God and "hallowing His name" is to read Psalms such as this one:

I will sing of the Lord's great love forever;

with my mouth I will make your faithfulness known through all generations.

I will declare that your love stands firm forever,

that you established your faithfulness in heaven itself...

Who is like you, LORD God Almighty?

You, LORD, are mighty, and your faithfulness surrounds you.

You rule over the surging sea; when its waves mount up, you still them...

The heavens are yours, and yours also the earth;

you founded the world and all that is in it…

Righteousness and justice are the foundation of your throne;

love and faithfulness go before you.

Psalm 89:1-14 (NIV)

Your Kingdom Come

What is the kingdom of God? What does it look like? When we read about the kingdom of God, there is always a sense of anticipation, of waiting in hope for something better than we are experiencing in our world. How can we or our children look forward to the kingdom of God if we don't know what it is or what it is like? Children need a growing understanding of God's kingdom. They will learn what the kingdom of God looks like by being around us, by hearing us describe it, and by sharing our excitement for a present and future restored kingdom. Like us, they need to understand that Christians are expected to have an impact on the world around them; the restoration and building of God's kingdom begins here and now. We are called to join Him in the restoration process. As parents we need to think of creative ways that our family can participate in making our homes and our world a better place with a goal of ushering in the restored kingdom of God.

I mentioned elsewhere that I use a timeline when I teach children in Sunday School. The timeline begins with "Nothing but God," and ends with "God's restored kingdom," with God's story in the middle. I always tell the kids that I can't wait for the restored kingdom to come. One Sunday, Connor raised his hand and asked me, "Why are you so excited for the restored kingdom?" It gave me the opportunity to tell the children what God's kingdom will be like when Jesus returns to earth as our King. I told them how we were created to be in His kingdom, similar to the Garden of Eden where there is no sin and death or pain and suffering. We know from God's Word that Jesus is coming back at some point in the future to establish His kingdom.

But what did Jesus mean when he told the Pharisees, "The coming of the kingdom of God is not something that can be observed, nor will people say, 'Here it is' or 'There it is,' because the kingdom of God is in your midst" (Luke 17:20b-21, NIV). That certainly is a different concept. When we pray "Your kingdom come, Your will be done on earth as it is in heaven," we are actually asking God to help us work with Him to build His kingdom not only within ourselves, but also in our spheres of influence. As we learn from the teaching of

Jesus in the Gospels, the values in God's kingdom are quite different from what we experience in the world we live in every day. Rightly so, God's kingdom is often referred to as an "upside-down" kingdom (for more on this subject see *Life in the Upside-Down Kingdom*, sermon series by Timothy Keller and *The Upside-Down Kingdom* by Donald B. Kraybill).

What are some things that are different in the kingdom of God?

- The "first shall be last; the last will be first."
- There is joy in giving, instead of receiving.
- Greatness comes through being a servant.
- "Blessed are the poor in spirit, for theirs is the kingdom of God" (Matthew 5:3).
- The fruit of my life comes through brokenness. The grain of wheat must die before it can bear fruit (John 12:24).
- Jesus came for the "least" and the "lost."
- Love your enemies; repay evil with good.

Accomplishing these things does not come naturally to any of us, but these things can take place right now, right here. We are to ask Jesus to help us to value what God values and to love what He loves. We need to help others see through Jesus' eyes and pray that they will respond to life situations as Jesus would respond. These passages reflect the heart of God through the life of Jesus and His teachings, and our children need to see these values modeled in our home and be given opportunities to live these things out through family activities and projects. This will take time, but we need to see ourselves as on a family journey where God can transform the hearts of our children as we model and teach them His love.

Are you trying to bring God's kingdom into your home or your Sunday School class?

Your Will Be Done on Earth, as It Is in Heaven

This is a hard one to ask! It involves choosing God's "upside-down kingdom" rather than responding from our natural vantage point, which, without God, spirals down to a "the survival of the fittest" mentality with constant battles in the home. When being like Jesus is the goal and desire for each member of your family, the kingdom of Heaven can come down to earth. This is what Jesus is asking us to pray for and desire.

A growing understanding of the love of God through Jesus is the foundation for transformation and becomes the motivation for each of us to want to be like Him. Based on the understanding of His unconditional love for us, there should be a gradual transformation in our lives and in the lives of our children. The result will be a desire to choose God's will in every life situation. Transformation is one of the mysteries of God's work in our lives, but it starts with the desire of our hearts to know Him and to do His will. We start by being open about our relationship with God and then praying for this process to happen in the lives of our children.

Can your children see that desire in your heart to be like Jesus? Are you choosing to respond in the realm of the "upside-down kingdom?" Are you guiding them in choosing the upside-down kingdom as well? Are you beginning to see changes in the way everyone is responding? For children, home is the practice field for real life as an adult. What happens in the home will greatly influence what they do outside the home.

I remember an amazing couple in our church in Colorado when Dave and I were young and beginning our own family—Dick and Margaret Patty. Dick was one of the founders of Overseas Christian Servicemen's Center, which is now Cadence International. Dick and Margaret were godly parents, ones that we all looked up to as role models. With four children, the oldest in early high school, Dick and Margaret agonized over the opportunity and decision to uproot their family in Englewood, Colorado, and move to Germany to lead the hospitality house ministry there. They finally decided to take the leap of faith and do it. They trusted God that this was His will for each member of their family and prayed accordingly.

Because of this decision, what resulted in the lives of two of their children has been phenomenal. Joyce and Dave, the two oldest children, started a singing group called Malachi Singers, which began traveling to military bases all over Europe and the United States in the mid-1980s to early 1990s with the goal of reaching youth. Dave Patty and his wife Connie were one of three couples from Malachi Singers to found Josiah Venture in 1993, a ministry committed to helping local churches in Central and Eastern Europe reach young people for Christ. They now have 300 staff members working in 13 countries! Dave Schroeder, one of the performers with Malachi Singers, married Joyce and has now been the president of Cadence International for over 20 years. Together they have had an amazing ministry. Dick and Margaret were parents who modeled faith and desired to bring the kingdom of God to earth through their family. God has used them in ways beyond what they imagined.

Right now you might be thinking you could never have that much impact as a family on the kingdom of God. But I believe God starts small, and no one is insignificant to God. He wants to use all of us within our spheres of influence to bring His kingdom down to earth. We only need to pray, "God accomplish your purposes in my life, my family, and in the lives of each one of my children." God will do the rest.

Families that are committed to establishing God's kingdom on earth will begin to have an influence outside their homes and will further bring God's kingdom to earth. Look for opportunities where you can bring the kingdom of Heaven to earth. As a family, ask, "How can my family bring the kingdom of Heaven to earth in its circle of influence, the neighborhood, community, or world?" You might help someone in need by being a friend, helping someone with car trouble, visiting a shut-in, taking a meal to someone who needs it, volunteering for a non-profit, adopting a refugee, or going on a family mission trip. When families get to this level of transformation, their faith becomes powerful, and God does amazing things in and through them as His kingdom is established in their communities here on earth. Kids rarely stray from their faith when they have participated in bringing the kingdom of Heaven to earth in this way.

Give Us This Day Our Daily Bread

God wants us to ask Him for everything we need. He wants us to acknowledge that He is the source of every good thing. We are meant to walk in dependence on God our Father for everything—materially, physically, spiritual, emotionally, and relationally. So much of the time this goes against our nature. We want to be known as self-sufficient, strong, not needing help, and able to take care of ourselves. Weakness is not a virtue in our culture. Our self-worth, unfortunately, is tied to our self-sufficiency. But, instead, we should have the same perspective as Paul did when he said, "I will boast all the more gladly about my weaknesses, so that Christ's power may rest on me" (2 Corinthians 12:9b, NIV).

Can our children see that we live dependently on God and that He is the source of our strength? As a family do you acknowledge that every good and perfect gift comes down from the Father of the heavenly lights? (James 1:17), and that everything we have ultimately belongs to God and comes from God? Do we recognize that He is entrusting us with everything we have, whether it is a lot or a little, so we may be a blessing to others? Do we recognize that everything we are and everything we have is ours because of God's gracious involvement in our lives?

American values promote hard work, self-sufficiency, and a can-do, tenacious mentality. These are some of the qualities that have made our country great, but unless we recognize God's role, we can develop a false sense of security and pride. Are we teaching our children to value what God values? "But seek first his kingdom and his righteousness, and all these things will be given to you as well" (Matthew 6:33, NIV). Are we teaching our children that God has blessed us so we can be a blessing to others, and that no blessing is too big or too small to share with someone else?

It has been an aspiration of mine to be a generous person, and my growth in this area is because of my experience spending time with someone who is generous. Almost everything I have learned about generosity has come from being with my dear friend, Leslie. If you were to spend time with her, you would soon see that she is very content; she knows everything she has comes from God. Money and belongings don't make her happy, but she always seems to have plenty. She generously shares all she has with those around her. She is a happy person who lives in complete dependence on God for everything.

From being around people like Leslie, I have observed that contentment is something that precedes generosity, and gratefulness is intertwined in both contentment and generosity. Gratitude is a feeling of appreciation or thanks to God. My biggest growth in gratefulness came several years ago when I read *One Thousand Gifts: A Dare to Live Fully Right Where You Are* by Ann Voskamp. This has become one of my favorite books. I keep my *One Thousand Gifts* journal handy all the time so I can write down even the simplest things that amaze me and bring me joy. What I didn't expect was that the result of gratefulness would be joy.

Is your family growing in recognition of and dependence on God for your daily needs in all areas of life? Are you grateful and growing in generosity, knowing that it is God who will give your family everything you need when you diligently work with Him in the job He has provided for you? Once again, our children will learn as we model these things in our lives. Consider having a family journal, maybe a page posted on the refrigerator where everyone can write down things they are thankful for in their world. Included would not just be possessions, but also acts of kindness between family members and experiences of blessings through no effort of our own. When we begin to see how much we have to be thankful for and how many blessings we really possess, we will begin to see how generous we can be toward others.

And Forgive Us Our Debts, as We Forgive Our Debtors

We all know the three hardest words to say are "I was wrong." Sin is not easy to acknowledge, but it is critical we do so if we are to have a relationship with God. "If we confess our sins, he is faithful and just and will forgive us our sins and purify us from all unrighteousness" (1 John 1:9, NIV).

Are you teaching your children to take responsibility for the things they do wrong? Do your children see you take responsibility for your wrongdoings? It all begins here, and the home is the perfect training ground for understanding and practicing forgiveness. In this area, we are all players on the field. For some children (and adults), forgiveness is harder than it is for others, but it is definitely easier in the long run if we begin when our children are young. If we cannot accept responsibility for our sin, we cannot be forgiven of it. It's as simple as that.

Do our children understand that Jesus died for their sin and that God's forgiveness needs to be acknowledged as a gift to us, believed, embraced, and received? Do our children see the connection between being forgiven and forgiving others? Jesus is saying that being forgiven should naturally lead to forgiving others. This may take a while for children to understand, but I have found that children mid- to upper-elementary school understand Jesus' parable of the unmerciful servant in Matthew 18:21-35, which so clearly illustrates this principle. Children get it. But it is hard to practice and will take time and effort to guide them.

Can we be forgiven if we don't forgive others? The true test for understanding the gospel is our willingness to forgive others who sin against us.

We should not confuse forgiveness with reconciliation. They are two separate things. As a child growing up, I was taught that forgiveness automatically results in a restored relationship (reconciliation), and that they were one and the same. In my childhood home, if we weren't OK with each other, it meant we hadn't forgiven each other. This led to a feeling of guilt and shame if I still felt violated and could not go back into a normal relationship easily. I was well into adulthood before I realized that while not all relationships can be fully reconciled, I can still forgive and not hold the offence against the person who wronged me. It takes two to reconcile, that is, to understand the perspective of the other person and to get to the root of the issue. Not everyone wants to go to those lengths for a relationship, but I can still forgive and release them from the debt they owe me. We also need to understand that forgiveness is sometimes a journey, and it may take a long time. Sometimes it may even be a daily or hourly thing, but God knows if we are trying and asking for help.

In this area, do your children see you acknowledging your mistakes and asking for forgiveness? Have they experienced your forgiveness? Have they seen you forgive someone who has wronged you? Can they see your efforts to reconcile the relationship? Dan Allender says in his book, *Bold Love,* "A forgiving heart hungers for a restored relationship" (p. 161). Finally, are your children connecting the gospel to forgiveness, realizing that if they don't forgive others, God will not forgive them? These lessons do not always come easily and can best be learned by walking alongside our children to help them give and receive forgiveness. The home is a great laboratory to prepare our children for conflict resolution in future relationships outside of the home.

The resources that have helped me the most with forgiveness over the years are:

1. *Bold Love*, Dr. Dan B. Allender (I recommend the whole book, but I am especially referring to Chapter 7, "Hungering for Restoration")

2. *Boundaries,* Dr. Henry Cloud, Dr. John Townsend (Chapter 14, "Resistance to Boundaries," under the heading *Unforgiveness*)

3. *The Bondage Breaker,* Neil T. Anderson (Chapter 12, "Steps to Freedom in Christ," Step 3 Bitterness vs. Forgiveness)

And Lead Us Not Into Temptation, but Deliver Us From the Evil One

We know temptations are all around us, and we can easily succumb to them. We all struggle with temptation, and our children should understand that we are all in the same dilemma. They should also know that temptation is not a sin, but we sin when we give in to its desire (see James 1:15). This is a verse children should know and understand. We can teach them that we need to ask God to help us recognize temptation when it comes. God does not tempt us, but He does allow trials for our spiritual growth. He wants us to know He can deliver us from the evil one. We need to help our children see that temptation often occurs during difficult times in our lives. When hard times occur, we are frequently tempted to deaden the pain of the trials by escaping or engaging in sinful activities that can provide short term relief but will later leave us feeling guilty for the sinful choices we made. Some of these wrong choices may have long lasting negative consequences for our lives.

Here are some passages we need to help our children become familiar and claim as their own:

- When tempted no one should say "God is tempting me." For God cannot be tempted by evil, nor does he tempt anyone; but each person is tempted when they are dragged away by their own evil desire and enticed (James 1:13-14, NIV).

- Put on the full armor of God (Ephesians 6:10-17).

- No temptation has overtaken you except what is common to mankind. And God is faithful; he will not let you be tempted beyond what you can bear. But when you are tempted, he will also provide a way out so that you can endure it (1 Corinthians 10:13, NIV).

- In all this you greatly rejoice, though now for a little while you may have had to suffer grief in all kinds of trials. These have come so that the proven genuineness of your faith—of greater worth than gold, which perishes even though refined by fire—may result in praise, glory and honor when Jesus Christ is revealed (1 Peter 1:6-7, NIV).

I believe one of the most important responsibilities of parents is protecting their children from evil and the temptations that lead in that direction. We must be sensitive at all times to teachable moments and guide them in making right choices. Consequences for poor choices when they are young serve to help them to better think through decisions and avoid the traps of sin later in their lives. Our job is to give them the benefit of our life experiences and help them see the big picture of the harmful consequences they may face as a result of their choices.

By the time our children were in high school, we were guiding them to make their own decisions in various areas of their lives. I remember my husband, Dave, doing this very well. Many times the kids would present Dave with a dilemma they were facing, and he would help them see the probable outcome for each of their choices. With that input, he stepped back and allowed them to make their own decisions. After hearing his logical, experienced-based description of potential outcomes, they would usually make wise choices. This can be a scary time for parents, but it's necessary for the maturity of our children. This kind of openness and trust begins when children are very young by encouraging them to share their lives with us, and as they get older, letting them know we will not force them to make a decision, but will allow them to make their own decisions after considering our input. Our children should see us as trusted advisors, infinitely interested in every detail of their lives and always walking alongside of them, no matter what choices they face.

Our children should have an age-appropriate understanding that Satan is real, and that evil exists in the world. Pay attention to the questions your children ask about Satan or about good and evil. These questions can be a good way to discern whether they are ready for a little more reality in their lives. The concept of good and evil is ingrained in our humanity, and we cannot get away from its storyline. The battle between good and evil is part of almost all children's movies, and these movies may provide a good opportunity to have discussions about good and evil, and right and wrong choices. Our role as parents is to use every opportunity, even small daily events, to teach larger life lessons that will have long term impact on our children.

The hope we have in Christ is that He rose victoriously over sin and death and that He can and will deliver us and our children from evil. To me, one of the most amazing things is how frequently God uses our mistakes and our detours from His path for our good and the good of others (Romans 8:28). God's unconditional love and forgiveness for us is unfathomable. We can trust our Heavenly Father to deliver us from the evil one.

Final Thoughts

I hope by now you can see there is no getting around the fact that parents are the number one influence in a child's life, so the evaluation process has to start with us, as parents. In order to pass faith to our children, we have to continually evaluate ourselves, what we are modeling in our own lives, and what we are teaching our children by word and example. The questions we need to ask ourselves, with respect to the Lord's Prayer are these:

- Am I living out and incorporating this prayer in my home?
- Is it coming from my heart?
- How am I leading my children to understand what God values in our lives?

Even when we cannot see progress in our children's hearts, we can measure our own progress. We cannot do our children's part or God's part in transformation, but when we focus on our lives first, we can expect to see God working in our homes and see our children embracing the implications of The Lord's Prayer in their own lives. When we do our part, God will do the rest. He will draw our children to Himself in His own time and way. We must trust Him and continue on our journey to know and love Him more with a growing understanding of "the height and depth of God's love" that motivates us to want to be like Jesus. When we understand how deeply we are loved, that God delights in us, and that He gave everything for us, we will be motivated, not by duty, but by a genuine heart-felt desire to be like Him. This is the growing understanding of Christ's love that we want our children to experience so He can transform the desires of their hearts to be like Him. This is how the next generation will know Him. In the process, might it be, that we will experience a little of the kingdom of God in our home? That is my prayer for each of us!

Resources

Allender, Dr. Dan B. *Bold Love.* NavPress, 1992.

Anderson, Neil T. *The Bondage Breaker, Overcoming Negative Thoughts, Irrational Feelings, Habitual Sins.* Harvest House Publishers, 1990.

Cloud, Dr. Henry & Townsend, Dr. John. *Boundaries, When to Say Yes; When to Say No to Take Control of Your Life.* Zondervan, 1992.

How Majestic Is His Name, Children Desiring God curriculum.

Michael, Sally. *God's Names.* P&R Publishing, 2011.

Voskamp, Ann. *One Thousand Gifts: A Dare to Live Fully Right Where You Are.* Zondervan, 2010.

JESUS SAID ...

God's Perspective on the Value of Children

> "Whoever welcomes one of these little ones
> in my name welcomes me."
> Matthew 18:5, Mark 9:37, and Luke 9:48, paraphrase

I had read these verses many times in my life before I really grasped its significance! When we welcome the children in our lives *we welcome Jesus...Himself!*

Could Jesus have made the value of children more clear to us than it is in this verse? When we welcome and love the children in Jesus' name, on our life journey, whether they be our own children, grandchildren, the children in our churches or community, or even children we randomly come into contact with, *we welcome Him*—our Savior, our Creator, and the Creator of the universe—the Son of God!

So what does that say for the privilege and value of being parents? Sunday School teachers? Nursery workers? Youth workers? I believe we are important people in God's eyes! We are molding and shaping the leaders of the church of the next generation. God is using us to keep watch on future faith; we are—the keepers of the faith!

So, what does it mean to welcome someone? We greet them courteously. We receive them gladly, which reflects the English Standard Version of this verse, which says "whoever receives one such child in my name receives me" (Matthew 18:5).

Many people are drawn to children simply because they are so cute, but it is important that we see the value they have in God's perspective. Do we see the significance of building relationships with them? Teaching them? Modeling our faith for them? Discipling them? Do we really understand how important they are to Jesus? Are we gripped by the reality that they have the potential to be the *faith of the next generation*?

When I was a young mom with three beautiful children, I remember so well how my heart soared when my mother expressed joy in my children and was excited to have them in her care. I loved hearing her experiences with them when I picked them up and it delighted me to see her delight! It actually made *me* feel her love when she loved my children! In other words, she was welcoming and receiving me when she loved my children! Jesus feels welcomed and received by us when we value what He values, which is His children!

Now that I am a grandmother, the giver of love and admiration, I understand the other side too! Not only do I love my grandchildren because they are my amazing grandchildren! But because I also have a special love for their parents—my children! I love my grandchildren because I love my children, and I want to be a mirror of the love they have for their kids, just like Jesus wants us to mirror His love to the children He loves.

This verse says to me that everything I do for the children in my life I am doing for Jesus. What an amazing opportunity! A privilege, indeed! I love being the eyes, the hands, and the feet of Jesus and loving what He loves! Understanding this verse has been the basis for my ministry for the *faith of the next generation*.

Why did Jesus make sure we understand the value of children and reflect His Father's love for the children? There are several reasons confirmed throughout Scripture.

> One generation commends your works to another; they tell of your mighty acts. They speak of the glorious splendor of your majesty—and I will meditate on your wonderful works. They tell of the power of your awesome works—and I will proclaim your great deeds. They celebrate your abundant goodness and joyfully sing of your righteousness (Psalm 145:4-7, NIV).

He decreed statutes for Jacob and established the law in
Israel, which he commanded our ancestors to teach their
children, so the next generation would know them, even
the children yet to be born, and they in turn would tell
their children (Psalm 78:5-6, NIV).

In God's perfect design, he gave parents, grandparents, and the
community of faith the responsibility to tell the next generation the
knowledge they have of Him, so His Story, His love, and His grace
would be passed from *one generation to the next*, so *all* of His children, created in His image, would hear of His rescue plan from the
consequences of the Fall (the original sin that impacts all of us in our
relationship to God).

At that time the disciples came to Jesus and asked, "Who,
then, is the greatest in the kingdom of heaven?" He called
a little child to him, and placed the child among them.
And he said: "Truly I tell you, unless you change and become like little children, you will never enter the kingdom
of heaven. Therefore, whoever takes the lowly position of
this child is the greatest in the kingdom of heaven (Matthew 18:1-4, NIV).

Jesus is using a child as an object lesson to teach His disciples.
What does it mean to *become like little children?* Children are fully dependent on their parents. They are innocent and like a sponge.
They are waiting for teaching, guidance, and help to grow up in the
world where they were born. Human babies remain dependent on
their parents much longer than any of the animal species. But unlike
everything God created, we were made in the *image of God*, a clear
distinction from the animal kingdom. We are recipients of God's love
and He wants to engage with us. God wants us to see Him as our
perfect Father and desire the relationship that was ours before Adam
and Eve fell into sin, a relationship that is now available to us through
the life and death of Jesus.

It is like Jesus is saying to his disciples, "look at this child and how
he desperately needs and desires his parents for everything—this is

how I want you to desire Me, being humble and admitting your need for Me. Never forget the beauty in a child who represents the qualities required for you to know Me." In fact, Jesus says, "whoever humbles himself as this little child is the greatest in the kingdom of heaven" (Matthew 18:4, NKJV).

Children are a visible example of what God desires our love for Him to look like. Then Jesus says, and by the way, this is how I much I love children… "And whoever welcomes one such child in my name welcomes me. If anyone causes one of these little ones— those who believe in me—to stumble, it would be better for them to have a large millstone hung around their neck and to be drowned in the depths of the sea" (Matthew 18:5-6, NIV).

Wow! What a horrible consequence. We can see the fire in Jesus' love and passion for children, and the value He places on them! After all, children are God's idea, we all come into the world as babies and we remain children for a long time.

Once again, I'm reminded of a baby shower invitation that read, *"Every child is a new thought of God!"* I have been meditating on this thought ever since. It's so amazing! God thought about me before I was born, and wanted me exactly as He created me. Psalm 139 confirms it! He thought about each person throughout history and wanted them to be born in the uniqueness He gave them.

> You have searched me, LORD, and you know me. … For you created my inmost being; you knit me together in my mother's womb. … My frame was not hidden from you when I was made in the secret place, when I was woven together in the depths of the earth. Your eyes saw my unformed body; all the days ordained for me were written in your book before one of them came to be (Psalm 139:1, 13, 15-16, NIV).

I have contemplated this thought for a long time—could it be that each of us (without the stain of sin) represent a unique aspect of God's personality and temperament? One facet of a *huge* diamond? Not only should we desire to reflect His character, but maybe each of us, in a unique way, is reflecting His glory and personality. Thinking about this has given me a deep appreciation for all the people God puts on my path causing me to admire their strengths, respect our differences, and look for the unique way we each reflect God.

I find it so fascinating to observe little children, to see their unique personalities blossoming and developing. I believe God wants us to be students of His children, guiding them to be all He created them to be in Him. Children! What a joy they are!

So the next question is, "how do we welcome the children in Jesus' name"? Well, here is an example in the Bible of how *not* to welcome them. The account is in Matthew 19:13-15, Mark 10:13-16, and Luke 18:15-17!

> People were bringing little children to Jesus for him to place his hands them, but the disciples rebuked them. When Jesus saw this, he was indignant. He said to them, "Let the little children come to me, and do not hinder them, for the kingdom of God belongs to such as these. Truly, I tell you, anyone who will not receive the kingdom of God like a little child will never enter it." And he took the children in his arms, placed his hands on them and blessed them (Mark 10:13-16, NIV).

I remember listening to a sermon several years ago on this passage, and the message has stayed with me all these years. The pastor shared that the word *indignant* in Greek is the same word used when Jesus overturned the tables in the Temple court where buying and selling was taking place. Jesus was very angry the disciples turned away parents who were bringing their children to Him for His blessing. He was angry to the same degree He was when He made a whip out of cords, driving out the sheep and cattle, overturning tables, scattering all the coins of the people who were using the Temple court as a marketplace hindering access to God.

This was a righteous anger. And He made a strong point. Children are valuable to God! Don't turn them away. Welcome them in the name of Jesus.

This understanding has stayed with me over the years as I have endeavored to spiritually develop children in my home, and in the churches where I've worked. What does it mean to turn children away in our setting and culture? What do children need to be welcomed in our churches? Would Jesus be pleased with what we are doing in our churches? What are the results of our efforts? Are we continually evaluating what we are doing and changing directions when needed?

I hope this book has helped to provide answers to these questions so a healthy evaluation can take place in homes and churches. In short, welcoming our children means providing meaningful relationships, a strong sense of belonging, models of a living and active faith, stories of faith, a good understanding of God's redemptive story, opportunities to serve together with their community of faith, and to be loved unconditionally all their lives.

How excited are we to welcome Jesus? Our love and admiration of anyone in our lives will determine our level of excitement in welcoming them. The natural result of loving Jesus will be adopting His values; seeing with His eyes and responding the way He would respond. When we demonstrate our concern for the faith of the next generation by welcoming and serving children, we are welcoming Jesus. This is an awesome responsibility and indeed, a noble calling! My prayer is, *Help us Jesus to love You more and more, to share Your values, and joyfully love and serve Your children!*

Appendix

Activity: Adversity
By Karen Noal

FAMILY TIME
TRAINING

Teaching Goal:	Hard times can make us stronger and give us more faith depending on how we choose to handle the challenge.
Scripture:	James 1:2-3 Consider it pure joy, my brothers, whenever you face trials of many kinds, because you know that the testing of your faith develops perseverance.
	Genesis 37 and 39-45 Story of Joseph
	Genesis 50:20 You intended to harm me but God intended it for good to accomplish what is now being done, the saving of many lives.
	Psalm 34:18-19 The Lord is close to the brokenhearted and saves those who are crushed in spirit. A righteous man may have many troubles, but the Lord delivers him from them all.
Materials:	Stove
	3 saucepans half full of water
	2 raw carrots
	2 raw eggs
	1 tea bag or coffee beans
	3 empty bowls or cups

I. Play theme song

II. Pray

III. Review last lesson

IV. Lesson and discussion

✔ Words written in **bold** are when the leader is speaking. Feel free to use your own words.

A. ACTIVITY: **We are going to put three different food items in hot water to see how they react. The hot water is going to represent tough times.** Fill three regular size saucepans half full of water. Put the carrot in one pan of water, the egg in another pan, and the tea bag in the third pan. Turn each burner on high until the water boils then lower the temperature to maintain a low boil for about 15 minutes. (NOTE: It is possible for the tea bag to break if left boiling too long. To avoid this possibility, make sure that burner is turned down to low heat.)

Have this discussion while the water is boiling. **Do you know what adversity means?** *It means being picked on, hard times, being misunderstood, or suffering.* **Have you ever faced adversity? Has anyone ever treated you unfairly or said things about you that hurt your feelings or weren't true?** Listen to their response. Allow children to tell you about their own hurts. You may want to mention one of your own to help get them started.

B. In your own words, tell the story of Joseph from Genesis 37, 39-45. Discuss the times of adversity he faced:

    His brothers hated him.

    His brothers sold him into slavery.

    He was wrongly imprisoned because of Potiphar's wife.

    He was forgotten in prison after interpreting the cupbearer's dreams.

Joseph had many reasons to give up. Instead, he trusted God and made the most of each challenge. He spent years and years in situations that were tough, but he remained faithful and never gave up. God had a plan in which He wanted Joseph to be a part. He could have fulfilled His plan through anyone but since Joseph remained faithful, Joseph received the blessings in the end. Invite a volunteer to read Genesis 50:20.

If 15 minutes has not yet passed, continue the discussion, using this time to show how God has been faithful to your family through different challenges. After 15 minutes, check the food in each pan of water.

D. Let's check the food to see what's happened to each item after 15 minutes in boiling water. Remember, the boiling water represents hard times...adversity in life. Put the carrot in a bowl, the egg in a separate bowl, and spoon out some tea-water into another bowl. Feel the carrot. How does it feel? *It is now soft.* Break a fresh carrot to compare the difference. Peel the shell from the egg and tell me how it has changed since it's been boiled? *It has become hard.* Break an uncooked egg and compare. The tea has changed too but in a different way. Put the tea bag beside the cup of tea-water.

The carrot started out strong but after going through adversity, it became soft, and lost its strength. The life of King Solomon is similar to the carrot. At the beginning of his reign he was strong. He asked God for wisdom. He built God's Temple. But the challenges of possessions, power, and pleasure caused Solomon to become soft. He built altars to idols and foreign gods. (See 1 Kings 11:3-5)

Inside the eggshell was the soft, liquidy yoke and egg white. But after going through adversity, it became hardened. In the story of Moses, Pharaoh had a hard heart. He refused to let the Israelites go which caused his people to suffer death and sickness from 10 different plagues. (See Exodus 10:27 and surrounding.)

Look at the tea bag. The tea bag also went through the adversity of being boiled in hot water. Instead of changing from strong to soft like the carrot; or from fragile to hard like the egg; the tea changed the environment…the water. The water has turned into a drink that is a positive change for those who enjoy tea. Queen Esther changed her environment under adversity. She could have been killed for approaching the king, but she did anyway. She asked the king to save the Israelites and he did. (See the Book of Esther) Paul and Silas changed the environment when they were put in prison. Instead of becoming soft or hard…they introduced the prison guard to Jesus. (See Acts 16:29-32)

We want to be like Esther, Paul, and Silas when we face adversity… hard times…challenges. Don't become soft and weak like the carrot and Solomon. Don't become hard and defensive like the egg and Pharaoh. Instead, like the tea bag, use the challenges to change the environment, to help others, and respond in such a way that others see we are different…different in a good way because we follow Jesus.

Read James 1:2-3 and Psalm 34:18-19. God promised He would be there for us even in times of adversity. He even tells us to consider it *joy*. Remember, God is in the good times and the challenging times. He uses challenging times to make us stronger and to help our faith in him grow.

Close in Prayer

Pass It On: Make an extra copy of this lesson and pass it on to another family.

Activity: Knock Sin out of our Lives

FAMILY TIME
TRAINING

Teaching Goal: We need Jesus to take our sin away so we can be back together with God.

Scriptures: Romans 3:23—For all have sinned and fall short of the glory of God (NIV).

Hebrews 4:15—but we have one [Jesus] who has been tempted in every way, just as we are—yet he did not sin (NIV).

1 John 5:17—All wrongdoing is sin… (NIV).

Materials: Clear glass jar with wide mouth

Metal pie pan

Paper and pen

Cardboard toilet paper tube

Egg, hard boiled in shell

Masking tape

Broom

   I.   Play theme song
  II.   Pray
 III.   Review last lesson
 IV.   Lesson and discussion

✔ Words written in **bold** are when the leader is speaking. Feel free to use your own words.

A. ACTIVITY #1: Invite a volunteer to read 1 John 5:17. **A definition of sin is "doing wrong things." Things are wrong if they go against the teaching of God. God says do not lie. So if we lie, we are doing something wrong and that is sin. Can you give examples of other wrong things that are sins?** *Listen.* Invite a volunteer to read Romans 3:23. **Who is all?** Me, you, the preacher, everyone, except Jesus. **We have all sinned. Jesus is the only one without sin.** Invite a volunteer to read Hebrews 4:15.

Cut ten slips of paper. Write Adam & Eve, Pharaoh, and Peter on three different pieces of paper. **What sins or bad things did these people do?** *Listen. Invite a volunteer to write the answers next to the names.*

Adam & Eve	Broke God's rule	Genesis 3
Pharaoh	Did not listen to God	Genesis 7
Peter	Denied knowing Jesus	*Mark 14:66-72*

What sins or bad things do we do? *Listen.* Invite a volunteer to write the answers on slips of paper. Examples of sins: Lying. Bad words. Disobeying. Selfishness. Hitting. Stealing. Meanness. Greed.

Put the ten pieces of paper representing different sins into the pie pan.

What will help us not to sin? What will help us make good choices instead of bad choices?

Believe in Jesus as the one who teaches us what is right.

Know what Jesus teaches by reading the Bible.

Listen and obey God's Spirit who reminds us to make good choices.

Listen and talk with God through prayer.

Good friends who make good choices.

Learn at church.

Obey parents.

Being in the right place, with the right people, at the right time.

B. ACTIVITY #2: Fill the jar with water and place it near the edge of a table. Center the pie pan containing the pieces of paper listing different sins on top of the jar. Place the toilet paper tube in the center of the pan, which should also center the tube over the jar opening under the pie pan. Place the egg sideways on top of the toilet paper tube. The edge of the pie pan, *not the jar,* should stick out over the edge of the table.

The pieces of paper represent different sins in our lives. Sins are bad choices we make; choices God would not want us to make. The jar of water represents people—you and me. The egg represents God. If we are the jar of water and God is the egg, then what separates us from God? *Sin.* What we need is a sin buster. We need someone who can come into our lives and take the sin away so we can be back together with God. Who do you think can be our sin buster? *Jesus.* That's right. Jesus, represented by the broom, is our sin buster. Invite a volunteer to write "Jesus" on a piece of masking tape and put it around the broom handle.

For the Faith of the Next Generation

Step on the straw part of the broom, which should be placed on the floor directly under the pie pan that is sticking out over the edge of the table. Pull back on the broom handle approximately twelve inches. With your free hand, press down on the table next to the jar. This will add extra support to the table. Release the broom handle. The broom will act as a spring, which causes the handle to hit and knock the pie pan out of the middle, so the egg falls into the jar of water. The table will stop the momentum of the broom handle and keep it from hitting the jar. **Jesus knocks the sin out of our lives so we can be back together with God.**

Close in Prayer

Pass It On. Make an extra copy of this lesson and *pass it on* to another family.